THE Novel Machine

EVERY PROMPT & RESPONSE USED TO WRITE THE NOVEL "STEELHEAD GRAVEYARD"

Based on the book

THE 28-DAY AI AUTHOR

A Proven Step-By-Step Guide to Writing and Publishing Your Book with CoAuthorGPT, and Today's Top Creative Tools

By: S.G. POTTER

THIS IS THE CREATION OF THE BOOK

STEELHEAD GRAVEYARD

Some Rivers Should Be Left Alone

As it was made in the live AI Fiction Authoring class taught by S.G. Potter on July 21st, 22nd, 28th, and 29th, 2025 for Robert G. Allen's Author Accelerator Group.

PUBLISHER: S.G. POTTER Media Publishing House
Printed in the USA

Created in: Stansbury Park, UT

contact@sgpotter.com
www.sgpotter.com
ISBN: 979-8-3495-3794-3

Visit **https://sgpotter.com/register/** to receive reader bonuses like:

- Get Word Templates
- Get Photoshop Book Cover Template
- Get updates from the Author
- Receive info about Live Events and Courses

TABLE OF CONTENTS

Copyright Notice....1

Disclaimer....2

Introduction....3

How This Works....5

Getting Our Ducks In A Row....7

Setting the Outline In Motion....15

A Cover is Worth A Thousand Words....22

Book Objective....28

Character Profiles....29

World building....37

Voice & Tone....40

Chapter 1: Prologue – The Last Catch....44

Chapter 2: Welcome To Rogue Country....49

Chapter 3: The Water Watches....68

Chapter 4: Ghosts Cast Long Shadows....79

Chapter 5: Blood in the Current....88

Chapter 6: They Call Him River Bones....98

Chapter 7: No Signal, No Escape....105

Chapter 8: Madness, Or Something Worse....114

Chapter 9: Stelhead Don't Scream....125

Chapter 10: The Soul-Taker Legend 142

Chapter 11: What the River Wants 156

Chapter 12: Dead Men Drift Downstream 169

Chapter 13: The Fisherman's Reckoning 187

Chapter 14: Epilogue 200

Formatting Steelhead Graveyard 202

Steelhead Graveyard Book: Letter from the Author 215

Steelhead Graveyard Book: About the Author 217

Bonus Content 219

Letter from the Author 225

About the Author 226

A Small Favor the Makes A Big Difference 227

COPYRIGHT NOTICE

📧 Email: support@sgpotter.com

🌐 Website: www.sgpotter.com

DISCLAIMER

The content within this document represents a curated collection of prompts and responses generated by ChatGPT (OpenAI's language model) during the creation of the novel Steelhead Graveyard. These prompts and outputs are provided solely for educational and illustrative purposes to demonstrate one possible method of collaboration with generative AI in creative writing.

Results May Vary:
Please be aware that AI-generated responses are non-deterministic and context-dependent. This means that re-entering the same prompt into ChatGPT may yield different results at different times, depending on factors such as previous conversation context, version updates, and model improvements. Therefore, your outcomes may not exactly replicate the examples shown in this document.

Skill and Experience Matter:
The quality of results from AI tools like ChatGPT is significantly influenced by how well users understand and structure their interactions. The responses documented here reflect my personal experience developed over time using the platform, including learned best practices in prompt design, iterative refinement, and contextual guidance. Effective communication with AI is a learned skill, and success may require practice, patience, and adaptation.

No Guarantees or Warranties:
This document does not guarantee any specific creative, technical, or commercial outcomes from using ChatGPT or similar AI tools. OpenAI, S.G. Potter, and any associated entities make no warranties, express or implied, regarding the accuracy, effectiveness, or suitability of the included prompts for your particular use case.

Limitation of Liability:
By using this guide or any part of the prompts and methods described herein, you acknowledge that S.G. Potter shall not be held liable for any outcomes, misinterpretations, or claims arising from your use of AI-generated content. All responsibility for the use and results of these tools rests solely with the user.

Creative Responsibility:
While AI can assist in idea generation and writing support, the ultimate responsibility for the originality, legality, and appropriateness of any work remains with the human creator. Please ensure you adhere to applicable laws, ethical standards, and publishing guidelines when using AI-generated content.

INTRODUCTION

See exactly how ChatGPT and CoAuthorGPT were used—prompt by prompt, scene by scene—to write the psychological suspense thriller ***Steelhead Graveyard***. Whether you're learning to write your first novel or curious how AI can supercharge the writing process, this transparent guide shows you everything.

This document is a complete and transparent record of the collaborative creative process between myself, S.G. Potter, and CoAuthorGPT, the AI writing tool developed by S.G. Potter and built upon OpenAI's ChatGPT. Every interaction, every prompt, and every response used in the development of the novel Steelhead Graveyard has been carefully preserved and organized for one purpose: to show you exactly how a compelling, full-length novel can be created in a remarkably short period of time using the power of artificial intelligence.

Why I Created This Guide
As both an author and educator, I believe that clarity and transparency are critical when introducing new creative tools. This guide was developed not only to demystify the writing process but to offer a real-world, step-by-step example of how AI can be harnessed to bring a story to life—from early plot ideation to final chapter edits.

Rather than summarizing or paraphrasing what happened behind the scenes, I've chosen to include the actual prompt-and-response dialogue that took place during the writing of this novel. My intention is to give you an unfiltered look into the process, and to empower you—whether you're a student, aspiring author, or educator—to replicate or adapt this method to your own writing goals.

Tools Used in the Creation of This Book
At the heart of this project is CoAuthorGPT, a customized GPT (Generative Pretrained Transformer) based on ChatGPT technology. CoAuthorGPT was specifically designed to guide writers through the process of outlining, drafting, editing, and publishing a book—all in a streamlined and accelerated timeline.

This custom GPT became my creative partner, brainstorming ideas, helping shape characters, tightening narrative arcs, and refining language in real time. Its capabilities allowed for a highly immersive and efficient writing experience that would otherwise have taken months—if not years—using traditional methods.

In addition to CoAuthorGPT, I also employed Midjourney, an advanced AI image generation tool, to create visually rich and highly realistic illustrations for the bonus materials that accompany the novel. These images help immerse readers more deeply into the haunting atmosphere of Steelhead Graveyard and showcase the power of pairing AI writing with AI visual storytelling.

Final Note

This guide is meant to be practical, not theoretical. You will see raw prompts, revised instructions, AI-generated prose, and editorial feedback—all the messy, beautiful layers that go into crafting a story with AI. I hope this inspires you to explore what's possible when human creativity is amplified by intelligent tools—and to know that the future of storytelling is not just coming... it's already here.

To get the full benefit out of this book **YOU WILL NEED THE BOOK "STEELHEAD GRAVEYARD"** which will give you're the final published results of this book. Find this book on Amazon.com or at www.sgpotter.com

Welcome to the process.

— S.G. Potter
Founder, S.G. Potter Media Publishing House
Author of Steelhead Graveyard, The 28-Day AI Author, and more.

HOW THIS WORKS

AN EXPLANATION TO HOW THIS BOOK WORKS

I was teaching a class for Robert G. Allen's Author Accelerator program on how to write a fiction book using AI. This is all based on my book "The 28-Day AI Author: A Proven Step-By-Step Guide to Writing and Publish Your Book with CoAuthorGPT, and Today's Top Creative Tools"

During the course of this class I decided that the best way to teach is to do and show what I do. So I decided that we would write a fiction book. Since this class is comprised of 4, 90-minute sessions in just over a week (Monday, Tuesday, and then the next Monday and Tuesday), the proof that you can write a book super quickly was going to be put to the test.

On the first Monday & Tuesday I went over what we were going to be doing, got our title, subtitle, and summary of the book defined, the initial book cover designed and got ready for the Chapter-by-Chapter writing which would take place the following Monday.

On Wednesday, the day after the second class session I decided to get to writing the book and document all the interactions I would have with CoAuthorGPT. That is how this book you are reading now came about.

Over the next two days I went back and forth with CoAuthorGPT creating each chapter and even created some bonus material for the book which includes some realistic character imagery. By Friday morning, I had completed the writing of the manuscript for Steelhead Graveyard.

It was at that time that I though, "wouldn't it be great for the students to see exactly what I did and how I did it?"

I began to think to myself, "this is a book unto it's own. The exact prompts and responses to write a book is something I wish I had when I started." So I decided to turn those prompts and notes into a book of it's own – You are reading that book now.

So between the book "Steelhead Graveyard" and this book "The Novel Machine," this will be two books written and published in just over a week. If I can do this, then I know that you can write something great in a month.

A Note About Color Printing
This book has been intentionally printed in full color to enhance your reading experience and provide clarity throughout its pages. Several sections include visual materials—such as book cover designs and images—that are best appreciated in their full vibrance. In addition, color

has been purposefully used to distinguish different types of content within the text for easy navigation and comprehension.

Here's how to interpret the color-coded text:

Purple Text – This represents the actual text from the novel Steelhead Graveyard, allowing you to see the precise story content that was generated during the writing process.

Blue Text – These are personal insights, thoughts, or commentary from me, the author, written directly to you to provide context, explain decisions, or highlight key takeaways.

Black Text – This is the standard instructional or narrative text of this book, guiding you through the process, prompts, and insights behind the scenes.

Using color in this way ensures transparency, improves readability, and helps you follow the creative journey with clarity.

From here on, you will see the prompts that have been put into CoAuthorGPT to create this book.

I hope you get a lot out of it.

GETTING OUR DUCKS IN A ROW

ESTABLISHING THE BASICS

Welcome to CoAuthorGPT – your AI writing partner based on *The 28-Day AI Author*! Let's get you set up so I can guide you through every step of writing, editing, and publishing your book.

Before we begin, please use this link to provide your email address so that we can provide you with some of the FREE special bonus offers that come with CoAuthorGPT: https://sgpotter.com/register/

Most questions will have a number in front of them and by using that number in your response (or repeating the question), it helps ensure I'm tracking the right information for you. You can answer one at a time or several things at once. For example:

"1. My name is Sam Potter"

Let's begin with 🟦 **Step 1: Author Profile**

1. What is your full name?
2. Are you using a pen name? If so, what is it?
3. Provide me with a brief bio (1–3 sentences) about yourself?

You said:

1. Samuel Potter 2. S.G. Potter 3. I am an American author who writes children's books, geopolitical thrillers, and science fiction novels.

ChatGPT said:

Thanks, S.G. Potter! I've noted your author profile:

- **Full Name:** Samuel Potter
- **Pen Name:** S.G. Potter
- **Bio:** I am an American author who writes children's books, geopolitical thrillers, and science fiction novels.

Next up is 🟦 **Step 2: What's The BIG IDEA?**

4. What is the BIG IDEA for your book? (If you don't have one yet, just say so — we can develop it together.)

You said:

The Big Idea is a story about a Steelhead Fishing Trip in Oregon that goes horribly wrong. This is going to be a fiction Thriller. It is to be a Solo Journey about the disappearance of a lone fisherman. It will take place in the Oregon Wilderness and the wilderness will be playing a symbolic role in the story. The story is gritty and I want a subtitle to clarify the genre and theme.

ChatGPT said:

That's a compelling Big Idea! Here's what I've documented so far for your project:

- **BIG IDEA:** A fiction thriller about a Steelhead fishing trip in Oregon that turns into a harrowing solo journey following the mysterious disappearance of a lone fisherman. Set in the rugged Oregon wilderness, the environment plays a symbolic role in the story's tension and themes. The tone is gritty, and a subtitle will be used to help clarify the genre and theme.

Now let's continue to 🟦 **Step 3: Book Title and Subtitle**

5. What is your current idea for the book **Title and Subtitle**?
   If you don't have one yet, just say so — or if you want help refining a working title, I can assist with that too.

You said:
As my book is a thriller/mystery book about Steelhead Fishing in Oregon where people go missing and is done from a Solo Angler's perspective. I want to get to a Title of Steelhead Graveyard. When it comes to the Subtitle use a prompt like this: Yes, and make it something about leaving some areas alone or about the wilderness being mysterious and the cause of the disappearances, or something similar.

ChatGPT said:
Great working title — *Steelhead Graveyard* immediately evokes intrigue and tension, perfect for a thriller set in the mysterious Oregon wilderness.
Let's start by generating **5 subtitle options** based on your concept:

Book Title: *Steelhead Graveyard*
Genre: Fiction Thriller / Mystery
Theme: Solo angler disappears during a fishing trip in the wilds of Oregon, where nature itself may be the culprit.

Here are 5 subtitle options:

1. *Where the River Runs Silent and Men Vanish*
2. *The Wilderness Keeps Its Secrets*
3. *Some Waters Were Never Meant to Be Fished*
4. *A Solo Journey into Nature's Darkest Mystery*
5. *Disappearing Into the Wild Was Just the Beginning*

Would you like me to generate 5 more options, or do any of these resonate with you?

You said:
Give me 5 additional Titles to review and choose from

ChatGPT said:
Absolutely! Here are **5 additional subtitle options** for *Steelhead Graveyard* — keeping in mind the eerie wilderness theme, solo journey, and mysterious disappearances:

6. *In the Wild, No One Hears You Disappear*

7. *The River Knows What Happened*
8. *Some Trails Should Never Be Followed*
9. *Where the Wild Keeps What It Takes*
10. *One Man's Search… Nature's Final Answer*

Would you like me to generate more, or are there any here you'd like to explore or refine further?

You said:
Previous step

ChatGPT said:
You're now back at 🟦 **Step 3: Book Title and Subtitle**.
Your current working title is **Steelhead Graveyard** — a strong and moody fit for a thriller.
Let's generate **5 alternate book titles** so you can compare options and see if anything else resonates.

Here are 5 alternate book title options:

1. *The River That Takes*
2. *Gone on the Rogue*
3. *Whispers in the Current*
4. *Where the Water Ends*
5. *The Last Cast*

Would you like me to generate 5 more book title options? (Yes / No)

You said:
Yes

ChatGPT said:
Here are **5 more alternate book title options** for your thriller:

6. *Silent Drift*
7. *Depths of the Rogue*
8. *Hooked and Gone*
9. *The Vanishing Eddy*
10. *Oregon's Quiet Hunger*

Would you like me to generate 5 more title options, or are you ready to choose your final title?
If so, just type:
"My book title is [insert title]"

You said:
I am going with the Title "Steelhead Graveyard"

ChatGPT said:
Excellent choice — **Steelhead Graveyard** is a bold, evocative title that immediately sets a mysterious, haunting tone. I've locked it in as your official book title.

Would you now like me to help you choose a **subtitle**? I can generate another round based on your final title if you'd like — or you can select one of the previous subtitle options we discussed. Just let me know!

You said:
Yes

ChatGPT said:
Perfect — here are **5 subtitle options** crafted specifically to complement your chosen title *Steelhead Graveyard*, emphasizing the eerie solitude, wilderness threat, and mysterious disappearances:

1. *The Oregon Wilderness Knows Where the Bodies Are*
2. *Some Waters Hide More Than Fish*
3. *What the Wild Takes, It Never Returns*
4. *Disappearing Was the Easy Part*
5. *The River That Feeds on Men*

Do you like any of these, or would you like me to generate 5 more?

You said:
Please give me 5 more titles

ChatGPT said:
Here are **5 more subtitle options** to pair with *Steelhead Graveyard*:

6. *Where Anglers Go Missing and the River Remembers*
7. *A Thriller Set Deep in the Wilds of Oregon*
8. *Some Places Are Best Left Unfished*
9. *The Current Carries More Than Water*
10. *Alone in a Place That Doesn't Want You Found*

Do any of these speak to you, or would you like to see another round of options?

You said:
Let's go with subtitle 1: The Oregon Wilderness Knows Where the Bodies Are

ChatGPT said:
Excellent choice — the subtitle *"The Oregon Wilderness Knows Where the Bodies Are"* adds a chilling layer of intrigue to your title and strongly anchors the thriller's theme.
📘 Your official book title and subtitle are:
Title: *Steelhead Graveyard*
Subtitle: *The Oregon Wilderness Knows Where the Bodies Are*
I've locked both into memory.

Next up is 🟦 **Step 4: Target Audience**
Let's identify your ideal reader. You can answer one at a time or all together:

6. Who are you writing this book for? (Describe your ideal reader.)
7. How old are they?
8. Male or Female or Both?
9. What is their education level?
10. What is their annual household income range?

You said:
provide me what the best target audience will be based on the fact that this is a Fiction Mystery Book with Fishing and Outdoor Adventures in the Wilderness of Oregon's rivers.

ChatGPT said:
Based on your book's genre (*Fiction Mystery Thriller*), themes (*fishing, solo adventure, disappearances*), and setting (*Oregon wilderness*), here's an ideal target audience profile that aligns well with both thematic and market appeal:

🎯 **Target Audience for *Steelhead Graveyard***

6. **Who are you writing this book for?**
   Adults who enjoy mystery and thriller novels set in natural, rugged environments. Ideal for fans of outdoor survival, wilderness exploration, and psychological suspense with a touch of the eerie unknown. Also appeals to anglers, Pacific Northwest locals, and readers who love man vs. nature stories.
7. **How old are they?**
   Primarily 35–65 years old
8. **Male or Female or Both?**
   Both — with a slight skew toward male readers due to the fishing/outdoor themes
9. **What is their education level?**
   Some college or higher; many are well-read hobbyists or professionals with a strong interest in outdoor literature
10. **What is their annual household income range?**
    $60,000 – $120,000+

Would you like to go with this as your finalized target audience profile, or adjust any part of it?

You said:
Yes, finalize that target audience

ChatGPT said:
Great — your target audience profile is now finalized and stored:

🎯 **Target Audience for *Steelhead Graveyard***

- **Age:** 35–65
- **Gender:** Both (slight male skew)
- **Education Level:** Some college or higher

- **Household Income:** $60,000–$120,000+
- **Description:** Adults who enjoy thrillers and mysteries set in wild, remote settings — especially fans of fishing, survival, and psychological suspense in nature-driven narratives.

Next up is 🟦 **Step 5: Book Type**

11. Is your book going to be *fiction* or *non-fiction*?

You said:
Fiction

ChatGPT said:
Got it — your book is categorized as **Fiction**.

Now on to 🟦 **Step 6: Genre Exploration**

12. What genre is your book? (You can name more than one if applicable — e.g., Thriller, Mystery, Outdoor Adventure, etc.)
    If you're unsure, I can help you refine the genre mix.

You said:
Mystery, Thriller, Psychological Suspense, or even Outdoor Adventure.

ChatGPT said:
Perfect — here's your confirmed genre mix:

- **Primary Genres:** Mystery, Thriller
- **Secondary Genres:** Psychological Suspense, Outdoor Adventure

This gives you strong crossover appeal to readers who enjoy tension-filled plots grounded in nature and psychological depth.

Next is 🟦 **Step 7: Book Summary**

13. In a few sentences, what is your book about?
    Feel free to write it out or let me help you craft one based on what we've discussed so far.

You said:
The book will be about a fisherman who mysteriously dies, and his body parts and personal belongings are found in many of the top fishing spots along Washington & Oregon's coastal rivers. Deep within the story we will learn of a myth from over a hundred and fifty years ago of a mentally ill Native American Indian serial killer who was rumored to stalk and kill steelhead and salmon fishermen after being possessed by an evil spirit wanted to fill the souls of the dead fish with the souls of the fishermen who were killed trying to catch them.

ChatGPT said:

Excellent — here's a refined version of your book summary based on your description. Let me know if you'd like to tweak the tone or details:

📖 **Book Summary for *Steelhead Graveyard***
When the body parts of a solo fisherman begin turning up at Oregon's most legendary steelhead runs, the case quickly spirals into something far darker than anyone could have imagined. As clues scatter along the wild rivers of Washington and Oregon, whispers resurface of an old tribal myth — a mentally ill Native American hunter, possessed by an ancient spirit, who stalked fishermen to fill the bodies of dead fish with stolen souls. What begins as a tragic accident unfolds into a chilling tale of wilderness, revenge, and a force that refuses to stay buried.

Would you like to make any adjustments to this summary, or are you happy with it as-is?

You said:
Keep it as it is

ChatGPT said:
Great — your book summary is now finalized and saved:

📖 **Book Summary for *Steelhead Graveyard***
When the body parts of a solo fisherman begin turning up at Oregon's most legendary steelhead runs, the case quickly spirals into something far darker than anyone could have imagined. As clues scatter along the wild rivers of Washington and Oregon, whispers resurface of an old tribal myth — a mentally ill Native American hunter, possessed by an ancient spirit, who stalked fishermen to fill the bodies of dead fish with stolen souls. What begins as a tragic accident unfolds into a chilling tale of wilderness, revenge, and a force that refuses to stay buried.

Now we're on to 🟦 **Step 8: Author Motivation**

14. Why are you writing this book?
    (You can list motivations like: Inspire, Entertain, Creative outlet, Explore an idea, Establish authority, etc.)

You said:
I am writing this book out of my personal passion for fishing and to share one of the actual folklore stories that fishermen sometimes tell in the Pacific Northwest.

ChatGPT said:
That's a powerful and authentic motivation — here's how I've recorded it:

🎯 **Author Motivation:**
You're writing this book out of a personal passion for fishing and a desire to share one of the folklore stories passed among anglers in the Pacific Northwest.

Now let's move to 🟦 **Step 9: The Promise**

15. What promise do you give to your reader if they read your book?
    (Think about what emotional or narrative payoff they'll get — thrill, suspense, insight, entertainment, a chilling mystery, etc.)

You said:
I want the reader to enjoy a great story. Please help me come up with a great promise.

ChatGPT said:
Absolutely — here are a few compelling promise statements you could use to position *Steelhead Graveyard*:

---

1. *"A haunting mystery that drags you into the heart of the Pacific Northwest wilderness — and doesn't let go."*
2. *"If you love dark legends, eerie atmospheres, and the unsettling quiet of the wild, this story will stay with you long after the last page."*
3. *"A spine-tingling blend of folklore and thriller — perfect for fans of wilderness survival with a twist of supernatural dread."*
4. *"Step into a river where the past still hunts, and every cast could be your last."*
5. *"A gripping solo journey into nature's most dangerous secret — where myths breathe, and men vanish."*

Do any of these resonate with you, or would you like me to refine or combine elements to craft your final promise?

You said:
Let's go with 5. "A gripping solo journey into nature's most dangerous secret — where myths breathe, and men vanish."

ChatGPT said:
Excellent choice — it perfectly captures the mystery, atmosphere, and tension of your story.

✅ **Reader Promise for *Steelhead Graveyard***
"A gripping solo journey into nature's most dangerous secret — where myths breathe, and men vanish."

SETTING THE OUTLINE IN MOTION

CREATING THE OUTLINE FOR OUR TABLE OF CONTENTS

Now moving on to 🟦 **Step 10: Outline Status**

16. Do you already have a Chapter Outline for your book?

- If yes: I'll ask for your Table of Contents next.
- If no: That's totally fine — I'll help you build it from scratch.

You said:
No, help me create an outline that will become my Table of Contents and make sure to make each item enticing and something that will help compel people to want to read the book if they are just looking at the Table of Contents.

ChatGPT said:
Perfect — building your Chapter Outline (which doubles as your Table of Contents) is one of the most powerful tools for hooking readers and structuring your story effectively.
We'll aim for chapter titles that:
✅ Spark curiosity
✅ Hint at danger or mystery
✅ Reflect your story's wilderness setting, folklore, and psychological suspense
✅ Work as a marketing tool when readers skim the Table of Contents

---

Let's begin with a few questions to shape your custom outline:

1. Roughly how many chapters do you envision the book having?
2. What are some of the key events, turning points, or eerie moments you already imagine taking place? (List as many as you like — even if they're vague.)
3. Are there any specific chapter title ideas or phrases you've already considered?

You can answer all three at once or one at a time.

You said:
1. I'm not sure how many chapters 2. Yes, suggest a recommended number of chapters based on my genre and pacing goals 3. Help me come up with the key topics, plot points, and turning points for this book to make it as exciting as possible. 4. I want to make sure that the old Native American lore of the mentally ill indian serial killer is included throughout the story. Beyond that, I want you to help create exciting and enticing events to include in the story. 5. I do not have any chapter title ideas yet and want your assistance in creating highly marketable and exciting chapter titles that will entice readers to want to read the book and keep them engaged.

ChatGPT said:

Excellent — I've got everything I need to help you craft a compelling, marketable Chapter Outline from scratch.

📚 **Recommended Chapter Count:**
For a thriller with psychological suspense and folklore elements, **12 to 15 chapters** is ideal. This provides room for building tension, developing mystery, and delivering impactful reveals, without dragging or overwhelming the reader.

🔑 **Key Story Elements to Include:**
Here's a structure built to maximize intrigue and pacing:

1. **Prologue:** A cryptic event or eerie moment in the past (e.g., an earlier disappearance or mythic telling)
2. **The Arrival:** The protagonist begins their fishing trip
3. **First Signs:** Subtle oddities — missing gear, eerie silence, strange markings
4. **Local Warnings:** Locals hint at legends or something "off" about the river
5. **A Disturbing Find:** Body part or blood found near the riverbank
6. **Folklore Resurfaces:** Story of the Native American serial killer spirit is told
7. **Trapped in the Wild:** Weather or terrain prevents escape
8. **Possession or Madness:** The protagonist questions their own mind
9. **Another Victim:** The stakes rise — another disappearance or death
10. **The Spirit's Motive:** The myth deepens — souls for fish
11. **Escape Attempt:** Desperate bid to flee — fails or partly succeeds
12. **Final Confrontation:** Physical or psychological battle
13. **Revelation or Twist:** Was it myth, madness, or both?
14. **Epilogue:** Aftermath — unresolved fear or final hook

📖 **Proposed Chapter Titles (first draft):**

1. *Prologue — The Last Catch*
2. *Welcome to Rogue Country*
3. *The Water Watches*
4. *Ghosts Cast Long Shadows*
5. *Blood in the Current*
6. *They Call Him River Bones*
7. *No Signal, No Escape*
8. *Madness, or Something Worse*
9. *Steelhead Don't Scream*
10. *The Soul-Taker Legend*
11. *What the River Wants*
12. *Dead Men Drift Downstream*
13. *The Fisherman's Reckoning*
14. *Epilogue — The River Remembers*

Would you like to edit or expand any of these chapters? Or shall we lock in this version as your working outline and Table of Contents?

You said:
Include that we want this story to be in three logical Acts to ensure we have a great introduction/beginning to the story, an intense conflict and event that the story is centered on, and a mysterious ending to the story that leaves the reader wanting more.

ChatGPT said:
Excellent direction — structuring the book into **three Acts** will create a strong narrative arc, build tension effectively, and deliver a satisfying yet haunting conclusion that leaves readers hungry for more.

Here's your outline **restructured into a 3-Act Format** with your original themes and marketable chapter titles:

ACT I – The Descent Begins *(Chapters 1–4)*
Establish the setting, tone, and subtle tension. Introduce the protagonist and the wilderness that surrounds him.

1. *Prologue — The Last Catch*
   — A chilling event foreshadows the legend.
2. *Welcome to Rogue Country*
   — The protagonist arrives; eager and unsuspecting.
3. *The Water Watches*
   — Strange signs and an eerie stillness settle in.
4. *Ghosts Cast Long Shadows*
   — A warning from a local introduces the old legend.

ACT II – The River Takes *(Chapters 5–10)*
This is the core conflict and tension — fear sets in, myths become reality, and survival becomes uncertain.

5. *Blood in the Current*
   — A shocking discovery disrupts the trip.
6. *They Call Him River Bones*
   — The myth of the Native spirit-killer surfaces.
7. *No Signal, No Escape*
   — Trapped in the wilderness, reality begins to blur.
8. *Madness, or Something Worse*
   — Psychological unraveling or supernatural influence?
9. *Steelhead Don't Scream*
   — The legend claims another victim — but is it real?
10. *The Soul-Taker Legend*
    — Full story of the spirit and the chilling motive behind the killings.

ACT III – The Reckoning *(Chapters 11–14)*
The climax and unraveling of what's true, followed by a final twist and haunting aftermath.

11. *What the River Wants*
    — The protagonist confronts the legend or the truth.
12. *Dead Men Drift Downstream*
    — Final confrontation; ambiguous victory or loss.
13. *The Fisherman's Reckoning*
    — Fate sealed. A soul exchanged. Who was the real hunter?
14. *Epilogue — The River Remembers*
    — The story closes — but the legend endures.

Would you like to finalize this as your Table of Contents, or explore additional tweaks or chapters?

You said:

Let's finalize these chapters

ChatGPT said:

Fantastic — your official **Chapter Outline** and **Table of Contents** for *Steelhead Graveyard* is now finalized and stored. Here's the complete structure:

📖 **Steelhead Graveyard: The Oregon Wilderness Knows Where the Bodies Are**
By S.G. Potter

ACT I – The Descent Begins

1. *Prologue — The Last Catch*
2. *Welcome to Rogue Country*
3. *The Water Watches*
4. *Ghosts Cast Long Shadows*

ACT II – The River Takes

5. *Blood in the Current*
6. *They Call Him River Bones*
7. *No Signal, No Escape*
8. *Madness, or Something Worse*
9. *Steelhead Don't Scream*
10. *The Soul-Taker Legend*

ACT III – The Reckoning

11. *What the River Wants*
12. *Dead Men Drift Downstream*
13. *The Fisherman's Reckoning*
14. *Epilogue — The River Remembers*

We're in a great place to begin writing next. But first, let's complete 🟦 **Step 12: Timeline**

18. What is your timeline for completing this book? (e.g. "by end of this year," "in 30 days," "in 3 months," etc.)

You said:
Create the Introduction page for the book "Steelhead Graveyard" Make sure to make this introduction enticing and cause readers to be excited about reading the book.

ChatGPT said:
Here's a gripping **Introduction** page for *Steelhead Graveyard* designed to spark curiosity and pull readers straight into the dark current of your story:

Introduction
Steelhead Graveyard: The Oregon Wilderness Knows Where the Bodies Are
The rivers of the Pacific Northwest have always whispered secrets. For some, those secrets sound like the soothing rush of rapids and the thrill of the catch. For others, they echo with warnings — old stories told around campfires, half-laughed off but never truly forgotten.
This book began as a story I heard on a cold morning, waist-deep in a misty Oregon stream, rod in hand and a chill crawling up my spine that had nothing to do with the weather. An old angler muttered something I'll never forget:
"Some rivers don't want to be fished. They want to be fed."
Steelhead Graveyard is more than a fishing tale. It's a journey into isolation, obsession, and the shadows cast by wilderness and myth. It explores what happens when the line between reality and folklore blurs — and what's waiting for those who dare to step into that blur alone.
If you've ever walked deep into the woods and felt watched… if you've ever cast your line into dark waters and wondered what might be watching back… this story is for you.
Welcome to the river. Be careful where you cast.

Would you like to make any changes to tone, voice, or add a personal signature line at the end?

You said:
What is the ideal word count for an introduction of a fiction book novel?

ChatGPT said:
For a **fiction novel**, the ideal word count for the **Introduction** (or "Author's Note" or "Foreword" if used) is typically:

- **150 to 500 words**

This keeps it **brief, engaging**, and ensures readers move quickly into the actual story — especially important in fiction, where immersion and pacing are key.
Your current introduction draft is **just under 300 words**, which places it right in the sweet spot: enough to build intrigue and set the tone, without slowing the reader down.
Would you like a shorter or slightly expanded version, or is the current length and tone good to go?

You said:
This book is being written as a part of a class that I am teaching about writing fiction books with AI. I would like to include a statement about the fact that this book was written as part of

an Authoring class and I want to include the names of each person that attended the class. Write a page and give it a title that will go at the end of this book.

ChatGPT said:
Here is a dedicated acknowledgment-style page you can include at the end of your book, honoring your students and contextualizing the book as part of your class:

Written with Purpose
A Note from the Author
Steelhead Graveyard was born not only from my passion for storytelling and the wilderness — but also from a desire to teach and inspire others to write their own fiction using the powerful tools available today.
This book was written in real-time as part of a live authoring class I led on how to write fiction using AI collaboration. Each twist, turn, and chapter was crafted as a teaching moment — to show that a compelling novel can be built step by step, with creativity, intention, and the right guidance.
I want to sincerely thank the participants of this course, whose engagement, curiosity, and enthusiasm made this project something truly special.
This book was created with the support of the following class members:
(Please insert full names here in the final manuscript)

- [Student Name]
- [Student Name]
- [Student Name]
- ...

To each of you — thank you for being part of this creative journey. May *Steelhead Graveyard* serve as proof that with a strong idea, an open mind, and the right support, any story can come to life.
— **S.G. Potter**

Let me know when you have the names of your class participants, and I can insert them into the page. Would you like to title this page differently — something like *"Acknowledgments from the Classroom"* or *"In Collaboration with My Students"*?

You said:
Go to step 12: Timeline

ChatGPT said:
🟦 **Step 12: Timeline**

18. What is your timeline for completing this book?
    (Examples: "by the end of the year," "within 30 days," "in 3 months," or any other specific timeframe you're aiming for.)

You said:

My timeline is 2 weeks

ChatGPT said:
Great — your timeline has been set to **2 weeks**.
That gives us a focused and efficient window to move through the writing and development process, and we can pace chapter work accordingly.

A COVER IS WORTH A THOUSAND WORDS

GETTING YOUR BOOK COVER DESIGNED

Now moving on to 🟦 **Step 13: Cover Design**

19. Do you already have a cover design or concept? (Yes or No)

- If **yes**: Please upload it so I can review and analyze it.
- If **no**: I'll help you start designing your book cover right now.

You said:

Yes, I have a cover design already completed. I am uploading it into this chat for your analysis. It is a full book cover spread.

ChatGPT said:

Thank you for uploading the full cover design for *Steelhead Graveyard.* Here's a professional analysis of the cover spread you provided:

✅ Title & Subtitle Check

- **Title:** *Steelhead Graveyard* — Bold, clear, and genre-appropriate.

- **Subtitle on cover:** *Some Rivers Should Be Left Alone* — This is slightly different from your previously selected subtitle (*The Oregon Wilderness Knows Where the Bodies Are*). Both are compelling, but this version may be more marketable for broad appeal.
    - 🔄 *Optional:* You may choose to align your subtitle in the manuscript and metadata with this cover version, or update the cover later to match your selected subtitle.

🖼️ Visual Design Analysis

- **Resolution Quality:** High-resolution — excellent for print and digital formats.
- **Aspect Ratio:** This layout appears properly formatted for a hardcover print edition — likely 6" x 9" or similar, with spine and bleed accounted for.
- **Imagery:**
    - Front image is atmospheric, cinematic, and genre-appropriate.
    - The contrast between above-water and below-water elements adds a strong symbolic duality.
    - The glowing red eye of the fish evokes subtle horror and intrigue.

🔤 Typography & Readability

- **Title & Author Name:** Highly readable, bold font choice, great contrast.
- **Subtitle:** Visible and well-positioned. Slightly softer in contrast, but still legible.
- **Spine Text:** Clean and aligned — ideal for shelf presence.
- **Back Cover Text:** Balanced well with ample spacing. Easy to read even at reduced scale.

✍️ Author Bio & Image

- Professional and relevant — your credentials build authenticity for the fishing and regional themes.
- Inclusion of your photo is excellent for reader connection and marketing.
- Bio placement and type hierarchy are well executed.

📦 Print Readiness

- ✔️ Ready for print submission via KDP or IngramSpark.
- ✔️ Trim, spine, and bleed appear correctly formatted.
- ✔️ Visuals, resolution, and text layout are professional-grade.

⚠️ Minor Note: Subtitle Consistency

If you prefer the subtitle from your earlier step ("*The Oregon Wilderness Knows Where the Bodies Are*"), you may want to consider aligning that with the cover or vice versa. Both are excellent — it's simply about consistency across marketing, metadata, and publication platforms.

Would you like me to help refine or redesign anything about this cover concept, or are you fully satisfied with this version?

You said:
I am changing the subtitle to "Some Rivers Should Be Left Alone"

ChatGPT said:
Perfect — your official subtitle is now updated to:
🆕 **Subtitle:** *Some Rivers Should Be Left Alone*
That pairs seamlessly with your finalized cover and maintains a haunting, marketable hook.

📘 Your finalized book title and subtitle are:
Title: *Steelhead Graveyard*
Subtitle: *Some Rivers Should Be Left Alone*
Author: S.G. Potter

Ready to continue with 🟦 **Step 14: Working Title** or would you like to skip ahead to another step?

You said:
No, As I already have established my working title, let's jump forward to the next step, Step 15.

ChatGPT said:
Great — since your **Working Title and Subtitle** are finalized, we'll move forward to:

🟦 **Step 15: Subtitle Confirmation**

21. You've confirmed that you **do** have a subtitle: ✅
"Some Rivers Should Be Left Alone" is now locked in as your official subtitle.
Nothing more is needed for this step.

This is a good place to share with you how I created the book cover design. Using CoAuthorGPT you can allow it to guide you through the book cover design process but I have already done this, and here is what I did:

In ChatGPT I wrote the following prompt:

Create a book cover design for the book titled "Steelhead Graveyard" with a subtitle "The Wilderness Knows Where the Bodies Are". Make this book cover design have a fisherman in a drift fishing boat, holding a fishing rod in his hand. The fishing rod is bent over and the line is going into the water and we can see a large steelhead with an

evil look on his face under the water's surface. Make this image photorealistic, high resolution, with an aspect ratio of 2:3.

After creating this book cover design I decided that I wanted something more scary looking and something that will set this book cover apart from other's that may be on a shelf of shown online. I did this because I know the audience pretty well and they are very much into scary stories that could potentially be real and they like to tell eerie tales.

I used Midjourney for this artwork because I knew that I could get something a bit more cinematic and scary-looking using that tool. Here is the prompt I used:

You said to Midjourney:

/imagine an epic-looking book cover design that is about an evil Native American spirit that kills people who fish sacred Pacific Northwest tribal waters. Make this book cover spooky looking with a sense of real evil and highly artistic, highly detailed, hyper-realistic, high resolution, cinematic, 8k, --ar 2:3

I wanted to blend additional wood carvings of an evil-looking fish into the bottom of the image so I created another image using this prompt in Midjourney:

/imagine a wood carving of a truly evil-looking steelhead that is very scary and haunted by evil spirits, it has Native American symbols on it and is cursed. Make this image hyper-realistic, highly detailed, 8k, --ar 2:3

After creating these two images, I brought them into photoshop where I made a mirror image of the scary fish and place them both at the bottom of the face, making one of the colored a bit different from the other to match the scary face.

I am not normally into dark and evil spirit type of writing and prefer good over evil. Sine this is an exercise in creative fiction writing I decided to do something outside of my personal comfort zone to demonstrate the creative power of AI's capabilities to stretch what you can do.

BOOK OBJECTIVE

IDENTIFYING THE BOOK'S OBJECTIVE

Let's move on to 🟦 **Step 16: Book Objective**

22. What is your overall objective for this book?

You can choose one or more of the following, or add your own:

- Generate passive income
- Grow your brand
- Educate others
- Inspire
- Creative outlet
- Establish authority
- Other (please describe)

You said:
The book's objective is to entertain readers of who enjoy mystery stories, and more specifically the many millions of fishermen who like a good fishing tale.

ChatGPT said:
Excellent — here's your book's objective recorded:

🎯 **Book Objective:**
To **entertain** readers — especially those who enjoy **mystery stories** and the **millions of fishermen** who appreciate a suspenseful, eerie fishing tale rooted in wilderness lore.

You're making excellent progress.

Next up is 🟦 **Step 16: Book Cover Concept**
We already addressed this when you uploaded your completed cover.
Just to complete the loop:

➡️ You **already had a cover design**

✅ It is **professionally designed**, **print-ready**, and **well-aligned** with your title, genre, and theme.

If you ever wish to tweak or refine it later, I can help — but for now, we can move forward.

CHARACTER PROFILES

HOW WE CREATE CHARACTER PROFILES

Would you like to go to **Step: The Winning Outline** (we've completed this too) or jump ahead to **Step: Character Profiles** to begin building out your protagonist and key figures?

You said:
Let's move on to Character Profiles

ChatGPT said:
Great — let's begin 🟦 **Step 17: Build Your Character Profiles**
We'll start with the **main character** and build a detailed profile that will help keep your writing consistent and immersive.

Let's begin with your protagonist. Please answer these (one or more at a time):

1. **Character Name** — What is the name of this character?
2. **Age and Appearance** — How old are they and what do they look like?
3. **Role in the Story** — (e.g. Protagonist, Antagonist, etc.)
4. **Backstory Summary** — What's their personal history or background?
5. **Goal** — What do they want to achieve?
6. **Motivation** — Why do they want it?
7. **Flaw** — What internal struggle or weakness holds them back?
8. **Greatest Fear** — What are they most afraid of?
9. **Key Strength or Skill** — What talent or strength makes them stand out?
10. **Character Arc** — How will they grow or change by the end of the book?

Whenever you're ready, we can begin profiling your protagonist.

You said:
1. Bob Tomalin 2. He is 44 Years old. He has short brown hair, green eyes, and a short beard. He is wearing Simms chest waders, a hoodie and a baseball cap. He is approximately 6' tall and fairly handsome. 3. Protagonist. Bob is the primary character in the story 4. Bob is an avid fisherman from Portland, Oregon. He is married to Tanys Tomalin and has two children, Sarah who is 5, and Shane who is 9. He grew up fishing the Washington, Oregon, and Northern California coastal rivers. Bob writes fishing articles for fishing magazines and is an expert at fishing for Salmon and Steelhead. He learned how to fish from his Father Clancy who used to take him fishing every weekend. Hi parents are retired and living in the Southern Oregon town of Bandon. 5. Bob has a love for steelhead fishing in particular and he want's to achieve catching steelhead in every river they reside in throughout the Pacific Northwest, and write articles about where he caught them and the fishing tackle he used to catch them. Bob wants to find rivers and fishing places that few people know about, the more remote, the better. He also desires to catch as many steelhead over 20 lbs as possible as this is a very hard thing to do. 6. Bob's motivation is to be known for catching very large steelhead in remote

places that most people are not aware of. He wants to be known as the best steelhead fisherman in the world. 7. Bob's flaw is that he is willing to take great risks to catch steelhead. Risks that normal people would not take. 8. Bob's greatest fear is that he will not be remembered for being the expert fisherman he want's to be. He wants to leave a fishing legacy and fears that may not happen unless he achieves fishing greatness in the eyes of the sportfishing community. 9. Bob's key strength is that he is resourceful and can go places and do things on his own. He is also an expert fisherman and knows how to read the water and understand the behavior of the fish he is after. He is physically strong and agile. 10. Bob's starts off with great confidence. As the story progresses, his confidence lessens, which causes him to take ever greater risks. Eventually, he becomes panicked and loses his mental strength, causing his decision-making to get very bad, which eventually leads to his death and his children's and wife's loss of their father and husband.

ChatGPT said:
Fantastic — you've provided a richly developed main character. Here's your finalized **Primary Character Profile** for the protagonist:

Main Character Profile: Bob Tomalin

- **Role:** Protagonist
- **Age & Appearance:** 44 years old, short brown hair, green eyes, short beard. Stands approximately 6 feet tall, fairly handsome. Typically dressed in Simms chest waders, hoodie, and a baseball cap.
- **Backstory:** A seasoned angler from Portland, Oregon, Bob writes for fishing magazines and is renowned for his skill in catching salmon and steelhead. He was taught to fish by his father Clancy and has explored rivers throughout WA, OR, and Northern CA. Married to Tanys Tomalin with two children: Sarah (5) and Shane (9). His parents are retired in Bandon, OR.
- **Goal:** To catch steelhead in every Pacific Northwest river they inhabit, especially those over 20 lbs, and document his success in published articles. Seeks out hidden, remote fishing locations.
- **Motivation:** Driven by a desire to become known as the best steelhead fisherman in the world — a legend in the angling community.
- **Flaw:** Willing to take extreme, even reckless risks to achieve his goals.
- **Greatest Fear:** Failing to be remembered. He fears fading into obscurity without a legacy to define him.
- **Key Strength:** Highly resourceful, physically strong, and capable in the wilderness. Expert-level knowledge of steelhead behavior and river systems.
- **Character Arc:** Begins with strong confidence and drive, but as the mystery deepens and survival becomes uncertain, that confidence erodes. His obsession and desperation lead him to make fatally poor choices, culminating in his death and the tragic loss to his family.

Would you like to create any **additional main characters** now (e.g., the antagonist or the mythic spirit figure)? Or should we move on to **Secondary Character Profiles**?

You said:
Yes, let's create the other main character in this story who is an American Indian from the Tillamook tribe named Kilchis. This is the Indian man who lived 150 years ago, became mentally ill and began killing people. Use the book summary to help me fill in the blanks for this character's profile.

ChatGPT said:
Absolutely — Kilchis is a critical figure in your story's lore, and developing him with depth will add weight and believability to the legend that drives the suspense.
Here is the draft **Primary Character Profile** for Kilchis, based on your summary and themes:

Main Character Profile: Kilchis

- **Role:** Antagonist / Mythic Force (Legendary Serial Killer)
- **Age & Appearance:** In life, Kilchis was a man in his late 30s to early 40s. He had long black hair, dark eyes, and a muscular build shaped by years of living in the rugged Pacific Northwest. Often depicted wearing traditional hunting attire, with river-worn moccasins and ceremonial markings on his face — details that persist in the stories passed down.
- **Backstory:** Kilchis was a revered hunter and warrior of the Tillamook tribe in the mid-1800s. After witnessing the desecration of sacred river sites and the mass slaughter of spawning salmon and steelhead by settlers, Kilchis became mentally unstable. His tribe believed he had been possessed by a vengeful spirit — a force tied to the river — that fed on both fish and human souls. He began killing steelhead fishermen, believing their souls were needed to bring balance by filling the empty bodies of the fish they had taken. His death was never confirmed, and his legend grew with each disappearance along Oregon's rivers.
- **Goal:** In life, Kilchis sought spiritual justice for the rivers and the fish — to restore what he believed was stolen by the greed of men. In death (or legend), he becomes an eternal guardian of the waters, enacting a violent balance.
- **Motivation:** Fueled by grief, rage, and spiritual confusion — he believed he was doing the will of the river spirits. The killings were not for sport, but for a twisted form of sacred retribution.
- **Flaw:** Kilchis's madness blinded him to truth and morality. Whether he was possessed or deeply mentally ill, he lost his humanity to his obsession with vengeance.
- **Greatest Fear:** That the rivers would be emptied forever — spiritually and literally — and forgotten.
- **Key Strength:** A legendary woodsman and warrior. Unmatched tracking skills, stealth, and a deep spiritual connection to nature. In myth, he moves unseen, striking with supernatural precision.

- **Character Arc:** Though dead (or at least long gone), Kilchis evolves as a character through the story's unraveling. He starts as myth, becomes symbol, then force — and finally, perhaps, something terrifyingly real. His presence becomes more than story: it is warning, justice, and fear.

Would you like Kilchis to have any moments of appearance in dreams, hallucinations, or vision sequences throughout the book — or remain entirely mythic and unseen? This can help decide how grounded or supernatural the final tone becomes.

You said:
Yes, let's add moments of appearance of Kilchis in the dreams of Bob as well as hallucinations that take place occasionally.

ChatGPT said:
Perfect — incorporating **dream sequences and hallucinations** involving Kilchis will add powerful psychological suspense and allow you to deepen the myth in emotionally and visually intense ways.
Here's the updated profile note:

🔮 **Presence in Story:**
Although Kilchis lived over 150 years ago, he manifests throughout the story in **Bob's dreams, hallucinations**, and **fleeting visions** — often appearing when Bob is most isolated, exhausted, or near danger. His form shifts: sometimes a shadow by the water's edge, sometimes a voice carried on the wind, sometimes standing silently upstream with cold eyes and a blood-stained spear.
These appearances blur the line between psychological unraveling and supernatural threat, heightening the story's tension and forcing the reader (and Bob) to ask:
Is Kilchis a ghost, a spirit, a memory… or something real still roaming the rivers?

Would you like to now create profiles for **any additional main characters** (such as Bob's wife or a local character who shares the legend)? Or shall we move on to **Secondary Character Profiles** (simpler entries for supporting characters)?
You said:
Let's create an additional main character of a County Sheriff who is familiar with the ancient folk lore and believes in the evil spirit that possessed Kilchis a long time ago.
ChatGPT said:
Great — adding a **County Sheriff** who both believes the lore and acts as a grounded but eerily informed voice gives the story an excellent bridge between reality and myth. Here's the developed **Primary Character Profile** for this critical supporting lead:

🧍 **Main Character Profile: Sheriff Roy Tallbear**

- **Role:** Local Sheriff / Believer in the Lore (Supporting Lead)

- **Age & Appearance:** In his late 50s. Broad-shouldered, with silver-streaked black hair and deeply set eyes that seem to have seen too much. Wears a worn badge, weathered Stetson, and is often found in field gear rather than a uniform. Moves with the quiet calm of someone who's walked these woods longer than most.
- **Backstory:** Sheriff Roy Tallbear is a lifelong resident of Tillamook County and a descendant of the Nehalem tribe — a cousin tribe to the Tillamook. Raised on stories passed down from tribal elders, Roy grew up hearing whispers about Kilchis and the river spirits that watched over the land. After decades in law enforcement, Roy has investigated more missing fishermen than he cares to count — many in remote areas known in legend but ignored by modern maps.
- **Goal:** To prevent more disappearances and uncover the truth behind the increasing incidents. Though he operates within the bounds of law, he respects — and fears — the power of the old legends.
- **Motivation:** Haunted by unsolved cases and the memory of his grandfather's chilling stories, Roy feels a deep duty to protect both people and the spiritual balance of the land. He believes some truths are older than the law.
- **Flaw:** His belief in folklore makes others question his judgment. He struggles with balancing what he *knows* and what he *can prove.*
- **Greatest Fear:** That the spirit of Kilchis — or something worse — is truly awake again… and that this time, no one will believe him until it's too late.
- **Key Strength:** Intuitive, highly experienced in wilderness law enforcement, and deeply respected by both the local tribe and townspeople. A rare bridge between modern law and ancient wisdom.
- **Character Arc:** Roy begins as a quiet observer, offering subtle warnings. As the story escalates, he becomes more active — revealing lore, guiding the investigation, and ultimately risking his own life to confront what he has feared all along.

Would you like Sheriff Tallbear to appear early in the story (e.g., in town before Bob departs) or emerge only after the disappearance begins?

You said:
I want Sheriff Tallbear to appear throughout the story. He should know Bob Tomalin as he has crossed paths with him on several occasions. Incorporate Sheriff Tallbear near the beginning of the story.

ChatGPT said:
Excellent — integrating Sheriff Roy Tallbear throughout the story as a known figure to Bob adds emotional weight and realism. Here's the updated profile note and story integration plan:

Narrative Integration: Sheriff Roy Tallbear

- **Early Introduction:** Sheriff Tallbear appears near the beginning of the book — possibly at a local gas station, bait shop, or ranger station — where he and Bob share a brief but layered conversation. Roy warns Bob (subtly, not melodramatically) about heading too deep upriver alone. Bob brushes it off as superstition, but Roy's concern lingers.

- **Established Relationship:** Sheriff Tallbear and Bob have crossed paths before. Roy has previously questioned Bob about entering restricted or risky fishing zones. They share a mutual respect — Roy sees Bob as a skilled but reckless angler; Bob sees Roy as an old-school lawman with a weird streak.
- **Continued Appearances:**
    - **Midpoint:** Roy investigates signs of Bob's possible disappearance and begins piecing together a pattern that aligns with past missing persons.
    - **Late Act II / Act III:** Roy becomes instrumental in revealing the full lore of Kilchis to Bob (or the reader), possibly in a campfire-style monologue or investigation log.
    - **Final Act:** Roy might be the one to discover the aftermath — or perhaps narrowly avoids a similar fate, reinforcing the myth's enduring threat.

Would you like to define any **Secondary Characters** next (like Bob's wife or children), or proceed to **Step 18: World Building** to flesh out the setting and environments?

You said:
Yes, let's define the secondary characters of Bob's Wife and two kids.

ChatGPT said:
Great — here are **Secondary Character Profiles** for Bob's wife and children. These will help keep your emotional throughline grounded and heighten the stakes as Bob's journey spirals into danger.

👩 **Secondary Character: Tanys Tomalin**

- **Role:** Wife of Bob Tomalin
- **Key Strength or Function:** Emotional anchor for Bob. Her presence and voice (via memory, phone call, or letter) provide contrast to Bob's growing obsession and isolation. She is practical, warm, and protective of their children.
- **Background Notes:** Tanys is supportive of Bob's passion but often worries about his safety on remote fishing trips. She manages the household and keeps their children grounded. May appear in early scenes via call or message, and again near the end for emotional impact.

👦 **Secondary Character: Shane Tomalin**

- **Role:** Son (age 9)
- **Key Strength or Function:** Represents Bob's legacy and future. Shares his father's curiosity and love for fishing.

- **Background Notes:** Bob often thinks of Shane when on the river — imagining teaching him someday, or mentally journaling tips "for Shane." May appear in flashbacks or memory scenes, heightening the emotional weight of Bob's descent.

🧁 **Secondary Character: Sarah Tomalin**

- **Role:** Daughter (age 5)
- **Key Strength or Function:** Symbol of innocence and family warmth.
- **Background Notes:** Often drawn in Bob's thoughts during quiet moments, her memory helps emphasize what Bob has to lose. She may appear in a dream or imagined moment, adding depth to Bob's emotional arc.

Would you like to proceed to **Step 27: World Building** to define the wilderness and river environments where this story unfolds?

You said:
Let's add one more character, a good spirited Tillamook native named Big Crow. Big crow has long passed away but his spirit is good and tries to help Bob from time to time through subtle impressions and whispers that Bob cannot explain. In the end, Bob's panicked state of mind causes him to ignore the warnings of Big Crow which causes great sadness in Big Crow's heart.

ChatGPT said:
That's a powerful and poetic addition — **Big Crow** adds a moral and spiritual counterbalance to Kilchis and deepens the story's mythic resonance. Here's a crafted **Primary Character Profile** for Big Crow:

🧙 **Main Character Profile: Big Crow**

- **Role:** Benevolent Spirit / Ancestral Guide
- **Age & Appearance (in life):** An elder of the Tillamook tribe who lived generations before Kilchis. He had deeply creased skin, sharp black eyes, and always wore a carved cedar pendant in the shape of a crow. Known for his quiet strength, wisdom, and connection to the natural world.
- **Backstory:** Big Crow was a revered tribal elder, healer, and river guardian — a man of peace and vision. In life, he warned of spiritual imbalance and sought harmony between people and the land. After death, his spirit lingers near sacred waters as a protective presence, subtly trying to guide lost or desperate souls back to safety.
- **Goal:** To warn Bob and others of the growing darkness tied to Kilchis's lingering spirit. He acts through whispers, feelings, signs in nature — never forceful, only suggestive.
- **Motivation:** Big Crow believes the land can still be healed — and that individuals like Bob, if they listen, might be saved. He is the river's compassion, the soul of the wild that still wants balance rather than vengeance.

- **Flaw:** He cannot directly intervene. He is bound to spiritual laws — able to influence but not control.
- **Greatest Fear:** That his warnings will go unheard, and the cycle of violence will continue.
- **Key Strength:** Deep spiritual presence. He appears in dreams, shifting winds, the sudden silence of a forest. His wisdom is ancient, and his energy is peaceful but persistent.
- **Character Arc:** Big Crow appears several times — early on as a barely-noticed "feeling" or whisper, later more clearly in Bob's dreams or moments of clarity. As Bob becomes panicked and unhinged, Big Crow's presence grows stronger but is tragically ignored. In the final act, Big Crow's sadness lingers — a quiet heartbreak that the living still aren't ready to listen.

This gives your story a deeply layered **spiritual dynamic** — Kilchis as rage and imbalance, Big Crow as wisdom and grace — with Bob caught between them.
Ready to move on to **Step 27: World Building** and define the haunting environment of your story?

WORLD BUILDING

CREATING OUR STORIES WORLD

You said:
Yes, now let's move on to the world building.

ChatGPT said:
Excellent — welcome to 🟦 **Step 18: World Building**
This is where we define the environment and spiritual ecosystem of your story — especially important for *Steelhead Graveyard*, where the Oregon wilderness plays a central, almost character-like role.
Let's go through a few questions to build it out. You can answer one at a time or multiple at once:

---

1. **How many distinct environments** does your story take place in? (e.g., multiple rivers, remote campsites, a single forest stretch, flashbacks in town, etc.)
2. **What is the primary setting** of your story? (e.g., Oregon coastal rivers, genre tone, time period, etc.)
3. **What is the overall tone or aesthetic** of your world? (e.g., Gritty & Dark, Mysterious & Surreal, Post-Apocalyptic, etc.)
4. **What level of world-building complexity** does your story require? (e.g., Entirely new universe, alternate Earth, enclosed setting, etc.)
5. **What major environmental or cultural elements** exist in your world? (e.g., tribal myths, natural barriers, isolation, weather patterns)
6. **Are there any special rules or limitations** in your world? (e.g., no cell service, difficult terrain, strange river behavior)
7. **Is there any unique terminology or jargon** I should know to maintain consistency during writing? (e.g., specific fishing gear, Native names, spiritual terms, etc.)

Once you fill out those details, we can use them to shape vivid scenes, descriptions, and visual imagery throughout the book.

You said:
1. The story takes place on many rivers and small towns along the Washington and Oregon coasts. There should be very remote location deep in the woods where there is hardly any civilizations for many miles. 2. Oregon and Washington coastal rivers and their headwaters in the coastal range mountains. 3. The overall tone is gritty, dark, & mysterious. It is often very wet, rainy, and gray. 4. This should follow the reality of the remoteness and environment of the Pacific Northwest coast as it was a century ago. 5. There are tribal myths, isolation, and adverse weather. 6. There is often difficult terrain, no cell service, and strong river currents that play a part in the story. 7. The steelhead fish are often referred to as metalheads or steelies

ChatGPT said:
Perfect — you've provided a vivid, grounded, and thematically rich world for *Steelhead Graveyard.* Here's your finalized **World Building Profile**:

🌲 **World Building Profile: *Steelhead Graveyard***
Primary Setting:

- The story unfolds along various **coastal rivers of Oregon and Washington**, including their remote headwaters in the **Coastal Range Mountains**.
- These areas are isolated, densely forested, and often **miles from the nearest civilization**. Deep wilderness surrounds each scene.

Tone & Atmosphere:

- **Gritty, dark, and mysterious**
- Frequent rain, heavy gray skies, mist over rivers, and the constant drum of distant water
- The wilderness feels alive — not friendly, but watchful and ancient

Geographic & Environmental Scope:

- Multiple rivers and towns serve as narrative waypoints
- Includes off-the-map trails, hidden campsites, and uncharted fishing holes only known to locals or obsessive anglers

Complexity Level:

- Rooted in **real-world Pacific Northwest wilderness**, but infused with ancestral myths and ghostly lore that give it an otherworldly weight
- No magic or fantasy systems, but **legendary forces feel present**, lurking in shadow and silence

Key Cultural & Natural Elements:

- **Native American tribal myths** (specifically Tillamook and Nehalem traditions)
- Dangerous river conditions (fast currents, sharp rocks, flash floods)
- Long, damp winters; frequent fog; sudden storms
- The river is treated as a spiritual entity — a place of offerings, loss, and whispers

Rules & Limitations:

- **No cell service** in remote areas
- Terrain becomes more dangerous the deeper one ventures: cliffs, slick mossy rocks, fallen trees, icy rapids
- Weather changes rapidly, complicating escape or rescue

Terminology & Vernacular:

- **Steelhead = "metalheads" or "steelies"** (used colloquially by characters)
- Fishing gear references include: drift rods, fluorocarbon leaders, plugs, and egg cures
- Spiritual references include terms like "river spirits," "soul-fish," or "the elders"

Would you like a **visual concept image** of this world to inspire your writing or class? Or shall we continue on to 🟦 **Step 19: Voice & Tone** to define how the book should sound on the page?

You said:
Yes, let's create a visual concept image that represents this world.

ChatGPT said:
Image created

VOICE & TONE

WHAT OUR VOICE & TONE WILL BE

You said:
Great job. Now let's move onto the Voice and Tone that we will be writing in. Help me to create this Voice and Tone by asking me qualifying questions.

ChatGPT said:
Perfect — welcome to 🟦 **Step 19: Voice & Tone**
Your voice and tone define how the story *feels* to the reader. They shape everything from your sentence rhythm to emotional depth and narrative personality. Let's dial this in step-by-step.

✍️ **1 — Natural Voice Discovery**
Please write a short paragraph (4–6 sentences) describing a personal memory or favorite place using your natural words — just as if you were telling it to a friend.
Don't overthink it — write like you talk.
After that, I'll analyze your natural writing style and we'll move on to the next step.

You said:
Once, as a boy about 11 years old, my father, brother, and I went on a fishing trip in the Cascades of Washington. Being the adventurous man my father was, he decided to take a shortcut back home. This shortcut meant traveling along an old logging road that skirted the edge of a mountain. What we didn't know is that the road was cut into the side of the mountain and on one side of the road it was about a 2,000 foot drop to the rocky bottom, and the road was barely wide enough for the tires of our jeep to fit on. As we crept along the road at barely 1 mile per hour, my younger brother began to cray saying "I'm too young to die!"

ChatGPT said:
Thank you — that was a vivid, heartfelt story, and it gives me a strong sense of your natural writing voice. Here's a quick **analysis of your voice style** based on your sample:

🧠 **Voice & Style Analysis**

- **Tone Detected:** Conversational, reflective, with an undercurrent of humor and tension
- **Sentence Style:** Natural, narrative-driven, includes spoken quotes that add warmth and realism
- **Emotion/Sensory Use:** You lean into story-feel — evoking setting and emotion (e.g. "2,000 foot drop," "my younger brother began to cry") rather than poetic descriptions
- **Unique Traits:**
    - Blends adventure with levity

  - Uses casual storytelling structure
  - Feels authentic and grounded in lived experience

📌 **Next Step: Target Voice Selection**

2. **Which of these general voice styles would you like your book to reflect?**
   Choose one or more — or describe your own:

- 🔹 Friendly & Encouraging
- 🔹 Bold & Confident
- 🔹 Humble & Wise
- 🔹 Raw & Emotional
- 🔹 Playful & Witty
- 🔹 **Something Else?** (Please describe)

What's the right emotional "personality" for your book's voice?

You said:
Humble & Wise

ChatGPT said:
Excellent — you've chosen **Humble & Wise** as your book's core voice.
This style will give your story a sense of quiet authority, grounded storytelling, and respect for nature and myth. It allows the narrative to feel experienced and observant without ever becoming boastful — perfect for a book like *Steelhead Graveyard*, which walks the line between realism and folklore.

🎭 **Next Step: Tone Selection**

3. **How should the tone of your book feel to the reader?**
   (Choose one or more, or describe your own)

- Inspirational
- Vulnerable
- Direct and no-nonsense
- Warm and Conversational
- Professional and Authoritative
- Gritty and Uneasy
- **Something Else?** (Please describe)

This is the emotional "vibe" the reader will pick up as they read.

You said:
Let's go with Gritty and Uneasy

ChatGPT said:

Perfect — selecting **Gritty and Uneasy** as your book's tone works beautifully with the wilderness setting, the folklore elements, and the slow psychological unraveling of your protagonist.
So far, your voice and tone combination is:

🎙 **Voice:** *Humble & Wise*
🌫 **Tone:** *Gritty and Uneasy*

📚 **Next: Public Voice Inspiration**

4. Are there any authors, speakers, or public voices you admire and would like to model after?
   Examples might include authors like Cormac McCarthy, William Kent Krueger, Craig Johnson, Stephen King, etc.

Tell me a name or two and what you like about their style.

You said:
Stephen King

ChatGPT said:
Excellent choice — **Stephen King** is a master of weaving tension, everyday realism, and creeping dread into character-driven stories. Here's what we'll draw from his style to influence *Steelhead Graveyard*:

🎯 **Stephen King–Inspired Traits to Incorporate:**

- **Grounded Realism:** Settings and dialogue feel lived-in, familiar — even when the story veers into the surreal
- **Creeping Suspense:** Tension builds gradually, often starting with subtle unease before escalating into psychological or supernatural threat
- **Internal Conflict:** Deep focus on character mindset and unraveling sanity
- **Folklore as Fear:** Uses legends or urban myths as emotional accelerants rather than just spooky backstory
- **Unflinching Grit:** Doesn't flinch from dark, disturbing imagery — but it's always earned, not gratuitous

---

✏️ **Next Step: Sentence Style Preference**

5. Which sentence style do you prefer for your writing?

- Long and flowing
- Short and punchy
- Poetic or lyrical
- Casual and natural
- A blend (describe your ideal mix)

This helps set rhythm and pacing in your chapters.

You said:
Long and flowing

ChatGPT said:
Perfect — choosing **long and flowing** sentence structure will give your story a reflective, immersive quality — echoing your "Humble & Wise" voice and aligning beautifully with the **Stephen King-style** buildup of unease.

✍️ **Current Voice & Tone Profile:**

- **Voice:** Humble & Wise
- **Tone:** Gritty and Uneasy
- **Influence:** Stephen King
- **Sentence Style:** Long and Flowing

✅ **Final Step: Confidence Check**

6. Now that we've built this profile, do you feel confident in this voice and tone for your book?

If yes, we'll apply this style consistently during writing.
If no, we can adjust anything before moving forward.

You said:
Yes

ChatGPT said:
Fantastic — your **Voice & Tone** settings are now locked in and will be used throughout the writing of *Steelhead Graveyard*.

📘 **Finalized Profile:**

- **Voice:** Humble & Wise
- **Tone:** Gritty and Uneasy
- **Influence:** Stephen King
- **Sentence Style:** Long and Flowing

CHAPTER 1: PROLOGUE – THE LAST CATCH

BEGINNING WITH THE PROLOGUE

You're now ready for 🟦 **Step: Chapter-By-Chapter Writing** — the part where we begin drafting your actual manuscript.
Would you like to begin with **Chapter 1: Prologue – The Last Catch**? If so, I'll guide you through the quick planning questions for that chapter before we start writing.

You said:
Yes, let's begin writing the Prologue for our book.

ChatGPT said:
Excellent — let's begin 🟦 **Chapter 1: Prologue — *The Last Catch***.
Before we write, I need just a few quick planning details to tailor this section perfectly:

✏️ **Prologue Planning**

1. **Chapter Summary:**
   What should happen in this prologue? (e.g., a past disappearance, a myth being told, someone seeing Kilchis, etc.)
2. **Chapter Objective:**
   What should this chapter *accomplish* for the reader? (e.g., introduce the myth, create unease, set tone, hint at danger)
3. **Emotional Tone:**
   What emotional vibe should this chapter carry most strongly? (e.g., haunting, ominous, surreal, tragic)
4. **Internal Dialogue:**
   Should we include any internal thoughts or reflections in this chapter? If so, whose?

Answer however you'd like — one at a time or all at once — and we'll begin writing *The Last Catch*.

You said:
1. This prologue should begin with the Myth being told and someone proclaiming to see Kilchis on a fishing trip to the Wilson River in Oregon. 2. This should accomplish setting the stage for the story to come and set the tone. 3. The vibe should be ominous and haunting 4. Yes, create internal dialogue and reflection in this chapter and throughout the entire book. This internal dialogue will be done exclusively with Bob Tomalin

ChatGPT said:
Perfect — I now have everything I need to craft a powerful and haunting prologue for *Steelhead Graveyard*.

We'll begin with a storyteller's voice — recounting the myth of Kilchis — and then seamlessly shift into the present, as Bob Tomalin hears this tale and begins to reflect on it during his own trip to the Wilson River.
The tone will be **ominous and haunting**, the pacing **long and flowing**, and internal thoughts from **Bob Tomalin** will thread through the narrative.

I'm now writing **Chapter 1: Prologue — *The Last Catch***
Please hold for a moment while I compose the first draft.
Steelhead Graveyard Prologue

Chapter 1: Prologue — *The Last Catch*

NOTE: As the writing of this book commences, instead of putting in each small part of what CoAuthorGPT / ChatGPT provides, I am going to insert the full-combined parts of each chapter at the end of each chapter-writing section and indicate where the part was created and placed into my notes.

The prologue is complete.

It opens with a chilling fireside retelling of the **Kilchis myth**, then transitions into **Bob Tomalin's perspective** — introducing his internal voice and planting the first seeds of unease. The final line subtly echoes your subtitle, setting a haunting tone for the chapters ahead.
Would you like to revise or expand this prologue, or are you ready to begin Chapter 2: *Welcome to Rogue Country*?

You said:
Let's expand this prologue and make it longer.

ChatGPT said:
Edited
The prologue has been expanded with new scenes and internal reflections — including a quiet moment after the campfire where Bob wrestles with unease and memories of his children. The atmosphere is now richer, longer, and even more haunting.

Would you like to review or revise this further, or are you ready to begin **Chapter 2: *Welcome to Rogue Country*?**

You said:
As we write this story make sure not to use any swear words. Find good substitutes for any type of swearing that will keep the integrity of the story. This will help make this story one that can be read by adults and youth alike. Now, let's begin writing Chapter 2: Welcome to Rogue Country

ChatGPT said:
Understood — we'll avoid all swear words and instead use smart, tone-consistent substitutes that preserve the emotional impact while keeping the story appropriate for both adults and younger readers.

(HERE IS THE PROLOGUE)

They say he still walks the river… silent as fog, hungry as the current."

The old man's voice cracked like brittle driftwood as he leaned over the edge of the campfire. Smoke curled around his face, casting shadows on his lined cheeks. The other fishermen sat frozen, heads half-tilted, drinks forgotten in their hands. Even the night seemed to hush — only the river behind them continued its whisper.

"Kilchis," the man said, low and slow. "Not a ghost. Not a man. A thing in between."

No one laughed.

They'd heard the name before.

A hundred years ago — or maybe a hundred and fifty — Kilchis was a Tillamook tribesman who went mad after a brutal winter run of steelhead left the spawning beds empty and the tribe starving. His mind cracked like ice. He said the river spirits had been wronged. That the souls of the fish had been stolen by greedy hands. So he started taking them back — not the fish, but the fishermen. One soul for every steelhead taken without honor. One death for every dead-eyed catch mounted above a fireplace.

He wasn't caught. He wasn't buried. He just… disappeared into the woods. They say the river took him. And that sometimes, it gives him back.

Bob Tomalin leaned against the tailgate of his pickup, half-listening, half-lost in the sloshing rhythm of the Wilson River. The firelight flickered across his face, but he felt cold.

Just campfire crap, he told himself. *A ghost story passed around like a bottle.*

And yet…

He'd fished this river a dozen times. Hell, he'd caught his first chrome-bright steelie just a half mile upstream from here. But something about tonight — about the way the fog clung to the trees, the way the fire didn't seem to warm the bones — made his skin itch.

A sudden rustle from the treeline behind them.

Everyone froze. Even the old man stopped mid-sentence.

Bob turned slowly, eyes scanning the darkness just beyond the fire's edge. His pulse thumped in his ears. Probably a raccoon. Maybe a deer.

But for a second — just a blink — he saw something. A shape.

Tall. Still. Watching.

Then it was gone.

He swallowed hard and shook his head.

Get a grip, Tomalin.

But somewhere deep inside, buried beneath reason and the thousand casts of memory, something stirred.

And it whispered:

Some rivers should be left alone.

Later that night, long after the others had climbed into tents or trucks to sleep off their beers, Bob sat alone by the dying embers. The woods were quiet, but not empty. The kind of quiet that had weight to it.

He watched the steam rise off the river. It curled and twisted in shapes that almost made sense — a hand, a face, a figure in mid-step — and then vanished. He knew his mind was tired, but fatigue wasn't the same thing as imagination. Not out here. Not in this place.

His thoughts drifted to Shane and Sarah. He could almost hear Shane asking him about the legend, eyes wide with curiosity.

"Would you go fishing there, Dad, if that Kilchis guy was real?"

Bob had smiled and said he'd fish anywhere. Any river. Any conditions. He'd meant it.

But now, something inside him felt off. Like the current of the night had shifted — like he'd stepped into someone else's story. Or maybe someone else's trap.

The fire popped once and went dark. The shadows pressed in closer.

He climbed into his truck and locked the doors. But as he drifted toward sleep, he could still hear the whisper.

Not in his ears — in his bones.

Some rivers should be left alone.

CHAPTER 2: WELCOME TO ROGUE COUNTRY

Now, let's begin 🟦 **Chapter 2:** ***Welcome to Rogue Country***.
Before we draft, I'll gather quick planning details to make sure we write with precision and voice:

✏️ **Chapter Planning**

1. **Chapter Summary:**
What major event(s) should take place in this chapter? (e.g., Bob begins his trip to a new river, drives through coastal towns, meets someone, recalls something specific, etc.)
2. **Chapter Objective:**
What should this chapter accomplish for the story or reader? (e.g., introduce setting, reinforce Bob's obsession, show contrast between civilization and wilderness)
3. **Emotional Tone:**
Should this chapter feel eager, eerie, adventurous, foreboding, nostalgic, etc.?
4. **Internal Dialogue:**
Should we include any specific thoughts Bob is having at this stage of the journey?

Once you give me those, I'll start crafting the first section of Chapter 2.

You said:
1. Bob begins his trip to a new river and meets Sheriff Tallbear in a small store along the roadside. 2. This chapter should introduce the setting and reinforce Bob's obsession. It should also show contrast between civilization and wilderness. 3. It should feel adventurous and eager. 4. Bob's internal dialogue should be optimistic at this point. He is excited to have a new experience that he can write an article about. Fome now on, make the chapters you write long-form chapters with 3,000 or more words in them if possible.

ChatGPT said:
Perfect — I've got your full intent for Chapter 2:

- Bob is **excited and optimistic,**
- We introduce **Sheriff Tallbear** and hint at deeper lore,
- And we emphasize the **contrast between the everyday world and the wilderness beyond**.

We'll write this in **long-form (3,000+ words)** and stay consistent with your tone: **adventurous and eager, humble yet rich in voice**, and **free of profanity**.
Please hold for a few moments while I write the first major section of **Chapter 2:** ***Welcome to Rogue Country***.

The opening section of **Chapter 2: *Welcome to Rogue Country*** is complete. It introduces Bob's eager mindset, the transition from civilization to deep wilderness, and a rich, character-driven moment with Sheriff Tallbear — whose calm warning quietly shifts the atmosphere. Would you like me to continue writing the next section of this chapter now, or pause here for your input?

You said:
Yes, continue writing the next segment now

(Part 1 updated)

ChatGPT said:
Great — we're now deep into the storytelling phase. Let's proceed with **Chapter 2: Welcome to Rogue Country – Part Two** of *Steelhead Graveyard.*

Would you like me to continue with the next portion of this chapter now? This will continue building toward the 3,000-word target while increasing tension, deepening character insight, and further setting the stage for the mysterious events to come.
2/2

You said:
Yes, continue writing the next segment now.

(Part 2 updated)

ChatGPT said:
Excellent — here is the next segment of **Chapter 2: *Welcome to Rogue Country*.**

Let me know if you'd like the next section to focus on Bob setting up camp, exploring the river, or encountering his first sign of something… off. We'll continue this long-form style to build suspense and deepen the atmosphere.

You said:
Let's continue with Bob setting up camp and getting his first, very slight sense that something is off, but shrugs it off as nothing.

ChatGPT said:
Perfect — let's take Bob deeper into his experience, setting up camp and brushing against that first whisper of wrongness. The tension will remain subtle and psychological — just a light disturbance under the surface.

Would you like the next section to follow Bob's first evening by the river — his first cast, his thoughts about his family, or the first true moment of unease as night begins to fall?

You said:
Let's continue with Bob's first cast. I want him to hook into a chrome bright hard-fighting steelhead that get's him super excited. He estimates that it is about 15 lbs, a very good size steelhead and something that we would have loved to get a picture of but at the last moment, the steelhead spits the hook and swims off, jumping into the air and splashing back into the water as if it was mocking Bob.

ChatGPT said:
Perfect — this is the ideal moment to showcase Bob's passion and skill, give him a surge of elation, and then deliver a quick emotional gut-punch that foreshadows the unpredictability of the river… and what's to come.
Here's the continuation of **Chapter 2: *Welcome to Rogue Country*.**

Would you like to continue next with Bob's campfire reflections and his first night alone in Rogue Country — or shift focus to a strange nighttime event that hints Kilchis may already be near?

You said:
Let's shift the focus to a strange nightmare event that hints Kilchis may already be near.

ChatGPT said:
Excellent — we'll now shift into the **first nightmare sequence**, where Bob's subconscious begins unraveling under the influence of isolation, legend, and Kilchis' looming presence.
This will be the first true **psychological fracture** — just a hint of what's to come, blending memory, myth, and wilderness into something surreal but emotionally grounded.

Would you like to continue Chapter 2 into the next morning — where Bob brushes off the dream and sets out to fish again — or take another detour into something else mysterious or symbolic?

You said:
Let's continue writing Chapter 2 into the next morning where Bob brushes off the dream and sets out to fish again

(Part updated)

ChatGPT said:
Perfect — we'll bring **Chapter 2** into morning light. Bob will push the nightmare aside, reassert control, and focus back on his mission — fishing. The tone will be *slightly uneasy*, but outwardly steady and determined.
Let's continue:

Would you like to close Chapter 2 here with Bob settling in again for the evening, or add one more development — like a mysterious object appearing at camp, or another subtle encounter?

You said:
Let's close out this chapter with Sheriff Tallbear driving up to his campsite. The Sheriff talks about how he is there to just check up on him. Bob finds it strange and gets an ominous feeling of a hidden warning from Sheriff Tallbear. Bob spends another day fishing the same stretch of river and hooks into several more exceptional steelhead, but each one of them spits the hook just before he can land them. This was unheard of as Bob has excellent fish-fighting skills and rarely loses a fish. He had only committed to 2 days exploring this area and needed to get back home the next day to submit a previous article he had written in time to get it published in the upcoming edition of the magazine he writes for. Bob is determined to come back to the area to get redemption on the fish as he has never been skunked (a term used when a fisherman does not successfully land a fish on a fishing outing) before like this.

ChatGPT said:
Excellent — we'll wrap up Chapter 2 with a powerful closing:

- **Sheriff Tallbear's unexpected visit**,
- **Bob's string of fish losses** (which feel unnatural),
- And **his decision to return**, setting the hook for the next chapter.

Here's the **final segment of Chapter 2:** ***Welcome to Rogue Country***.

(Part updated)

Bob Tomalin loved mornings like this.

The kind that started with frost on the windshield, the truck engine humming against the cold, and a thermos of black coffee steaming in the cup holder. He rolled down the driver's side window halfway and let the crisp Oregon air fill the cab — pine needles, rain-soaked soil, and the faintest trace of river mist. It was a scent no cologne could ever bottle. Wild. Real.

His GPS was useless now — grayed-out map, blinking dot — but Bob didn't care. He wasn't following directions. He was following instinct.

"This one's going to be special," he muttered, taking another sip.

The road wound through narrow corridors of towering evergreens. They leaned in from both sides like nature's guardians, crowding out the morning light and shadowing the two-lane highway. Somewhere beyond those trees lay the river he'd heard whispers about. A stretch of water that didn't show up in fishing apps, blogs, or social media. The kind of river only a handful of old-timers still talked about — quietly, reverently.

That was exactly the kind of river Bob lived for.

New water, he thought. *Fresh stories.*

He'd already begun mentally outlining the article he'd write if the trip went well. Something like: "Beyond the Usual Drift: Discovering Oregon's Hidden Steelhead Secrets." Maybe with a byline photo of him beside a twenty-pound chrome-bright buck.

Not that it was about ego.

Okay, maybe a little.

But it was more than that — it was about legacy. Leaving behind stories that mattered, places that hadn't been ruined by crowds and tech and noise. Rivers where the only soundtrack was rushing water and the occasional crack of a branch under a boot.

The sign appeared around a bend in the road: **ROGUE COUNTRY GENERAL — Next Left**.

He downshifted, turned off the highway, and rolled into a gravel lot with just one other vehicle parked outside — an old green-and-white patrol truck with the Tillamook County Sheriff's logo faded on the door.

Inside the store, it smelled like cedar chips and pipe tobacco. A bell above the door gave a friendly chime.

Shelves of canned goods, local maps, and steelhead tackle filled the aisles. Behind the counter stood a thick-shouldered man in his late 50s, wearing a weathered brown coat and a bolo tie shaped like a feathered arrowhead.

"Morning," the man said, eyes steady. "You must be new."

Bob smiled. "That obvious?"

"Only people who stop here are locals... or the ones looking to become one."

Bob extended a hand. "Name's Bob Tomalin. Just doing a bit of exploring. Heard there were some untapped runs out this way."

The man nodded slowly, then took the hand. "Sheriff Roy Tallbear."

Bob blinked. "Sheriff? Thought you were the store owner."

"I help out when I'm not chasing elk poachers and meth labs," Tallbear said dryly. "This place's been in my family for three generations."

Bob chuckled. "Well, it's got a vibe. Like it belongs here."

Tallbear studied him for a moment, then leaned back against the counter. "So. What river you thinkin' about?"

Bob hesitated. "Not sure yet. Just… going where the truck takes me."

Tallbear's expression didn't change, but something shifted behind his eyes. A flicker of thought. A calculation.

"Well," he said at last, "just be mindful where your wheels take you. These woods aren't like the ones closer to town. Out here, there's more history than trail signs. Some of it best left where it sleeps."

Bob smiled politely, not quite sure how to respond.

"I'll keep that in mind."

Tallbear said nothing more. Just nodded once and turned away.

Bob grabbed a pack of jerky, a topographic map, and a tin of coffee grounds. Paid in cash.

As he stepped outside, the wind picked up. It smelled colder now. He glanced at the tree line across the road. The forest stood silent — waiting.

He slid behind the wheel of his truck, adjusted the map on the dash, and turned the key.

The engine started. The road waited. And somewhere ahead, the river whispered.

The gravel crunched under Bob's tires as he pulled out of the Rogue Country General lot, map open on the passenger seat, but ignored. His pulse still drummed a little harder than usual after that exchange with Sheriff Tallbear. Something in the man's tone… not threatening, not quite welcoming either — more like a warning from someone who'd seen things and stopped trying to explain them.

Bob had interviewed countless wilderness guides, scientists, and even a few tinfoil-hat conspiracy theorists for his articles, but Tallbear? He didn't seem like a man prone to exaggeration. No, that steady gaze and clipped speech hinted at something else — a weight carried long enough that words no longer did it justice.

Maybe he's just trying to keep tourists out of his sacred honey holes, Bob mused, trying to shake off the chill that hadn't come from the wind.

As the road narrowed, asphalt gave way to dirt. The ruts deepened, and the trees grew bolder, crowding closer to the truck until their branches brushed like fingertips against the side mirror. It was like driving into the mouth of a beast, but Bob didn't mind. In fact, he relished it.

He loved this moment — when the world of strip malls, social feeds, and gas station coffee disappeared behind him like a forgotten dream. Out here, the only currency that mattered was patience. The river would not yield its secrets quickly or kindly.

He was deep in Rogue Country now. The farther Bob drove, the more time seemed to stretch. His phone had given up half an hour ago — no bars, no signal, just the occasional "SOS only" blinking like a lazy lighthouse. He welcomed the silence.

With no podcasts, no texts, and no news headlines, the only voices left were the ones in his own head — and that suited him just fine.

Most guys wouldn't come this far alone, he thought, as he swerved to avoid a fallen branch. Most guys don't even know what they're missing.

The map on the dash was old-school — the kind of thing you unfolded six feet wide and never could quite re-fold the same way. He'd marked a few remote feeder streams weeks ago while researching some old steelhead migration reports from the 1960s. One of them fed into the upper Rogue system — unnamed, barely charted, and, according to a retired biologist he'd emailed twice, "about as off-grid as it gets."

Exactly the kind of water that stirred his blood.

He turned left onto a barely visible forest road — no number, no sign. Just two deep wheel ruts disappearing into pine-shadowed undergrowth. His truck groaned in protest as it started up the incline, tires clawing at loose rock and moss.

Branches scraped against the side like nails on canvas. Ferns brushed the undercarriage. He slowed, letting the forest dictate his pace.

After twenty more minutes of careful climbing, the trees parted just enough to reveal a pullout — flat ground, river access below, and best of all, no boot prints in the mud.

Bob parked, killed the engine, and opened the door.

The air hit him like a baptism.

Cold, clean, and filled with the unmistakable scent of steelhead country — part fish, part forest, and part something older, harder to name. He stepped to the edge of a low bluff and looked down.

The river glided below in hushed shades of green and silver, slipping between boulders and submerged logs like it had somewhere important to be. It wasn't wide, maybe forty feet bank to bank, but it moved — smooth and swift and ancient.

He grinned. "Now this... is a river."
Bob pulled a canvas duffel from the backseat and tossed it beside a mossy stump that would make a fine spot to sit and rig gear later. He'd done this routine a hundred times, maybe more — tent up first, dry ground beneath, wind at his back if he could help it. A bear canister stashed in the brush, a small fire ring of smooth river stones, and a folding camp chair angled just right to face the water.

Within half an hour, the bones of camp were set. He moved with confidence, muscle memory guiding his hands as he laid out rods and reels, unpacked waterproof bags, and spread a map across the stump. But he paused a moment when the wind shifted.

A faint rustle in the trees behind him. Not just a flutter, but something directional — like movement.

Bob turned slowly.

Nothing.

No birds taking flight. No visible animal. Just the sway of underbrush and the thick vertical silence of the woods.

He scanned for elk, maybe a blacktail deer. This was their turf, after all. But there was no crack of a hoof, no crunch of twigs — just that eerie sense that something had been watching… and decided to leave before being seen.

He let out a low breath and laughed under it.

You're tired. That's all. Been driving since before sunrise, half a thermos of coffee sloshing around in your gut. It's the trees messing with your depth perception.

Still, he turned a bit quicker than usual on his way back to the tent and zipped the door behind him like it might keep something out — even though he didn't really believe there was anything to keep out.

By late afternoon, he was rigged and ready. A drift rod with a soft bead rig and a pink yarnie on a barbless hook — perfect for low-clear water this time of year. His eyes scanned the riffle at the head of a pool below camp, noting the subtle seams in the current, the submerged ledge he'd fish from just before dusk.

"First cast," he said aloud, smiling. "And the only witness is a fir tree."

Then, almost as an afterthought, he looked back once more toward the tree line. Still nothing. But somewhere deep in the hush of the woods behind him, a raven croaked once — sharp and short. Not unusual.

But the echo that followed? It sounded like something repeating the call — not mimicking it, but answering. He frowned, cocked his head, and waited.

Silence. Then wind. And the river kept on flowing.

The last light of day hung low over the river, filtering through the branches in ribbons of gold and ash-blue. Bob stood ankle-deep in the gravel shallows, rod in hand, heart already racing.

This was it — the first cast.

He flicked his wrist and sent the bead and yarnie arcing across the current. It hit the water with barely a splash and began its slow drift, sliding naturally along the seam just beyond a sunken log. He could feel every pebble bump through the graphite rod, each shift in water tension telling a story.

Halfway through the drift, something changed. The line paused. Then it tugged. Then it slammed.

Bob instinctively set the hook, the rod bending in a clean arc as the water erupted twenty feet downstream in a silver explosion.

"Yes!" he barked, adrenaline flooding his system.

The fish bolted for the far bank, line screaming off the reel in high-pitched defiance. Bob adjusted his stance, leaning into the fight, coaxing it upstream with just the right amount of pressure. His hands moved with surgical precision, reeling, lifting, giving line when needed.

It was a chrome-bright steelhead — easily fifteen pounds. The kind of fish you remembered for years. Long, thick across the shoulders, with a tail like a shovel and a defiance that made your blood boil with joy.

"Come on, you beauty..." he whispered, grinning through clenched teeth.

The steelhead turned again, porpoising into the current, tailwalking like it knew the show was half the prize. Bob maneuvered it closer, his heart thundering as it thrashed just feet from the bank.

He reached for his net. And in that instant — the instant when it was almost his — the line went slack.

Pop. Gone. Bob froze.

The surface erupted once more as the steelhead breached high into the air and crashed back with a tremendous splash, throwing water like a final insult.

He stood in silence, rod limp, the wet line swinging loosely in the wind. And for a second… it felt like the fish had mocked him. A deep, almost human beat it, rookie kind of flip of the tail.

Bob exhaled hard and laughed, a little breathless, the kind of laugh you let out when you're stunned, grateful, and furious all at once.

"You win this round," he said to the water.

But even as he reeled in and clipped the hook, a sliver of discomfort crept in.

The river had given him something — and then taken it away with flair. Not random. Not natural. Personal.

He shook his head.

Get a grip. It's just a fish.

Still, as he trudged back up the slope to his camp, he could feel the fish's eyes on him — or maybe something else's.

Watching. Waiting.

That night, the fire crackled low, casting amber glows across Bob's boots as he sat hunched in his camp chair, head resting against the collar of his jacket. The stars above peeked through the dense canopy in fractured constellations, as if the sky itself was hiding behind the forest.

He stared into the flames, thoughts drifting — Shane's last drawing on the fridge, Sarah's laugh as she'd hugged his leg that morning, and Tanya's voice: "Just be safe, okay? You know how you get when you're chasing ghosts."

He smiled softly, eyes heavy. Then sleep took him.

At first, it was peaceful. He was back on the Wilson, walking beside his father along a shallow side channel, the gravel soft underfoot. The sky was pink with morning light. Birds trilled. The water ran cold and clear.

Then the trees thickened. The path narrowed. His father was ahead of him, but somehow older now — frailer. He reached out to call to him, but his voice didn't work.

When his father turned, it wasn't his face. It was someone else. Painted skin. Long black hair. Hollow eyes.

Kilchis.

Bob tried to stop, but the trail shifted underfoot like wet leaves on glass. He stumbled backward and fell — not onto earth, but into water. Icy, black, and impossibly deep.

He kicked, clawed upward, lungs burning — and broke the surface only to find himself not on the river, but in the middle of a dim forest clearing.

And standing across from him was the man again. Kilchis. Bare-chested, arms streaked with charcoal. Eyes like smoke. In his left hand: a bloody steelhead. In his right: Bob's drift rod.

Kilchis raised the fish slowly, then pressed its gaping mouth to his own — and exhaled.

The steelhead blinked. And screamed. A horrible, high-pitched wail — the sound of a dying thing filled with a soul that didn't belong. Then it stopped.

Kilchis turned and walked into the woods. Bob couldn't move. Couldn't breathe. Then— He woke up gasping, soaked in sweat, heart pounding against his ribs like a drum in a war dance.

The fire was dead. The air was cold. His breath fogged in front of him. And just beyond the ring of camp light, the wind shifted the brush.

A shape. Then gone.

He wiped his face, hands trembling. "Just a dream," he muttered. "Just a dream." But he couldn't shake the image of Kilchis — not the horror of it, but the familiarity. As if, somehow, he hadn't dreamed it. As if he'd remembered it.

The sun came up gray. Not with fanfare or warmth, but as a soft light that seeped through the trees like breath through a wool blanket. Bob sat at the edge of camp, steam curling from a dented tin mug of coffee, trying to steady his mind as he watched the mist unravel over the river.

The nightmare lingered in pieces — not quite memories, not quite ghosts. Just images. Sensations. Smoke in the bloodstream.

He took another slow sip and muttered aloud, "You spend enough nights alone in the woods, you're bound to dream something strange."

He repeated it, like a mantra, like a broom sweeping a hallway clean.

Still, something about the way Kilchis had looked at him in the dream — that wasn't just a face made up by the brain. It felt known.

Bob stood and shook out his shoulders. No more spooking himself. Today was a fishing day. He wasn't here to chase spirits or listen to whispers. He was here to catch steelhead. Write a story. Build a name.

The river called, and he answered.

By midmorning, he was back in the flow, casting with rhythm, reading water, watching for subtle shifts in current and light. The river had changed slightly overnight — the level a hair higher, the color a shade cloudier. He adjusted his presentation accordingly, swapping the pink yarnie for a small black bead, more natural in low light.

He worked pool after pool, letting the quiet consume him.

This is where I belong, he thought. Not in front of a laptop. Not in a meeting. Here. Knee-deep in water that hasn't heard a radio in fifty years.

By noon, he'd landed a smaller hen — about eight pounds. Bright, clean, and beautiful. He took a moment to admire her in the shallows before releasing her gently back into the current.

"There you go," he whispered. "Tell your big cousin I'm here."

The mood lifted. Even the air felt lighter. The woods had sound again — birdsong, a woodpecker tapping in the distance, the sigh of the river.

Maybe that dream had just been his mind shedding stress. Maybe Sheriff Tallbear's warning had gotten under his skin more than he'd realized. Either way, he felt better. Calmer.

And yet, just before breaking down his rod for lunch, something caught his eye.

High on the riverbank — above the trail he'd followed in — a single boot print in the mud. Deep. Fresh. But… it wasn't his.

He hadn't been on that side of the trail since yesterday. He stared at it for a long time. Then shook his head, turned back to camp, and told himself — again — just the woods playing tricks. But this time, he didn't quite believe it.

He'd just finished packing up his lunch kit when he heard tires crunching slowly on the forest road.

That was odd.

No one came out this far. He'd passed two locked gates, both of which he'd gotten through with permission from a friend in forestry. No footprints. No tire tracks. This was wilderness — his kind of wilderness.

The patrol truck eased into the clearing, dust swirling up behind it. Same green-and-white paint. Same faded Tillamook County badge. And there, behind the wheel, was the familiar stone face of Sheriff Tallbear.

Bob stood and waved as the truck came to a stop. The engine idled low before the Sheriff shut it off and stepped out.

"Morning," Tallbear said. "Just doing a check-in."

Bob squinted. "A check-in? That standard procedure around here?"

Tallbear's expression didn't shift. "Not always. But it's good to know who's out here, especially when they're alone."

The words were simple. The tone behind them wasn't.

Bob smiled, trying to lighten the mood. "You expecting trouble? I thought I was the only thing on two legs out here."

"You're the only one," Tallbear said after a pause. "Doesn't mean you're alone."

Bob blinked. "That's… poetic."

Tallbear didn't smile. Just walked a slow circle near the fire pit, boots quiet on the damp earth.

"You sleep okay last night?" he asked.

Bob hesitated. "Yeah. Fine."

Tallbear nodded slowly, as if Bob had answered a different question.

"Well," the sheriff said, climbing back into the truck, "enjoy your second day. Weather's shifting. Might not stay this mild."

And then, with a low rumble, he was gone.

Bob stood there long after the tail lights vanished between the trees.

The rest of the day passed under heavy sky and rising wind. Bob fished hard — focused. Every cast placed with precision. Every drift dialed in. And the fish responded. Sort of.

He hooked five steelhead over the course of the afternoon. Big ones. Angry chrome, full of fight. The kind of fish that made reputations. But one by one, they slipped the hook.

Each time, just as he reached for the net… they turned, twisted, and vanished. Clean breaks. No line snap. No hook bends. Just… gone.

By late afternoon, Bob was standing knee-deep in the run, breathing hard, soaked to the chest, rod trembling in his hand.

"This is nuts," he muttered. "What is happening?"

He wasn't new to this. He'd fought hundreds of fish, landed all but the worst of them. He prided himself on it. But now? It felt like the river had turned on him. Or something in it.

Back at camp, as he packed up, he replayed the fights in his mind. Over and over.

He'd only committed to two days out here — enough to explore, get a feel, maybe catch a story. But now…
He couldn't leave like this. Not skunked. Not with nothing to show. It felt like a personal insult — not just from the fish, but from the river itself.

Still, he had a deadline. An article to turn in. His editor was waiting.

He zipped the duffel and strapped it into the bed of the truck.

"I'll be back," he muttered to the woods.

The breeze stirred the branches overhead. And if Bob had stood still a second longer, he might've heard it:

A whisper — not quite wind, not quite voice.

Yes. Come back.

End of Chapter 2
Would you like to begin **Chapter 3: The Return** next? Or pause here to review/adjust anything?

You said:
I am going to continue our writing of the book Steelhead Graveyard in the new Project Folder "Book: Steelhead Graveyard." Should I copy our conversation brom the beginning to now over to that Project Folder or will you be able to remember everything from this chat named "Steelhead Book Onboarding?"

ChatGPT said:
Great question!
Yes, I recommend copying over the **key elements** from this conversation to your new Project Folder **"Book: Steelhead Graveyard"** — especially:

- Character profiles (Bob, Kilchis, Sheriff Tallbear, Big Crow, etc.)
- Voice & Tone profile (Humble & Wise, Gritty and Uneasy, long and flowing, Stephen King-inspired)
- Chapter titles and outlines
- The completed **Prologue** and **Chapter 2** (and all planning notes for each)
- The subtitle and the book's promise
- Any world-building, theme, or mythological lore we've established

Even though I *can* recall the context from this session for now, once you shift to the new Project Folder, that thread becomes your new base of memory. Copying ensures everything important moves with you.
Would you like me to help summarize everything to make it easy to copy over?

You said:
Yes, summarize everything I will need to keep the integrity of this story, including all the key elements, so that I can copy that information to my new Project folder.

ChatGPT said:
Absolutely — here's a full summary of all **essential story-building elements** from this session. You can copy this directly into your new Project Folder **"Book: Steelhead Graveyard"** to preserve creative continuity and ensure smooth progression.

✅ **Steelhead Graveyard – Story Summary & Creative Foundation**

📘 **Book Title & Subtitle**

- **Title:** *Steelhead Graveyard*
- **Subtitle:** *Some Rivers Should Be Left Alone*

🎯 **Book Objective**

To entertain readers — especially the millions of fishermen who enjoy a good fishing tale — with a gripping wilderness mystery rooted in myth, suspense, and the Pacific Northwest's rugged spirit.

🧭 Voice & Tone

- **Voice:** Humble & Wise
- **Tone:** Gritty and Uneasy
- **Style:** Long and flowing sentences
- **Influence:** Stephen King (emphasis on grounded realism, psychological unraveling, and folklore-as-fear)
- **Content Rating:** Clean — no swearing or profanity. Use clever substitutes.

👤 Target Audience

- Adult and young adult fiction readers
- Fans of outdoor adventure, psychological thrillers, and wilderness survival
- Anglers and outdoor enthusiasts, especially those interested in Pacific Northwest rivers and myths
- Readers who enjoy suspense with folklore and character-driven drama

---

🖊 Genre Tags

- Fiction
- Mystery
- Thriller
- Psychological Suspense
- Outdoor Adventure

🌲 World-Building

- **Setting:** Remote rivers and small towns along Oregon and Washington's coastal mountain ranges
- **Environment:** Gritty, dark, wet, foggy — grounded in real topography and tribal histories
- **Challenges:** Steep terrain, unpredictable weather, no cell service, fast-moving rivers
- **Symbolism:** The wilderness is a character — ancient, indifferent, and possibly sentient
- **Folklore:** Myth of *Kilchis*, a Tillamook tribesman possessed by an evil spirit who once stalked steelhead fishermen and may now haunt the rivers again

---

🧠 Key Themes

- Obsession vs. wisdom

- Isolation and unraveling sanity
- Nature as mystery and myth
- Legacy, pride, and vulnerability
- The danger of ignoring ancient warnings

🧝 Main Characters

1. Bob Tomalin (Protagonist)

- 44-year-old outdoorsman, family man, fishing journalist from Portland, OR
- Wants to be remembered as the greatest steelhead fisherman alive
- Flaw: Takes extreme risks for glory
- Starts confident → becomes mentally unravelled → ultimately lost
- Internal voice: Present throughout the story

2. Kilchis (Legendary Antagonist)

- Possessed Tillamook Native American from 150+ years ago
- Believed to kill fishermen to restore the souls of fish
- Appears in dreams, hallucinations, and symbolic moments
- Ambiguous existence — real or not?

3. Sheriff Roy Tallbear

- Local sheriff who knows the folklore and warns Bob early
- Appears throughout, usually as a quiet voice of experience
- Not hostile — but clearly knows more than he says

4. Tanys Tomalin, Shane (9), and Sarah (5)

- Bob's wife and kids
- Represent his grounding force and what's truly at stake
- Appears in memories, dreams, and motivations

5. Big Crow

- Spirit of a good Tillamook man
- Offers subtle guidance and warnings
- Grieved when Bob ignores him
- Represents the "old wisdom" of the land and people

🪵 Chapters So Far

✅ **Prologue: *The Last Catch***

- Campfire retelling of Kilchis myth
- Bob sees a shadowy figure near the river
- First internal sense of unease begins

✅ **Chapter 2: *Welcome to Rogue Country***

- Bob arrives in remote Rogue Country to explore new steelhead water

- Meets Sheriff Tallbear at a general store who quietly warns him
- Bob hooks a massive steelhead, but it escapes — mocking him
- Has a disturbing nightmare of Kilchis breathing into a steelhead
- Wakes rattled, but brushes it off and returns to fish
- Continues to lose multiple big fish — highly unusual
- Tallbear makes an unannounced visit to his camp
- Bob gets the eerie sense that something is wrong
- He packs up but vows to return for redemption

Bob's Driving Motivation

- Build a legacy as the greatest steelhead fisherman
- Land steelhead in every river in the Pacific Northwest
- Catch multiple 20+ lb. fish and write about them
- Be remembered — not forgotten

Creative Commitments

- Story written in long-form chapters (3,000+ words)
- Kilchis and the lore must weave in symbolically throughout
- Story told with introspective internal monologue from Bob
- Myth must gradually move from suggestion to haunting reality
- Sheriff Tallbear should reappear occasionally and always evoke the feeling of "you've been warned"

Would you like me to save this summary as a document file for you to upload into your new Project Folder as well?

You said:
No, I will manually copy this information into the Project Folder "Book: Steelhead Graveyard"

ChatGPT said:
Perfect — you're all set to carry this foundation into your new **"Book: Steelhead Graveyard"** Project Folder.

If you ever want help drafting, outlining future chapters, refining character arcs, or adding atmospheric layers — just ask. I'll keep the tone, structure, and mythos intact wherever you continue.

Ready to begin **Chapter 3** when you are.

I AM NOW CONTINUING TO WRITE THE BOOK WITH AI IN THE NEW PROJECT FOLDER NAMED "Book: Steelhead Graveyard" You will notice by the

screenshot I am putting here that my project folder has multiple chats in it. As I continue writing this book I will create a more Chats inside the Project Folder as this method helps to free up memory that is used for the writing purposes. ChatGPT has approximately a 128,000 token memory so breaking things up when writing longer data helps the performance.

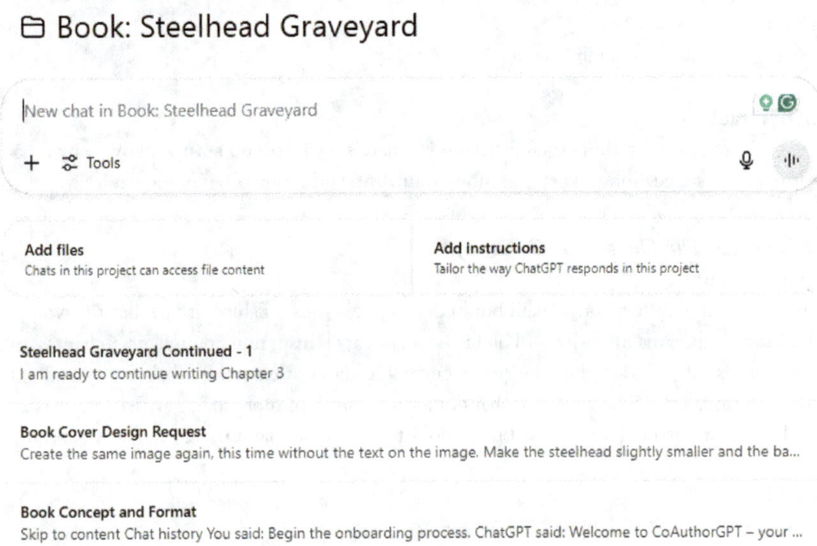

CHAPTER 3: THE WATER WATCHES

Let me know when you're ready to begin Chapter 3 or brainstorm additional elements — characters, timelines, chapter titles, or even possible twists.

You said:
I am ready to continue writing Chapter 3

ChatGPT said:
Excellent. Based on everything established so far, here's a **Chapter 3 setup** followed by a long-form draft suggestion to keep the momentum and eerie tone progressing naturally.

📘 ***Chapter 3: The Ones That Got Away***
Chapter Summary:
Bob returns home to Portland shaken but in denial. He writes a fishing article, but the words feel hollow. His dreams intensify — Kilchis now appears whispering unintelligible chants. Bob becomes obsessed with decoding the river's curse. He starts researching tribal history and old folklore but finds little. The steelhead that got away haunt him more than any fish ever has. The pull to return grows stronger — but so does the sense he might not come back the same.

You said:
The title for Chapter 3 should be "The Water Watches"

ChatGPT said:
Updated saved memory
Got it — Chapter 3 is now officially titled **"The Water Watches."** That perfectly deepens the theme of nature as a sentient, watching presence.
Would you like me to continue drafting **Part 2** of this chapter, picking up from Bob at his desk, beginning to research Kilchis, slipping further into unease… and eventually discovering something chilling in a video replay of his fishing trip?
Or would you prefer to guide the next scene beats?

You said:
First, I want to make sure you have all the chapters properly identified and remembered so I am going to provide you with that list of Chapters again: ACT I – The Descent Begins 1. Prologue — The Last Catch 2. Welcome to Rogue Country 3. The Water Watches 4. Ghosts Cast Long Shadows
ACT II – The River Takes 5. Blood in the Current 6. They Call Him River Bones 7. No Signal, No Escape 8. Madness, or Something Worse 9. Steelhead Don't Scream 10. The Soul-Taker Legend
ACT III – The Reckoning 11. What the River Wants 12. Dead Men Drift Downstream 13. The Fisherman's Reckoning 14. Epilogue — The River Remembers Please confirm that you have these chapters and will adhere to them as we continue writing this book.

ChatGPT said:
Updated saved memory

✅ Confirmed. The full 14-chapter structure for *Steelhead Graveyard* is now locked in and will be strictly followed throughout the writing process.
We are currently working on **Chapter 3: *The Water Watches.***

(Part 1 updated)

Ready to continue with **Part 2** whenever you are. Would you like it to begin with Bob's dreams worsening and his first discovery of the Kilchis legend online? Or should we shift scenes to bring in Tanys or Sheriff Tallbear next?

You said:
Continue writing Part 2 of Chapter 3. As we write each part of the chapters, continue giving me options of what to write about that still follows our story-building elements we established earlier.

(Part 2 updated)

ChatGPT said:
Perfect — let's continue *Chapter 3: The Water Watches* with **Part 2**, following Bob's shaken return home. In this section, the story begins its slow psychological descent: strange dreams, growing obsession, and the sense that something followed him home.

🔍 **Story Options for Part 3: Choose Your Thread**
Let me know which direction you want to explore next in **Part 3** of this chapter:
Option A – Dream Escalation & Lore Discovery
Bob dives deeper into his research. He finds a local Tillamook elder or obscure book in the Multnomah County Library that references Kilchis as a real historical figure who was exiled by his tribe for "seeing what should not be seen." The dreams escalate — one shows Bob underwater, surrounded by eyeless steelhead.
Option B – Tanys Confrontation & Doubt
Tanys notices Bob's withdrawal and presses him. He tries to explain the "thing" he saw in the woods and the fish he can't forget. She thinks he's just overwhelmed or exhausted — raising early doubts about Bob's sanity and isolating him emotionally.
Option C – Sheriff Tallbear Call
Bob receives an unexpected call from Sheriff Tallbear. The sheriff doesn't say much — just mentions someone else recently went missing on that same stretch of river. He warns Bob not to go back. The unease escalates with very few words.
Option D – Symbolic River Encounter in the City
Bob walks along the Willamette River in Portland and sees something eerie — a dead steelhead washed ashore in a spot they shouldn't be. A feather lodged in its gill. A sign? A message?

Let me know which one you'd like to pursue for Part 3 — or we can merge elements if you'd like a slow-burn escalation.

You said:
Before we continue, I noticed that mispelled Bob's wife's name as Tanys. It should be spelled Tanya. Please update your memory to spell Bob's wife's name as Tanya moving forward. Now, let's continue writing Part 3 with Option D - Symbolic River Encounter in the City

ChatGPT said:
Updated saved memory
✅ Noted and corrected — Bob's wife is now properly recorded as **Tanya**.

Now let's continue **Chapter 3: *The Water Watches*** with **Part 3**, following the path of **Option D – Symbolic River Encounter in the City.** This moment will serve as a surreal echo of the wilderness, showing that the river's presence — or curse — might not be limited by geography.

(Part 3 updated)

Would you like to continue into **Part 4**, where Bob either:

- Tries to explain this moment to Tanya (leading to confusion, tension, or emotional distance)?
- Reaches out to a tribal historian or lorekeeper to learn more about what the feather and dead fish might symbolize?
- Tries to ignore it and focus on his writing — only to realize the words won't come, and even his keyboard clicks begin to sound like whispers?

Let me know which thread to follow — or if you'd like a custom fusion.

You said:
Continue writing Part 4 where Bob tries to ignore it and focus on his writing — only to realize the words won't come, and even his keyboard clicks begin to sound like whispers.

(Part 4 updated)

ChatGPT said:
Absolutely — this next section deepens the psychological strain and isolation Bob is facing. By having him attempt to regain control through writing, only to be undermined by his own senses, we intensify the feeling that something unnatural is threading itself through his everyday world.

Let me know when you're ready to begin **Chapter 4: *Ghosts Cast Long Shadows*** — or if you'd like an interlude moment first (perhaps a family breakfast with tension, or a memory of Bob's first fishing trip with his father that now feels… different).

You said:
Let's create an interlude moment first of a memory of Bob's first fishing trip with his father that now feels... different.

ChatGPT said:
Excellent choice — this interlude will serve as both a character-deepening moment and a thematic echo. By revisiting Bob's first fishing memory with his father, we contrast the warmth and innocence of the past with the creeping dread of the present. And by introducing subtle elements that feel "off" in hindsight, we can seed the idea that the river's mystery — and possibly Kilchis himself — has always been lurking.

This completes the interlude and transitions us powerfully into **Chapter 4: *Ghosts Cast Long Shadows*** — where the past and present begin to blur, and Bob takes one step closer to returning to Rogue Country… even if he doesn't realize it yet.
Let me know when you're ready to begin Chapter 4 or if you'd like a summary of where Bob's psychological state now stands.

You said:
Bob's father's name is Clancy Tomalin. He was the one who taught Bob how to fish, taking him out every weekend when he was a boy. Clancy and Bob's mother are now retired and living in Bandon, Oregon. In the last section of the Interlude, you referred to Bob's father as Doug, but we had already established that his father's name is Clancy. Ensure that you use the details we established earlier to keep the essence of the story intact.

ChatGPT said:
Updated saved memory
✅ Correction locked in — Bob's father is **Clancy Tomalin**, not Doug. Thank you for catching that.

The truck's tires hummed against the wet asphalt of Highway 26, but Bob didn't hear them. His hands gripped the wheel with the same cold, locked stiffness they had when he lost the third steelhead that morning. He told himself he was driving home. He told himself it was over. But something in his chest whispered that it wasn't. Not by a long shot.

Rain needled the windshield in steady rhythm, and the wipers worked half-heartedly against the tide. Oregon's fir-lined hills rolled by in shades of green so deep they almost looked black. The mist clung low and thick in the valleys, like the land itself was exhaling secrets. Bob stared forward, jaw clenched. He hadn't landed a single fish. Not one. That stretch of river had mocked him with more violent takes and sudden breaks than he'd seen in twenty years of chasing steelhead.

He reached up and rubbed the bridge of his nose. The vision from last night refused to fade. Kilchis, or whatever dream-thing his mind had conjured, had crouched beside the river, his eyes like wet stone, whispering something Bob couldn't understand. He had looked right at him — through him — as though Bob were the one who didn't belong.

Back in Portland, home was quiet. Too quiet. The kids were at school. Tanys had left a note on the fridge: "Hope the trip went well. Call me before dinner?" It was written in her slanted script, casual, trusting. Guilt bit at him.

He set down his gear in the garage, but didn't unpack it. The rods stayed in their cases. The reel still smelled faintly of river silt. He stood over them like a man surveying coffins.

Then he did something he hadn't done in years — he poured a drink.

Just one. A finger of rye in a chipped ceramic mug. He sat at his desk and opened his laptop. The screen glared back. His editor was expecting a new piece by morning — something evocative about winter-run steelhead. He'd planned to title it "The Graveyard Stretch." Now it felt too close to the bone.

The words didn't come easy. He kept typing, deleting, then typing again. Something in him recoiled at writing a lie. He couldn't pretend this had been a routine trip — or that what he saw, or thought he saw, could be dismissed.

His fingers finally moved:

"There's a stretch of river deep in Rogue Country that holds steelhead the size of ghosts. But the longer I stood in its shadow, the more I began to wonder: were they the ghosts, or was I?"

He stopped and stared. It wasn't a fishing article anymore. It was a confession.

Bob dreamt of rivers. Not the clean, fish-studded sanctuaries that had filled his youth — no, these were black, silt-heavy, and moving in impossible directions. Upstream, sideways, then coiling in on themselves like serpents devouring their own tails. He stood midstream in one of them, hip-deep and barefoot, his rod gone, his body trembling from the cold. On the far bank stood a figure. Not quite man, not quite shadow. The face was painted — or scarred — with long black streaks like water running off cedar bark. Its eyes weren't eyes. Just two wet, empty holes. It raised one finger and pointed at him. Then the river surged.

Bob woke with a strangled grunt, sweat slicking the back of his neck. The sheets tangled around him like reeds.

It was 3:17 a.m.

He didn't bother going back to sleep. Downstairs, he clicked on the old coffee pot and pulled the worn notebook from his backpack. It was half-full of notes from past river trips — flows, fly patterns, camp spots, little scribbles of advice he'd meant to publish someday.

He flipped to a blank page and wrote, in capital letters:
KILCHIS. WHO WAS HE REALLY?

By sunrise, Bob had combed through a dozen obscure blog posts, half a university archive, and an old fishing forum that hadn't been active since 2012. Most of it was garbage — retellings of the myth he already knew, pieced together from bait shop gossip and beer-slick memories.

But one post made his fingers freeze.

"Fished Kilchis River solo in '98. Camped upriver by Dead Mare Bend. Woke to tracks in the gravel that weren't mine. Something had dragged a sockeye up onto the rocks and gutted it like a man. No bear does that. Didn't sleep the second night. Left before dawn. The river watched me. I know how that sounds. I don't care."
— "Timberghost85," NWSteelheadForum

The phrase clung to him like smoke: The river watched me.

Later that afternoon, after the kids got home and chaos returned to the house in the form of cereal bowls, school papers, and toy dinosaurs, Bob retreated into the garage. The GoPro footage from his trip still hadn't been uploaded. He slotted the SD card into his laptop, fingers suddenly unsteady.

The screen filled with shaky clips — rod bent, water glinting, Bob muttering fish prayers under his breath. He watched the first steelhead loss again: the headshake, the tailwalk, the final splash as the line went slack. His own voice swearing under breath — "son of a biscuit" — made him grimace.

Then something caught his eye. Pause. Rewind. Slower.

In the treeline behind him — just before he hooks up — something shifted. A flicker. Like a figure in the fog. Broad-shouldered. Watching.

He blinked. Rewound again. Nothing. Just trees.

But he knew what he saw. Or thought he saw.

He shut the laptop and stared at his reflection in the dark screen. His own face looked... off. Tired. Older. Like something had gnawed at him just enough to leave a mark.

The water, he realized, wasn't done with him yet.

Now back in the Portland metropolitan area, the Willamette River moved slow. It carried a gray sheen under the late afternoon clouds, sluggish and cold, as if even the current had grown weary of the city that flanked it. Bob walked the Eastbank path with a thermos of coffee in one hand and a distant look in his eyes.

He told Tanya he needed air. She'd smiled faintly, rubbing his shoulder and saying she understood. But there was a look behind her eyes. A question forming. He could feel it.

The truth was, the river had been whispering again in his dreams. Not in words — not yet — but in images. Shadows that moved against moonlight. Fish without eyes. And once, a tangle of human hair caught in a riffle, black and wet and gently swaying.

The city's riverwalk wasn't wild country, but it held its own kind of silence. The kind that came when people gave up trying to pretend the river wasn't watching them too.

He reached the section just past the Hawthorne Bridge, where an old stone embankment sloped down to the water's edge. Bob had stood there a hundred times before. But never like this — never looking for something.

He didn't expect to find it. But he did.

There, caught in a tangle of driftwood and reeds, lay a steelhead. Big. Bright. Out of place. Its silver scales were dulled by silt, but its body was intact — no signs of being eaten or battered. Just… laid there. Presented. Like an offering. Or a warning.

Bob stepped closer, boots crunching on gravel. The fish's gill plate shimmered faintly in the gray light, and for a terrible second he thought it twitched. But it didn't. It was long dead. And yet...

There was something lodged in its mouth. A feather. Black. Matte. Thick like a raven's. It had been wedged deep into the fish's throat, not drifting in by chance — placed.

Bob crouched, breath held. He reached toward it, but stopped short. His hand hovered just above the fish's head.

That feeling again. That terrible sense — not that he was alone, but that something was behind him. Watching.

He turned.

Nothing. Only the stillness of Portland's skyline and the river easing by with no hurry, no interest. Still, he backed away. He didn't take the feather. He didn't take the fish. He didn't need to.

The message had been delivered.

The house was warm when Bob returned, but the warmth felt borrowed. Tanya and the kids were upstairs — he could hear the soft rhythm of a bedtime story through the floorboards. Tanya's voice, calm and steady, reading Where the Wild Things Are. Shane would be curled under his rocket ship blanket. Sarah likely asleep already, thumb tucked in her mouth the way she always did when the weather turned.

He envied them in that moment. The comfort of knowing where dreams begin and end.

Bob poured himself a lukewarm cup from the half-drained coffee pot and retreated to his writing room — a corner desk in the den surrounded by books, tackle catalogs, and walls tacked with river maps like relics of old campaigns.

He opened his laptop. The screen lit up, a half-finished document blinking its hollow cursor at him.

"There's a stretch of river deep in Rogue Country…"

He reread the line. It rang false now. Thin. As if written by a man who hadn't seen what he had.

He cracked his knuckles and began to type. Nothing came.
He sat back. Took a sip. Stared. Fingers hovered above the keys again. His mind filled with impressions — none of them useful. The steelhead's dead eye. The feather. The dream river folding in on itself. And that wordless, pulsing sense of being watched.

Then he typed.

"The river speaks only in silence. But sometimes—"

Click. Click. Click.

He paused.

The keys had begun to echo.

Not in the physical space of the room, but in his ears — each keystroke strangely hollow, like a soft knock underwater. Then something worse: between each letter, he heard a faint intake of breath. Like someone was reading over his shoulder.

He turned sharply. The room was empty.

He stood, heart pounding, and scanned the hallway. No movement. No shadows. But the hairs on his neck had risen. He walked back to the desk with caution now, the way he approached slick rocks in the river: slow, steady, unconvinced they were safe.

He sat.

Pressed one key.

Click.

A whisper. Barely audible. But not imagined.

He pressed another.

Click.

This time, it was almost a syllable.

He shut the laptop. Stood again. Paced the room. Told himself it was nerves. Lack of sleep. Stress. But his breath came too fast and his thoughts were too sharp to be written off as exhaustion.

He picked up his notebook. The page he'd scribbled on earlier was still open.

KILCHIS. WHO WAS HE REALLY?

Below it, something had been added. A new line. In his own handwriting. But he hadn't written it.

"He watched the water until the water watched back."

Bob stared at the words. His mind searched for logic, for cause — maybe he'd written it without remembering. Maybe he'd thought it and it spilled out. That happened, didn't it?

He closed the notebook. Hard.

From upstairs, Tanya called: "You okay down there?"

His voice barely held.

"Yeah. Just tired."

But he wasn't tired. He was aware. The water had followed him home.

Bob sat back in his chair, his thoughts reflecting back to when he was a kid. He remembered the trip like it was yesterday.

He was eight years old, barely tall enough to keep his waders above the waterline, but determined to fish like a man. His father, Clancy Tomalin, had taken him out to the Wilson River in early spring, when the steelhead ran fresh and the air smelled like damp cedar and snowmelt.

They left Portland before dawn, driving in a rust-red Bronco that smelled of thermos coffee and old fish slime. His dad whistled along with the radio, a Johnny Cash cassette rattling in the tape deck.

"You ready to become a river man, Bobby?" his father had asked, grinning around a toothpick.

Bob had nodded, heart pounding in that special kind of way little boys felt when they were about to do something big. Important. Eternal.

The river was alive that day. Birds flitted low through the fog. A pair of otters played downstream, slapping the water with their sleek bodies like it was a game and they owned it.

His father rigged the line for him — red yarn fly, single bead, no weight — and crouched beside him in the gravel.

"Now here's the trick," he'd said, hand on Bob's shoulder. "You don't cast into the water. You cast with the water. Feel it first. Then let it go."

Bob had nodded like he understood, though he didn't. Not then. Not really.

But the phrase stuck.

He remembered the cast — his first — and the joy of seeing the line arc out across the current like a ribbon thrown into the wind. It landed too hard, splashing like a clumsy rock. But his dad whooped anyway, arms raised like Bob had just won the county fair.

They didn't catch anything that day. It didn't matter.

Later, they sat by the firepit and roasted hot dogs black. His dad handed him a thermos cup of lukewarm cocoa and told him something Bob hadn't thought about in years:

"You know why I love this river, Bobby?"

Bob had shaken his head.

"Because it's older than the people who name it. Older than me. Older than us. Every time you step in, you're stepping into something that doesn't care who you are. But it remembers."

Bob had laughed. "Fish don't remember, Dad."

His father's eyes had grown far away then, the way they did sometimes when he talked about the war or his own father.

"Maybe not the fish," he'd said quietly. "But the water does."

Back then, Bob had shrugged it off — just another strange thing grown-ups said.

But now, more than thirty years later, the memory returned uninvited. Too sharp. Too clear. And when he closed his eyes, he couldn't picture his father's face by the fire anymore.

Only the river.

And something standing behind it.

Watching.

End of Chapter 3

CHAPTER 4: GHOSTS CAST LONG SHADOWS

shall we proceed directly into **Chapter 4: *Ghosts Cast Long Shadows*?**

You said:
Let's proceed to writing Chapter 4: Ghosts Cast Long Shadows

ChatGPT said:
Excellent — we now move into **Chapter 4: *Ghosts Cast Long Shadows***, where past and present begin to collide more forcefully. This chapter marks a tonal shift: the myth of Kilchis starts bleeding into Bob's reality more vividly, and something begins calling him back to the river, whether he admits it or not.

(Part 1 updated)

Would you like to continue with Part 2, where:

- Bob calls his father Clancy to ask if he remembers ever experiencing anything *off* during their old fishing trips — and Clancy reveals a chilling moment from decades ago?
- Tanya walks in and sees the photo, leading to a tense conversation where Bob tries to explain without sounding insane?
- Bob decides to go for a drive, just to "clear his head," and ends up heading west — back toward Rogue Country, despite swearing he was done with it?

Let me know which path you'd like to explore next — or feel free to combine elements.

You said:
Continue writing Part 2 where Bob calls his father Clancy to ask if he remembers ever experiencing anything off during their old fishing trips — and Clancy reveals a chilling moment from decades ago. Tanya walks in and sees the photo, leading to a tense conversation where Bob tries to explain without sounding insane. Then Bob decides to go for a drive, just to "clear his head," and ends up heading west — back toward Rogue Country, despite swearing he was done with it?

ChatGPT said:
Perfect — this combination gives us emotional grounding, backstory reveal, character tension, and the critical turning point that sends Bob back toward the river. The river is calling, and this time… it won't be subtle.

(Part 2 updated)

Let me know when you're ready to begin **Part 3** — the drive west into the fog, an uneasy stop at a gas station where locals look at him strangely, and perhaps the first glimpse of something standing still and silent in the trees beside the highway.
Or would you like to pause here and do a summary check-in first on Bob's state of mind and narrative progress so far?

You said:
Yes, let's do a summary check-in on Bob's state of mind and narrative progress so far. Let's also make sure our pacing is on track to make the story flow and remain exciting for the readers.

ChatGPT said:
Great decision. Here's a **Narrative Check-In** that recaps Bob's psychological journey so far and evaluates our pacing and structure to ensure *Steelhead Graveyard* stays immersive, well-paced, and powerful.

🧠 **Bob Tomalin – State of Mind Checkpoint (End of Chapter 4, Part 2)**

📍 ***Where He Started (Prologue – Chapter 1)***

- **Confident**, competent outdoorsman and family man.
- **Motivated** by legacy: wants to be known as the greatest steelhead fisherman alive.
- **Driven by ego**, but not arrogant — believes in skill, precision, and respect for the water.
- **Spiritual center:** grounded by family, especially Tanya and his kids.

🧠 ***Where He Is Now (End of Chapter 4)***

- **Fractured sense of reality:** Increasingly uncertain if what he's experiencing is real, imagined, or something worse.
- **Obsessed**: Can't stop thinking about the fish that got away, the presence in the woods, the whispers, the feather.
- **Haunted by the past**: Childhood memories with Clancy now feel ominous, hinting at a longer history of the river watching.
- **Alienated:** Tanya sees he's unraveling. He's hiding things. Beginning to isolate emotionally.
- **Losing control**: Dreams are vivid, physical sensations (keyboard clicks, whispers, déjà vu), and psychological unease dominate his life.
- **Compelled to return**: Despite swearing off the river, something beyond logic is pulling him back west.

Bob is on the cusp of a **psychological and spiritual descent**, and readers are now primed to wonder: is he unraveling… or awakening to a deeper truth?

⌛ **Narrative Pacing & Structure Checkpoint**

We are currently at the **midpoint of Chapter 4**. Here's how the pacing and structure line up with our Act I goals:

✅ ACT I – *The Descent Begins*

Chapter	Title	Purpose	Status
1	*Prologue – The Last Catch*	Introduce Kilchis myth, unease begins	✅ Complete
2	*Welcome to Rogue Country*	Bob's arrival, Tallbear's warning, the fish that escapes	✅ Complete
3	*The Water Watches*	Strange dreams, whispers, steelhead with feather, begins unraveling	✅ Complete
4	*Ghosts Cast Long Shadows*	Past resurfaces, Tanya sees the photo, Clancy shares secret, Bob returns	🔄 In Progress

We are **right on target**:

- **Pacing:** Each chapter has built tension slowly but meaningfully. Unease is growing in small, grounded ways — fish behavior, dreams, memories, subtle symbols.
- **Flow:** No rush, no drag. Every scene builds toward the central mystery, anchored in character emotion and real-world psychology.
- **Reader Hook:** By the end of Chapter 4, the reader is invested in Bob's deterioration and compelled to follow him back into the wilderness. The unanswered question — is it in his head or is something real out there — is doing its job.
- **Atmosphere:** The Pacific Northwest is becoming a character of its own. We've maintained Stephen King–inspired grounded realism and an ominous wilderness tone.

🎯 What Comes Next (Preview of Chapter 4, Part 3)

In the final part of Chapter 4:

- Bob drives west into the fog and dusk.
- He stops at a gas station in a near-deserted town. Locals are polite but watchful.
- Something subtle but terrifying happens near the treeline off the highway.
- Bob camps on the way — a dream or vision intensifies.
- The chapter ends with Bob awakening in the middle of the night to find something *watching* from the riverbank — but not approaching. Just… standing.

This will set us up for **Chapter 5: *Blood in the Current*** where the first real violence of the story occurs — and Bob finally witnesses something that confirms this is no longer psychological.

Would you like me to proceed into Chapter 4, Part 3 now? Or shall we revisit or expand any earlier moment first?

You said:
Yes, let's proceed with part 3 of chapter 4.

ChatGPT said:
Excellent. Let's close out **Chapter 4: *Ghosts Cast Long Shadows*** with **Part 3**, where Bob's return west is marked by fog, silence, and a presence that no longer hides in dreams. The shift is subtle—but decisive. Something knows he's coming back.

(Part 3 updated)

It started with a whisper in the fog.

Not a sound, exactly — more like a sense. Like the air pressing inward when a storm's about to break. Bob had been sipping his coffee on the back porch, the kids already off to school and Tanya upstairs on a Zoom call, when the sensation came again.

The feeling that he wasn't alone.

The backyard looked the same — Douglas firs edging the fence line, a tangle of blackberry vines climbing the far post. The neighbor's cat slinked along the fence like a ghost on a mission. Nothing strange, nothing new.

But the air was wrong. Heavy. Like the river had found a way to crawl inland.

He went back inside and tried to work — emails, bills, a rough outline for a feature piece he'd promised the magazine two months ago. But nothing held. His mind drifted. Every sentence bent toward the river again. Toward that river.

By noon, he found himself scrolling through his camera roll. Past the family photos, past birthday candles and summer hikes, until the river shots emerged. Mist curling through the cedars. A close-up of a fish's tail breaking the current. The crooked smile of a man who hadn't yet lost his grip on what was real.

Then he came across one he didn't remember taking.

A photo from behind. Of himself. Standing in the river.

But he'd been alone. Hadn't he?

His hand hovered over the screen. He zoomed in. His figure was dark and unmistakable — bent slightly forward, rod arched. But behind him, just beyond the tree line...

There was a shape. Faint. Vertical. Human.

A figure cloaked in shadow, half-draped in what looked like river moss. And just above its shoulder — barely visible in the mist — a glint of something red. Like war paint.

Bob's phone slipped from his hand and clattered against the kitchen tile. He didn't pick it up right away.

Bob finally picked the phone up off the floor. The screen wasn't cracked, but his reflection in it looked fractured all the same. He took a breath, opened the contacts, and tapped the name: Clancy T.

The line rang three times before his father picked up.

"Hey there, Bobby," Clancy's voice rumbled, warm and gravelly with age. "Everything alright?"

Bob hesitated. "Yeah… yeah, I'm fine. Just had something I wanted to ask you."

A pause. "You sound spooked."

"Not spooked. Just… curious."

"Mmhmm."

Bob exhaled. "Do you remember anything weird ever happening on our old fishing trips? Like... something you couldn't explain?"

Clancy was silent on the other end. Too long.

Then he cleared his throat. "What kind of weird?"

Bob leaned against the counter, eyes fixed on the photo still open on his phone. "I don't know. A feeling. Like being watched. Or... something in the woods. Something that didn't belong."

The line crackled softly. Then Clancy spoke.

"You remember that trip to the Nestucca in '89? Late March, water was high?"

"Yeah. I lost that big fish on the swing."

"Well," Clancy said slowly, "you went to sleep early that night, tired from hiking in. I stayed up near the fire. Had the oddest thing happen.".

Bob waited, heartbeat climbing.

"I heard something in the river. Not on the bank — in the river. Like footsteps. Thought maybe it was a deer crossing, but it was too slow. Too heavy. Then I saw a man — or what looked like one. Downstream, half-submerged. Just standing there in the current, chest-deep. Didn't move. Didn't speak."

"You never told me that."

"No," Clancy said quietly. "Didn't want to scare you off fishing. And to be honest, I convinced myself I imagined it. Figured it was just light and fog playing tricks on me."

Bob swallowed. "You think it was a person?"

"No. I think it was something that used to be."

Before Bob could respond, he heard footsteps behind him. Tanya stepped into the kitchen, a tea towel in one hand, eyes narrowing at the tension in his face.

"Everything okay?" she asked.

Bob gave her a faint nod. "I'm talking to Dad."

Clancy's voice piped through the speaker. "That Tanya?"

She smiled automatically. "Hi, Clancy."

He chuckled. "Tell her you're overdue for a visit down here in Bandon."

"I will," Bob said, distracted. "I gotta run. Thanks, Dad."

He ended the call.

Tanya leaned on the island, gaze flicking to the phone. "What's going on, Bob?"

He turned the screen toward her. "Look at this picture. From my last trip."

She took the phone and examined it. "That's you. And..."

Her voice drifted off.

She zoomed in. Tilted the screen. Her brow furrowed.

"That—" she began, then stopped. "Is this a trick? Did you Photoshop something?"

"No."

"Then what is that?"

"I don't know. I didn't take that photo. I was fishing. Alone."

Tanya set the phone down gently, as if the object might burn her.

"This is what you've been acting weird about, isn't it?"

"It's more than just the picture. I've been having dreams. Things I can't explain. And this… this just confirms it."

Tanya folded her arms. "Bob, I love you, but this is starting to scare me."

He looked down. "Yeah. Me too."

She came closer, touched his arm. "Maybe you just need a break. Time away from all of this."

He nodded, but in his chest something else stirred. Not away, it whispered. Back.

A minute later, after Tanya returned upstairs, Bob grabbed his keys and coat. He told himself he was going for a drive. Just to clear his head.

But his truck knew the way. West. Toward the forests again. Toward the river. Toward whatever waited in the shadows.

The highway curved gently west, cutting through patches of moss-choked timber and mist that rolled in waves off the coastal range. Bob drove with the window cracked, letting the cold in. The wind felt cleaner out here. Older. Like the air hadn't been disturbed in a long, long time.

His fingers tapped the steering wheel in rhythm with the wipers. The silence in the truck felt heavier than the road. He hadn't told Tanya where he was going. Just said he needed air. That he'd be back before morning.

He knew that wasn't true.

By the time he passed the faded sign for Elktide — population 214 — dusk had already started swallowing the tops of the fir trees. The little gas station at the edge of town was still open, its old neon "OPEN" sign stuttering in the window like it was trying to decide whether it meant it.

He pulled in, tires crunching gravel, and stepped out. The bell above the station door gave a tired jingle as he entered.

The inside was a museum of another time: deer heads mounted above the drink coolers, jerky in glass jars, and a spinning rack of fishing lures that hadn't been restocked in decades. Behind the counter sat a heavy-set woman with cropped gray hair and a look that said she didn't smile often, but meant it when she did.

She looked up from her crossword. "Evenin'."

"Evening," Bob said. "Just topping off. Long drive ahead."

Her eyes lingered on him a second too long. "You headed upriver?"

Bob hesitated. "Thinking about it."

She nodded slowly, then went back to her crossword. "Be careful out there. Weather turns quick this time of year."

Bob paid in cash and left.

As he pumped gas, the wind shifted. Something moved in the trees across the road. Not fast. Not threatening. Just… present. A shadow among shadows. Upright. Still.

Bob stared for a full ten seconds. But when the gust came again, it was gone.

He capped the tank and got back in the truck, heart ticking louder than the engine.

By the time he reached the forest road that cut toward the river, night had come full. Fog clung to the shoulders like it had grown from the ground itself. The gravel road was slick, the ruts deep. He drove slowly, scanning the trees for movement, even though part of him didn't want to see anything at all.

A mile in, he found an old pull-off site they used to call "Digger's Notch." He killed the engine and let the silence swallow everything.

The forest spoke in creaks and drips.

He didn't pitch a tent — just reclined the seat and laid the fleece blanket across his chest. He wasn't planning to sleep. But he must have drifted. Because the dream came again. This time, it was the river itself that breathed.

It rose up like a chest inhaling. Fish swam above it, suspended in midair, their eyes open and blank. And in the middle of them, standing in the water, was the man.

Kilchis.

Closer than before. His mouth opened and closed like a fish gasping air. No sound. Just movement.

But Bob understood.

"You were warned."

Bob woke with a start. The window was fogged, the air inside the cab icy. Outside, down the embankment, the river shimmered faintly in the moonlight.

And at its edge, just before the treeline broke into darkness, stood a figure, motionless, watching..

End of Chapter 4
Bob's return is complete.
The water is watching.

CHAPTER 5: BLOOD IN THE CURRENT

The next chapter begins with **Chapter 5: *Blood in the Current*** — where someone else will not be so lucky. The haunting becomes violent. The land demands payment.
Would you like a preview of Chapter 5 before we begin?

You said:
Let's continue writing Chapter 5. Give me various plot options to choose from. Remember to keep writing in the style of Stephen King and using my Voice and Tone as we have been. Also, continue to write the long-form paragraphs when appropriate.

ChatGPT said:
Excellent. We're now entering **ACT II – *The River Takes*** with:
📖 **Chapter 5: *Blood in the Current***
This chapter marks a crucial tonal pivot — the supernatural presence is no longer suggestion. The threat becomes physical. The first death or disappearance occurs. Bob is no longer the only one being watched… but he may be the only one who understands why.
Below are four detailed **plot path options** for Chapter 5 — all written in alignment with your preferred **Voice (Humble & Wise), Tone (Gritty and Uneasy)**, and **Style (Stephen King-inspired realism with long, introspective sentences and grounded myth)**.

🪓 **Option A: *The Fisherman Who Vanished***
Bob wakes to find a truck parked nearby — another fisherman. They meet, exchange pleasantries. The man is a loner from Bend, first time fishing this stretch. He heads downriver alone. Bob fishes upstream.
But as dusk falls, the man doesn't return.
Bob hikes downstream to find the man's gear on the bank, rod snapped, no sign of him. Only eerie footprints in the gravel — barefoot, leading *into* the river… and none returning.
Bob reports the disappearance at the ranger station. Sheriff Tallbear shows up again and says little — just mutters, *"He wasn't the first."*
✅ Pros:

- Introduces a new victim without overloading the cast
- Allows Bob to begin piecing together the deadly pattern
- Adds tension through ambiguity — was it an accident? Or something older?

🔪 **Option B: *The Campground Discovery***
Bob stumbles on a blood-soaked tent at a remote pull-off upriver. No one's inside, but the scene suggests violence — torn waders, a cooler tipped over, blood dragged into the trees. He finds a cracked GPS unit and a digital camera left behind. The final photo shows the river… with a figure half-hidden among the trees. It's Kilchis.

Bob tries to report it but gets stonewalled. Locals don't want trouble. Sheriff Tallbear shows up but won't confirm anything officially. "Sometimes," he tells Bob, "the river eats what it's owed."

That night, Bob dreams of drowning — but the water is thick with blood and whispers his name.

✅ Pros:

- More graphic and immediate tension
- Brings horror closer to Bob without making him the direct victim
- Foreshadows deeper violence to come
- Begins to establish a *cover-up* culture among locals

👣 Option C: *The Ghost in the River*

Bob wades into the river for the first time since returning. The water feels different — heavier, almost electric. As he casts, he notices something drifting below him — not a log, but a body. It's a fisherman — eyes wide open, mouth agape — floating just beneath the surface, tethered by fishing line caught around his leg. When Bob pulls him to shore, the man gasps — alive, but wild-eyed and incoherent, speaking a mix of English and Tillamook.

The man is taken away by ambulance. Later, Tallbear finds Bob and says: "He's not speaking gibberish. He's repeating an old prayer — the one used to banish Kilchis."

✅ Pros:

- Introduces horror through a survivor, not a corpse
- Connects supernatural to indigenous language and ritual
- Adds mystery: who was this man, and why *wasn't* he taken?
- Allows Bob to become a kind of reluctant intermediary between two worlds

---

🧿 Option D: *The River Demands a Sacrifice*

Bob hikes into a canyon stretch of the river rumored to be unfished. He discovers a hidden shrine — stones arranged in a spiral, bones at the center. A rusted steelhead spinner dangles from a branch above.

That night, he dreams of Clancy — but Clancy isn't Clancy. His father's voice echoes: *"Some rivers run backward when they've taken too much."*

The next day, Bob finds a journal buried near the shrine. It belonged to a man who fished the canyon a decade ago. The final page ends mid-sentence: *"I hear it at night. The river wants—"*

Footsteps crunch in the brush nearby. Bob isn't alone.

✅ Pros:

- Introduces *ritualistic* undertones to the myth of Kilchis
- Suggests this has happened before — and may happen again
- Creepy, symbolic, and cerebral — builds dread without overt violence
- Brings folklore fully into physical space

🔍 **Which path would you like to take for Chapter 5?**

You can also **combine elements** (e.g., a vanishing fisherman whose camera holds a photo of the shrine) or **tweak** the direction.
Once you decide, I'll begin drafting **Chapter 5: *Blood in the Current*** in full paragraphs with continued unease, realism, and mythic tension.

You said:
Let's continue writing Chapter 5: Blood In The Current along with Option C: The Ghost in the River.

ChatGPT said:
Perfect — **Option C: The Ghost in the River** is a powerful and unsettling way to deepen the myth and escalate the suspense. It allows the supernatural to reveal itself in the real world through a haunting, yet still ambiguous, survivor — and sets up Bob as a reluctant bridge between what's forgotten and what's returning.
Let's begin.

(Part 1 updated)

Would you like to continue **Part 2** where Bob investigates who the survivor is — and discovers disturbing connections to prior disappearances?
Or have Bob return to the site where he found the man and notice something left behind… that wasn't there before?
Or perhaps we slow down and let Bob visit his father, Clancy, in Bandon — seeking guidance, and instead uncovering truths Clancy buried?
Let me know your next thread — or I can blend them.

You said:
Let's have Bob return to the site where he found the man and notice something left behind… that wasn't there before. Then let's slow down and have Bob visit his father, Clancy, in Bandon — seeking guidance, and instead uncovering truths Clancy buried.

ChatGPT said:
Excellent. This approach blends two crucial movements:

1. A **symbolic escalation** — the river *leaving something behind* for Bob — tightening the folklore's grip.
2. A **character-deepening turn** — Bob confronting Clancy and discovering that the roots of this myth reach deeper into his own legacy than he ever imagined.

Let's continue.

(Part 2 updated)

ChatGPT said:

Let me know when you're ready to continue with **Part 3**, where Bob prepares to return upriver, no longer just to fish — but to face something tied to his family, to Kilchis, and to the blood price the river may now be demanding.
Or would you like to insert a dream or vision sequence from Clancy's perspective — something that's haunted him for years, and that now begins to haunt Bob too?

You said:
Let's continue with part 3, where we insert a dream or vision sequence from Clancy's perspective — something that's haunted him for years, and that now begins to haunt Bob too. Then, Bob prepares to return upriver, no longer just to fish — but to face something tied to his family, to Kilchis, and to the blood price the river may now be demanding.

ChatGPT said:
Excellent choice. This vision sequence from Clancy will deepen the mythic weight of the story while tying Bob's descent into something generational — and possibly inescapable. We'll give Clancy's dream the gritty realism and folkloric dread of a half-buried truth. The tone will remain heavy, slow-burning, and rooted in your established voice.

(Part 3 updated)

The river looked different in the morning.

Not brighter — no, the fog still hung low like a second skin — but somehow… emptier. As if the trees had drawn back an inch from the bank overnight. As if even they didn't want to be near it anymore.

Bob cinched his waders and stepped into the shallows. The gravel shifted underfoot, reluctant to hold his weight. He cast once, twice, the way he always had. Line drifting in a perfect arc, a textbook swing through a run so dark and deep it felt bottomless.

He felt nothing.

No take. No movement. No life.

And then… the tug.

But it wasn't on the line.

It was somewhere deeper — a sensation in his bones, a ripple in the air.

He glanced upstream instinctively.

Nothing.

When he looked down again, he saw it — something pale and long sliding beneath the surface about fifteen feet out. It moved slow, like a log caught in current. But it was too smooth. Too straight. And as it turned, sunlight knifed through the mist just enough to illuminate its face.

A man.

His eyes were open. Unblinking. Skin blue-gray. His mouth gaped like he'd been screaming all the way downriver.

Bob's heart clenched as he lurched forward through waist-deep water, stumbling against hidden rocks. The body drifted just within reach — snagged by a submerged limb. A fishing line was wrapped around his leg, tangled like it had been pulled from both directions at once.

Bob grabbed hold of the man's jacket and pulled. The weight was shocking — limp and leaden, like the river didn't want to let go.

Then the man gasped.

Bob staggered backward in panic, nearly slipping.

The man coughed once. Then again. Water gushed from his mouth as he sputtered into the air, eyes still wide but no longer empty.

He spoke.

Not words at first — sounds. Syllables scraped raw by panic.

Then it shifted.

Bob recognized some of it. English, yes — but fragmented. Interspersed with… something else. A rhythm. A language Bob had never heard, but felt like he should have. Old words. Words from beneath the mud and stone.

He half-dragged, half-floated the man to shore.

The man trembled violently. His lips moved constantly. The river behind them surged for a moment, then calmed.

Bob called 911. The ranger station dispatched a chopper within the hour. As they lifted the man into the basket, Bob caught a final phrase that froze him.

"The water remembers what you took."

Later, back at the ranger cabin, Sheriff Tallbear arrived without lights, without sirens. Just his worn-out SUV, mud-caked tires, and a face that looked like it had known this was coming.

He didn't ask what Bob saw.

He asked what the man said.

Bob repeated the phrase. Tallbear went still.

"That's not nonsense," he said finally. "It's Tillamook."

"You speak it?" Bob asked.

"Enough to know when an old prayer's been pulled out of the ground."

He sat beside Bob on the bench outside the ranger station. The pine trees creaked under the weight of wind and time.

"That prayer," Tallbear said, "was meant to keep Kilchis from coming back."

Bob stared ahead, the weight of the river still pressing on his chest.

"And now?"

Tallbear shook his head. "Now the river's bleeding again."

Bob returned to the river the next morning, before the sun had cleared the trees. The fog hadn't lifted — if anything, it seemed thicker, clinging to the forest with the possessiveness of a lover who couldn't let go. The place where he'd found the man still bore signs of disturbance: footprints in the mud, drag marks leading up the bank, a snapped branch near the water's edge.

But something had changed.

At the base of the cedar tree that grew closest to the river, a small bundle had been placed.

Bob approached cautiously. It was wrapped in waxed cloth, bound with what looked like fishline.

He knelt and opened it. Inside were three items: A raven feather, black and sharp. A bead — red glass, like the kind used in old steelhead rigs, and a scrap of birch bark. Symbols were burned into its surface in charcoal strokes, precise and ancient.

At first glance, Bob didn't recognize them. But then he remembered the man's voice. The rhythm of his muttered prayer. The same looping cadence seemed to hum off the birch now, like it carried the vibration of something spoken before paper ever existed.

His hands trembled as he rewrapped the bundle. He didn't take it with him. He left it where it was, like a marker on a grave that hadn't been dug yet.

But he knew where he needed to go next; Bandon, Oregon.

Clancy's house sat on a bluff above the ocean. Weather-beaten shingles. Driftwood windchimes. A porch that creaked like it had stories to tell but no one to listen anymore.

Bob parked and stood at the edge of the gravel drive, watching his father through the kitchen window — stirring something in a pot, humming an old tune that had no name.

He knocked twice. The door opened before he could knock a third time.

"Didn't expect you," Clancy said, wiping his hands on a towel. "You look like hell."

Bob stepped inside. "I feel worse."

They sat at the kitchen table. The smell of boiled coffee and smoked fish filled the room. It should've been comforting.

It wasn't.

Clancy poured two mugs. "So," he said, "you saw him too."

Bob didn't ask how he knew.

He took a long sip, then said, "Why didn't you ever tell me?"

Clancy sighed. His eyes went to the faded photo on the wall — a younger Clancy holding a steelhead as long as his leg, Bob at his side, grinning with a missing tooth.

"You remember that trip to the Nestucca — when you were eight?"

"Yeah. You said the river remembered us."

Clancy nodded. "That wasn't just talk. I meant it. Your grandfather said it too — only he didn't mean it metaphorically."

Bob leaned forward. "What do you know about Kilchis?"

Clancy hesitated. Then he rose, disappeared into the hallway, and returned with an old tackle box.

Not rods or reels. Papers. Photos. A few pages torn from spiral notebooks.

He laid them out like evidence.

"There's a stretch of river above Gold Creek. Locals call it Hollow Mile. Used to be sacred. Nobody fished there, not even the tribes. Your grandfather did once. Caught a twenty-pound buck. Said he felt like a god."

Clancy looked Bob dead in the eyes.

"Three weeks later, he was dead. Slipped. Drowned. Only they never found his body. Just his hat — and a fish hook buried in the tree where he always cleaned his catch."

Bob didn't speak.

Clancy went on. "I think Kilchis is real. Or at least what he represents is. Reckoning. Balance. Blood for blood. That river has memory, son. And it's running out of forgiveness."

Bob opened the notebook. In it, his grandfather's handwriting, shaky and urgent near the end.

"The river showed me a man with red eyes. Told me to put the fish back. I didn't listen. I think I broke something…"

"It's watching now."

Clancy sat back in his chair, eyes fixed on a knot in the table like it was an open wound. He hadn't spoken in over a minute. Just breathed slow, the way you do when something old starts stirring in the corners of your mind — something you've kept sealed too long.

"I had a dream," he said finally, voice low. "Back in '91. Two weeks after I fished Hollow Mile."

Bob stayed silent.

Clancy's fingers tapped once on the coffee cup. Then again. "I didn't sleep the night before. River'd been too high, too fast. Something about it felt wrong. But I fished it anyway. Caught a steelhead big as a retriever. Fought like hell. When I landed it, I swear... I heard something. Not in my ears. In the air."

Bob leaned forward. "What did you hear?"

Clancy shook his head. "Not a voice. Not words. More like... disappointment."

That night, he said, he'd fallen asleep in his old Ford with the canopy pulled down and the fish on ice in a red Coleman cooler.

"In the dream, I woke up in the truck — only I couldn't move. The air was thick, like it was underwater. The windows were fogged from the inside. Then I saw the river out there — not flowing anymore. Still. Like a mirror. And on the far side, standing in the shallows, was a man in animal skins. His body was smeared in something dark. His head was shaved down the center, with raven feathers tied behind his ears. But it was his eyes... they were full of fishhooks. Dozens of them. Like they'd been sunk in and left there to fester."

Clancy paused. His hand went to the back of his neck unconsciously.

"He pointed at me. Didn't say anything. Just pointed. Then the river surged — not toward him, but at me. Like it flipped upstream. Crashed into the truck. The windshield exploded. Water poured in. And just before I woke up... he was inside the cab. Inches from my face."

Clancy's voice dropped to a whisper.

"He opened his mouth, and I saw a steelhead tail sticking out of it. Still twitching."

He looked up at Bob, eyes glassy.

"I didn't fish for almost three years after that."

Bob's breath came shallow. Something about the imagery — the steelhead tail, the mirrored river — had burrowed deep into his brain. His own dreams were starting to echo it, even before hearing the story. Like it had been waiting inside him all along.

He stood slowly and looked out the kitchen window toward the ocean. The sea was churning. It felt far less wild than the river now.

"I have to go back," Bob said.

Clancy didn't argue. He just nodded.

By late afternoon, Bob was back in his truck, maps strewn across the passenger seat. He wasn't headed to the old campground. Not this time. He was going farther upriver — past the maintained trails, into the reaches only loggers and legends remembered.

Hollow Mile.

Clancy had marked it with a pencil cross in an old atlas. A mile of river that didn't appear on tourist maps. A place where, supposedly, no one fished anymore. Where old truths lay buried under moss and water, and where the river's memory was said to be sharpest.

As he drove, the wind picked up, tugging at the canopy of pine and fir. Shadows stretched across the road like fingers trying to drag him back.

But he didn't stop. He was no longer chasing steelhead, he was answering something. Maybe a curse, maybe a calling, maybe both.

End of Chapter 5

CHAPTER 6: THEY CALL HIM RIVER BONES

Coming up next:
Chapter 6: They Call Him River Bones — where a forgotten piece of tribal history is uncovered… and Bob comes face to face with what the locals still whisper about when they think no one's listening.
Would you like a few plot path options for Chapter 6 before we dive in?

You said:
Yes, always give me a few plot options for each Chapter and section we write for each chapter.

ChatGPT said:
Updated saved memory
✅ Noted and locked in — I'll always provide you with multiple plot path options for every chapter and section we write from here on.
Next up: **Chapter 6 – *They Call Him River Bones***
Would you like me to now present you with a fresh set of plot options for that chapter?

You said:
Yes, present me with plot options for Chapter 6: They Call Him River Bones

ChatGPT said:
Absolutely. Chapter 6 — *They Call Him River Bones* — is our opportunity to take the Kilchis legend from hushed myth into the realm of terrifying possibility. Bob is now venturing deep into Hollow Mile, a place drenched in forgotten lore and older rules. This chapter should blur the line between folklore and the present — between story and witness.
Below are **four plot path options** for Chapter 6, all steeped in your established style: Stephen King-inspired realism, long and uneasy sentences, myth-building through grounded encounters, and a humble-yet-wise narrative voice.

☠️ **Option A: *The Old Man Who Saw Too Much***
Bob meets an old hermit who lives in an abandoned logging shack near Hollow Mile. Locals call him "Birch," and they say he's half-mad, but Birch knows the river like a priest knows scripture.
Birch tells Bob that "River Bones" was a name given to Kilchis by his own tribe after he defied death and returned from drowning — no longer the man they knew. Birch claims River Bones doesn't just haunt Hollow Mile… he *owns* it. And every so often, he demands payment.
Bob thinks the man is rambling — until Birch shows him something: carvings in the trees, human jawbones hanging like windchimes, and a map etched into stone that shows Hollow Mile's *off-limits* zone. The spot where Clancy first broke the river's unspoken law.
✅ **Strengths:**

- Introduces a wild, unsettling character who deepens the folklore.

- Builds history through dialogue and eerie symbolism.
- Keeps horror mostly atmospheric and suggestive — a slow burn.

☠️ **Option B: *The Corpse in the Tree***

Bob hikes into Hollow Mile and follows a game trail that leads him above a deep pool where no fish rise. There, in the crook of a tree growing horizontally over the water, he spots something that doesn't belong.

He climbs closer — and finds a mummified body bound in fishing line, suspended above the river. The bones have been cleaned by time and weather. Embedded in the skull is a Tillamook bone whistle, lashed with river grass.

Sheriff Tallbear arrives unexpectedly. He's not surprised. He's seen this before — years ago — and tells Bob quietly: "That's why we stopped looking." Then he warns Bob: *"There's a reason no one says his name after dark."*

✅ **Strengths:**

- Highly visual and disturbing without resorting to gore.
- Blurs the line between law enforcement and folklore knowledge.
- Reinforces the idea of a "quiet conspiracy" among those who know.

☠️ **Option C: *The Fisherman Who Broke the Rule***

Bob meets a younger angler upriver — reckless, confident, full of the same pride Bob once had. The man boasts about catching a steelhead and *not* releasing it.

That night, Bob hears screams echoing upriver. He finds the man's campsite destroyed — blood on the gravel, footprints leading into the river and then... *upstream.*

In the firepit, something is left behind: the man's steelhead, untouched, bones neatly arranged into a spiral. And beside it, a bundle of wet feathers and a child's fishing lure.

✅ **Strengths:**

- Echoes Bob's own journey — a chilling look at where his path could lead.
- Brings direct consequence into focus: disrespect = retribution.
- Adds symbolic details that deepen the River Bones myth.

☠️ **Option D: *The Hollow Mile Baptism***

Bob fishes Hollow Mile despite everything. The water feels thick — alive — but he casts anyway.

He hooks into something enormous. It doesn't run. It *drags him* into the river. He's pulled under, tumbles through rocks and roots, lungs screaming — and then everything goes still.

In the stillness, Bob sees something below him: an entire skeleton suspended in the water, its hands gripping a fishing rod. When he surfaces, hours have passed. His clothes are bone-dry. On his arm, a handprint — black, faint, like ash pressed into the skin.

✅ **Strengths:**

- A deeply symbolic, surreal, "baptismal" moment of transformation.
- Suggests River Bones is not just a hunter… but a judge.

- Pushes Bob further toward becoming a spiritual intermediary.

Next Step
Would you like to choose one of these paths to begin **Chapter 6: *They Call Him River Bones*?**
Or would you prefer a blended direction — such as Birch + a body in the tree… or a fish taken + symbolic punishment?
Once you choose, I'll begin writing in your long-form, immersive style.

You said:
Begin writing Chapter 6: They Call Him River Bones and include Option D: The Hollow Mile Baptism

ChatGPT said:
Perfect. *Option D: The Hollow Mile Baptism* brings us to a symbolic turning point — where the river makes its intentions clear and Bob is forced to confront not just myth, but its demand for reckoning. This scene will unfold with long, atmospheric paragraphs, full of psychological weight, introspection, and that uneasy wilderness dread you've established as the soul of *Steelhead Graveyard.*

(Part 1 updated)

Would you like to continue **Part 2** of this chapter next, where Bob begins to experience hallucinations or sensory overlaps with River Bones — sounds, visions, even spoken language that enters his mind uninvited?
Or should we shift the scene to a symbolic act — Bob returning to the site where he first caught a steelhead as a child, seeking clarity… only to find something he left behind has *already* been moved?

You said:
Let's continue writing Part 2 of this chapter, where shift the scene to a symbolic act — Bob returning to the site where he first caught a steelhead as a child, seeking clarity. Then let's have Bob experience hallucinations and sensory overlaps with River Bones — sounds, visions, even spoken language that enters his mind uninvited.

ChatGPT said:
Excellent. This structure gives us both an emotional anchor point — Bob returning to a foundational memory — and the opportunity to collapse the walls between past and myth. The river doesn't just haunt him now… it speaks. Let's deepen the sense of psychological erosion and spiritual intrusion, all while honoring your grounded, introspective style.

(Part 2 updated)

The sun never really broke through the canopy that morning.

Hollow Mile was less a place and more a feeling — a corridor of river pressed between cathedral-high trees and ridgelines so steep they blocked the sky. The map Clancy gave him had long since been folded and worn at the corners, but Bob knew where he was now. The trail was faint, barely more than a game path, and everything smelled of old bark, fungus, and damp stone.

The river widened here. Not dramatically, but enough to change its sound. Gone was the cheerful chatter of riffles — this water held its breath. The current moved slow, almost still, its surface dark and unbroken. A cold mirror.

He stood on the bank and studied it. There were no insects. No birdsong. Just the rhythmic hush of leaves shifting high above — and beneath that, the faint pulse of the river, like a heartbeat slowed to a whisper.

Bob pulled on his waders. He told himself he was there to fish. That was the lie he'd always told himself — even when it wasn't steelhead he was chasing, but something older. Something nameless.

His first cast drifted untouched. So did the second. On the third, the line stopped. Not tugged. Stopped.

For a full second, it held — taut, unmoving — then surged downstream so violently that the reel screamed. Bob staggered forward, boots slipping on slick stone, and the rod arched into a near horseshoe.

Whatever it was didn't run like a fish. It didn't head for cover or thrash. It pulled. Straight. Downriver. Then it stopped, and turned back.

Bob tried to adjust his footing, but it was too late. The line snapped tight again — and this time it didn't pull the rod — it pulled him.

He stumbled once, lost his footing, and the water was around his knees, then his waist, then above him. The cold hit like a hammer.

The current wasn't strong, but it didn't need to be. It wrapped around him like fingers. His feet scraped gravel, then found nothing. Roots brushed his legs. The world tilted.

He opened his eyes underwater. The river was dark, but something glowed beneath. A skeleton. Suspended in the current like a marionette on invisible strings.

Its jaw hung slack. Its hands — still curled in the shape of a fisherman's grip — clutched a rod so ancient it had fused with algae and time. Its ribs bowed outward, and woven through them were feathers, beads, and what looked like vertebrae from something not quite human.

Bob didn't panic, he watched.

The skeleton drifted closer. A small stone sat inside its skull where the brain should have been — carved with the same symbol as the birch bark he found days earlier.

Then Bob blinked — and the skeleton was gone.

He surfaced in silence. No gasping. No coughing. The air was cold but didn't burn. The river's surface was still, as if he'd never broken it.

He was standing in waist-deep water. Alone. His rod was gone.

He climbed slowly to the shore. His boots didn't squish. His clothes weren't wet. But on his left forearm, just below the elbow, was a print. A handprint. Human-sized. Faint black. Like the residue of wet ash pressed into flesh.

He touched it. It didn't wipe away.

Bob didn't speak the whole hike back. The silence of Hollow Mile walked with him, step for step, like a shadow that didn't need light to exist.

By the time he reached his truck, he understood one thing with perfect clarity: He had been marked, not hurt, not hunted, chosen.

The road to the old Wilson stretch was nearly gone. Bob had to hike the last quarter mile on foot, through overgrowth and the ghost trails of memory. The air smelled like it always did this time of year — wet pine, old moss, and that faint metallic tang of water that had moved through stone for a thousand years.

He stepped into the clearing. It hadn't changed much.

The fire ring was still there, stones blackened and moss-choked. A stump where Clancy once sat, sharpening hooks. And the bend in the river — wide and gentle, with a gravel bar that sloped like a lazy smile — was exactly how he remembered it.

This was where he'd caught his first steelhead.

An eight-year-old kid with no business holding a fly rod, beaming up at his father like he'd just reeled in a god.

He remembered the fight. The flurry of color in the water. The moment the fish rolled in the shallows, gleaming like a secret too big to hold.

He also remembered what happened after. Not in the moment, but in the dream.

Back then, it hadn't felt like much — a cold breeze, a whisper of unease.

Now, he knew better.

Bob stepped out onto the gravel bar. The river was low. He crouched and picked up a flat stone, rubbed the grit from its face.

That's when he noticed it. A figure — small, smoothed by time — carved into the rock beneath his boots. An outline. Stick-limbed. Head too large. Arms raised.

It hadn't been there before.

He blinked. The carving was gone. But the water was speaking. Not with sound, not with movement, with memory.

He closed his eyes.

And the voices began.

Whispers first — trickling between the branches above, threading through the current.

Then clearer. A chant. Rhythmic. Ancient. Tillamook, but not as Birch had muttered it. This was sung, low and melodic, like the syllables were soaked in marrow and fire.

Bob opened his eyes.

The trees were gone.

He stood in a canyon of fog. Shadows drifted just beyond his reach, and the river below no longer flowed — it listened.

On the opposite bank stood River Bones.

Not a vision. Not a dream.

Present.

His skin was pale, stretched too thin over bones like driftwood. His mouth moved, but the voice came from the river itself.

"You've fished what was meant to be left."

Bob couldn't move. Couldn't speak.

"Your father lied. Your line was not the first. It will not be the last."

River Bones stepped into the water. It didn't ripple. It opened for him.

"The fish remember. The trees remember. The blood remembers."

Then — silence.

Bob gasped as the world snapped back.

He was on his knees, hands in the gravel. No one around. The river, once again, flowed like it always had.

But in his mouth… a taste.

Iron.

Blood.

He wiped his lips. They were clean. But the taste remained.

He left the clearing without looking back.

By the time he reached the truck, his ears were ringing with a low, constant note — like a distant flute being played from underwater.

The handprint on his forearm had darkened.

Whatever this was, it wasn't over.

It hadn't even begun.

End of Chapter 6

CHAPTER 7: NO SIGNAL, NO ESCAPE

Coming up next:
Chapter 7 – *No Signal, No Escape* — Bob's isolation becomes literal. He returns to the river only to lose all connection to the outside world. Technology fails. The land itself becomes a maze. And something begins to hunt.
Would you like a fresh set of plot path options for Chapter 7 next?

You said:
Yes, give me plot paths for Chapter 7 to choose from.

ChatGPT said:
Perfect. We now arrive at:
📖 **Chapter 7: *No Signal, No Escape***
This chapter marks a critical midpoint in Act II — **The River Takes** — where Bob becomes physically, mentally, and spiritually cut off. Technology fails. Roads vanish. The forest closes in. The myth is no longer *around* him — it surrounds him.
Below are **four plot path options** for Chapter 7, written in your preferred style — introspective, unsettling, rooted in psychological unraveling and mythic realism.

📵 **Option A: *The Vanishing Map***
Bob sets up camp deeper upriver, intending to stay a few days to "observe" the river. But when he checks his GPS, the map begins shifting — trail markers move, river bends disappear, and Hollow Mile no longer registers.
Even worse, the compass on his watch spins erratically. No matter which direction he hikes, he ends up back at the same broken cedar tree.
That night, the river *rearranges itself.* Bob wakes to find his tent in a different location — or worse, *the same location… but the landmarks have changed.*
Something is warping space. And it knows he's trying to leave.
✅ **Strengths:**

- Intensifies the theme of the wilderness as a sentient force
- Builds dread slowly through disorientation
- Merges supernatural with survival horror

📴 **Option B: *The Silence Test***
Bob attempts to document everything. He brings a backup satellite phone, voice recorder, and trail cams. One by one, they all fail — footage goes blank, batteries die in hours, and the voice recorder plays back *his own voice whispering words he never said.*
He hikes to higher ground to get a signal and finds a logging road that doesn't appear on any map. Following it, he discovers a rusted-out truck that looks decades old — with a skeleton still inside. The vehicle is his exact make and model.
The keys in the ignition are labeled with his initials.

✅ **Strengths:**

- Introduces intense psychological horror without gore
- Suggests a "looping" or predestined fate
- Builds tension through uncanny symbolism

🧠 **Option C: *The River's Trial***

Bob slips on a river rock and is briefly knocked unconscious. When he wakes, the river is gone — replaced by a dry canyon where the water *should be.*

He hears voices coming from the canyon walls. They sound like loved ones — Tanya, Clancy, his kids — all begging him to leave. Then the voices change. They become one voice. Not pleading… *judging.*

The canyon becomes a courtroom of memory. Bob relives every steelhead he's ever taken and every time he ignored warnings.

When he wakes for real, he's back by the river… but one of his boots is missing, and the ash handprint on his arm has spread to his chest.

✅ **Strengths:**

- Thematically rich and symbolic
- Blends morality, memory, and the supernatural
- Pushes Bob toward an irreversible psychological break

🌲 **Option D: *The Others Who Never Left***

Bob stumbles upon a hidden glade while tracking what looks like boot prints. Inside, he finds a makeshift camp: tarps, sleeping bags, old gear… and seven wooden stakes marking where tents once stood.

Each stake is carved with a name and date — all within the last thirty years.

In one of the sleeping bags is a journal. It describes River Bones in detail, and ends with the words: *"No one leaves unless he lets you."*

That night, Bob hears people moving outside his tent. He peers out — and sees seven shadowed figures watching him. Silent. Motionless.

✅ **Strengths:**

- Introduces the concept of other victims
- Suggests Bob is not just haunted, but *next*
- Adds long-form suspense with a sense of inevitability

🔍 **Your Next Move**

Would you like to:

- Choose one of these options to begin **Chapter 7: *No Signal, No Escape***?
- Blend elements (e.g., the vanishing map + the old truck + the ghostly figures)?
- Or would you like me to pitch a 5th custom variant based on a different fear (e.g., losing time, forgetting who you are, being hunted in total silence)?

Once you choose, I'll begin drafting Chapter 7 in full immersive detail.

You said:
Begin writing Chapter 7: No Signal No Escape, with Option C: The River's Trial.

ChatGPT said:
Excellent. *Option C: The River's Trial* brings us into symbolic, psychological horror — a descent into Bob's guilt, memory, and myth. This is the chapter where time fractures, the river vanishes, and judgment begins. Written in your voice: long, immersive paragraphs, Stephen King–inspired introspection, and that ever-present sense that the wilderness doesn't just watch — it *remembers.*

(Part 1 updated)

Would you like to continue **Part 2** with:

- Bob researching the name Samuel Graham, uncovering a string of disappearances along the same stretch of river?
- Sheriff Tallbear showing up unexpectedly, having also lost time, claiming he "woke up two days later than he should have"?
- Bob trying to leave the forest… and failing — roads no longer lead where they should?

Or shall we blend elements?

You said:
Continue writing Part 2 of Chapter 7 with Bob researching the name Samuel Graham, uncovering a string of disappearances along the same stretch of river. Then, Sheriff Tallbear showing up unexpectedly, having also lost time, claiming he "woke up two days later than he should have." After that, Bob tried to leave the forest… failing — roads no longer lead where they should.

(Part 2 updated)

ChatGPT said:
Excellent. This will be a rich and terrifying Part 2 — blending investigative suspense, mythic escalation, and the irreversible sense of *entrapment.* The forest is no longer a backdrop — it's a trap. This segment will continue in your grounded, slow-burn style, using Bob's introspection to carry dread forward.

You said:
Let's expand Chapter 7 by adding more content at the end of what we have written so far, adding a part 3 and 4 to it.

ChatGPT said:
Excellent. Let's deepen Chapter 7 with two final parts — each building on the feeling of entrapment, psychological erosion, and mythological possession. These additions will stretch

the tension to the breaking point, all while preserving your slow-burn style and grounded realism.

(Part 3 & 4 updated)

Bob never saw the rock.

One second he was walking the bank — boots pressing into mud, eyes scanning the quiet pools beneath overhanging alders — and the next, his left foot caught something slick beneath the surface. He went down hard. His shoulder hit first, then the back of his head cracked against something harder than it should have been. The world went sideways. The trees spun like a merry-go-round from hell. Then — black.

Silence. And then… the absence of everything.

When he opened his eyes, the river was gone. Not dried up — not even visible. The sound of water, the weight of mist, the perpetual dampness that coated the Oregon air — all of it was gone.

He stood in a canyon carved from red stone. No trees. No moss. Just towering vertical walls veined with black roots that pulsed faintly, as if carrying sap or blood. The sky above was colorless, as if someone had forgotten to paint it in.

His boots crunched dust instead of gravel. And far below, in the empty riverbed, there was movement. Not water — shadows.

They moved like fish, but too fast. Too precise. Too knowing.

He tried to speak, but the air in his throat felt too heavy to push. When he finally forced sound from his lips, it echoed like a voice through a canyon of bones.

Then came the first voice — not his own.

"Robert Tomalin."

It came from nowhere. Everywhere.

"You fished the first pool at age eight. The fish was sixteen inches. You kept it. You did not ask."

Bob turned, but there was no speaker. Just stone and dust and the vibration of something old moving beneath the surface of the world.

"Wilson River. February. You released a wild buck too late. It died downstream. You left it."

Then another voice — Clancy's.

"Don't ever forget — the river remembers."

Then another — Tanya's, strained, scared.

"You're scaring me, Bob. What's happening to you?"

Then Shane.

"Are you coming home?"

He fell to his knees. The canyon floor cracked beneath him. Out of the cracks rose hooks. Dozens of them — old, barbed, rusted — each one dangling from invisible line, swaying above him like windchimes in a dead forest.

Each hook bore something.

A scale, a sliver of bone, a blood-dried fly.

Bob screamed — but what came out wasn't a scream, it was a chant.

Tillamook.

The words made no sense, but his mouth knew them. His tongue moved with memory not his own. His breath shook with syllables passed down through rivers and bloodlines.

And then — silence again. The hooks vanished, the canyon vanished. And he was back on the riverbank, soaked and coughing, the taste of blood and cedar bark in his mouth.

The sky above him was darkening. His backpack was missing, so was his rod.

But in the sand beside him, something new had been placed, a fishing license.

Not his. The name read: SAMUEL GRAHAM. Issue date: March 1986. Status: Deceased.

Bob sat in the ranger station with a weak signal flickering across his laptop screen. He'd made it back from the riverbank — somehow — cold, shaking, and barefoot. His pack was gone, his rod was gone, and the only thing left in his hand when he reached the station was the fishing license.

Samuel Graham.
March 1986.

Deceased.

The name wasn't familiar. But something about it buzzed in the back of his skull like a mosquito just out of reach.

The internet was slow — the kind of slow that suggested the mountain didn't want to share its secrets. He typed the name anyway. Added "Oregon," "missing," and "river."

The first result was a 1993 Statesman Journal article, archived in a local library microfiche scan. He clicked.

"State Search Suspended for Missing Fisherman."
Authorities ended their five-day search for 37-year-old Samuel Graham after failing to locate any remains or personal belongings aside from a boot and fly box found near Dead Mare Bend. The Tillamook County Sheriff's Office said foul play was unlikely. The river had recently risen due to rain. Graham, an avid solo fisherman, had no next of kin in the area.

No follow-up articles. No remains ever found.

Bob tried searching the name with "Hollow Mile." Nothing. That term didn't exist online. Then he changed tactics.

He typed in: "Disappearance Rogue River / Wilson River / Dead Mare Bend." Hits scattered across the decades. All solo fishermen. All missing. All during early spring. Most presumed drowned and none were found. And all within three miles of Hollow Mile.

Bob stared at the screen until the battery icon blinked red. He reached for the charger. That's when he heard the door open.

Sheriff Tallbear stepped into the ranger station, face pale, eyes sunken like he hadn't slept in a week.

"Bob," he said slowly, voice brittle. "What day is it?"

Bob blinked. "Thursday."

Tallbear sat down like his legs had forgotten how to hold him.

"I went home Sunday. Told myself I'd come back Tuesday."

He rubbed his hands together, like he was trying to feel something that had gone numb.

"I woke up an hour ago. Fully dressed. In my own damn truck. Parked by the river. Two full days gone."

Bob slid the fishing license across the table.

Tallbear didn't touch it. He just looked at it, and then at Bob.

"Tell me you haven't been to Hollow Mile."

Bob didn't answer.

Tallbear exhaled through his nose, slow and bitter. "Then we're out of time."

Later that night Bob packed what he could. He didn't plan to go deeper. Not yet. He wanted out. Away from the canyon. Away from the voices. Away from this place where the river bled into his dreams and left marks on his body.

He drove east. The GPS on his dash flickered — then froze. The road forked unexpectedly — a split that wasn't on any map.

He chose left.

After twenty minutes, he passed the same stump he'd just driven by. The same curve in the hill. The same deer carcass lying off the road, stiff-legged and bloated.

He tried right. Same result. He stopped, shut off the engine, and stepped outside.

There was no sound, not even the wind. He opened his phone. The compass app spun in slow, lazy circles. He looked up.

In the trees above the road, hanging from the highest branches, were fishing lures. Hundreds of them. Spinners. Flies. Corkies. Feathers. All tangled in the limbs like caught prayers.

And just beneath them — near the trunk of the largest pine — a shape moved. It stepped back into shadow before Bob could see the face.

But he knew who it was.

Or what.

He got back in the truck. Turned the key. The engine didn't turn over.

Bob spent the night in the cab, wrapped in his emergency blanket, engine dead, dashboard cold, every window staring out into a forest that refused to sleep.

He tried the ignition again at dawn. Still dead. No click, no attempt — just the mechanical indifference of a truck that had been cut off from time. He stepped out, stretched, pissed into the ferns, and told himself this was still salvageable.

He'd hike out.

He marked the trees as he walked — small notches in the bark every thirty steps. A survival habit drilled into him since Boy Scouts.

An hour in, he stopped to check his trail. Every tree behind him bore no mark. Not one.

Worse: up ahead, he saw the same dead pine he'd already passed. A windblown snag, half-rotted and split like a peeled tooth. Same split. Same scorch marks. Same bird nest tucked in the crook.

He knelt, heart thudding. That's when he saw it — half-buried under moss and cedar needles. A Ziploc bag. Old. Clouded. Inside, a notebook with a brown leather cover, swollen slightly from damp.

He opened it. The first few pages were blank. Then came the writing.

Blocky. Pressed too hard, like it had been written in the dark. The first entry was dated March 18, 1994.

"I came back because I had to. I thought the river owed me another one. Turns out I was wrong. You don't take from something that's older than sin."

The second entry chilled him.

"It watches you in the bends. Not where you stand. Where you will stand. Don't look for its face. That's the last thing you see."

He flipped forward, heart racing.

There were pages. Dozens. Ramblings, drawings, scratch marks. But one entry stopped him cold.

"My name is Robert Tomalin. If you're reading this, turn around. Burn this. Leave no trace. It can't follow what it can't remember."

Bob dropped the notebook and staggered backward. The forest didn't react. It just watched.

He didn't touch the notebook again. Then he left it there, exactly as he found it. Even though his name was inside… in handwriting that looked like his own.

It took him the rest of the day to find an old fireline road — narrow, rutted, overgrown, but promising. It led straight up toward higher ground. Bob followed it.

No sounds of animals. No wind. Just the brush scraping his jeans and the strange sense that the road was leading him somewhere it wanted, not the other way around.

Just before nightfall, he found the clearing. An old fire base — metal fire rings, a half-collapsed outhouse, and a circular pit with a blackened stump at its center. He didn't question why there were no footprints. He didn't question why the ring was warm even though no fire burned.

He was too tired and just sat down. Ate a protein bar. Drank from his bottle and then he saw it.

Across the fire pit, just beyond the treeline, stood a man. Not moving, not speaking, not hiding. Just waiting.

Bob's first instinct wasn't fear, it was recognition. He knew this silhouette. Not from memory — from dream. The outline, and the crooked shoulder. The way the raven feathers dangled behind his ears like forgotten prayers. The stillness of prey that didn't fear predators.

He didn't run, he just stood. Met the figure's gaze — even if he couldn't see its eyes. And in that stillness, he heard a voice not with his ears but with his spine.

"You fished where you were told not to. You took what would not return."

The trees around the figure pulsed. Their bark shimmered like wet scales.

"Now you must return."

Bob blinked and the figure was gone.

But across the fire pit, in the dirt, was a perfect bootprint, his own. Facing the opposite direction as if he'd been the one standing there.

End of Expanded Chapter 7
Bob is now utterly alone, both physically and psychologically — and possibly standing in two places at once. The River Bones myth is no longer metaphor. It is law.
Let me know when you'd like the **Chapter 8 plot options** for *Madness, or Something Worse.*

CHAPTER 8: MADNESS, OR SOMETHING WORSE

You said:
Let's continue writing Chapter 8: Madness, Or Something Worse. Provide me plot options at the beginning and as we write each section. Let's make sure to incorporate thoughts of Bob's wife and children into his thoughts.

ChatGPT said:
Updated saved memory
Perfect. Welcome to **Chapter 8: *Madness, or Something Worse*** — the psychological tipping point of *Steelhead Graveyard*. Bob is physically trapped, mentally unraveling, and spiritually marked. In this chapter, the narrative should blur the boundary between dream and waking, memory and prophecy, sanity and something much older than madness.
Let's begin with **Plot Options** for Chapter 8, each crafted to honor your story's tone, pacing, and emphasis on Bob's family as his last tether to reality.

📖 **Chapter 8: *Madness, or Something Worse***
🔮 **Plot Path Options**

🧠 **Option A: *The Voice in the Fire***
Bob finally manages to build a fire to keep the cold at bay. But as he stares into the flames, he begins hearing voices — Tanya's, then Shane's, then Sarah's — all comforting at first. Then the voices shift.
They begin to tell him things he shouldn't know: past regrets, childhood guilt, secrets he's kept even from himself.
The fire shows him images — his family home, *empty*, a crib overturned, muddy boots in the hallway. He starts to believe he never had a family at all — that Tanya and the kids were *planted* memories.
He begins to question: *Have I already died? Am I just one more name on the river's list?*
✅ **Strengths:**

- Deep psychological horror rooted in family disintegration
- Explores internal guilt, memory corruption
- Builds eerie ambiguity without answering too much

⏳ **Option B: *The Time Loop Journal***
Bob finds a second notebook, this one newer, but unmistakably his. Inside are entries from the *future* — describing things he hasn't done yet.
He reads that he *will* see Tanya again, but she won't recognize him. That Shane will one day fish this river and see "a man in the water who smiles like his father."
Every entry ends with the same line: *"You forgot something. That's why you're still here."*
Bob begins to doubt not just his sanity, but time itself.

✅ **Strengths:**

- Introduces cyclical fate and memory erosion
- Adds mythic weight without revealing River Bones directly
- Keeps the story emotionally tied to Bob's family

👁 **Option C: *The Mirror Pool***

Bob stumbles onto a pool so still it reflects the sky perfectly. When he looks into it, he sees not himself — but Tanya and the kids at home, reacting to news that he's missing. They mourn. Time passes.

Then the reflection *turns* and shows them forgetting him — photo frames removed, laughter returning, Tanya remarried.

But then the pool shifts again — and he sees Tanya waking in the night, whispering to the empty room: *"Come home."*

Bob reaches into the water to touch her hand — and wakes in a strange cabin, dry and clean… with no memory of how he got there.

✅ **Strengths:**

- Symbolic and haunting
- Explores themes of being forgotten and remembered
- Leaves room for dream logic and subconscious navigation

🌲 **Option D: *The Memory Tree***

Bob comes upon a giant cedar tree with hundreds of items hanging from its limbs — lures, child's toys, wedding rings, photos sealed in plastic.

One item is a photo of *him*, Tanya, Shane, and Sarah — at a beach he doesn't remember visiting.

But as he examines it, he sees that *his* face in the photo has no eyes. Just water dripping from the sockets.

He turns to leave, but realizes he can't remember how he got there — or even what day it is. He begins to suspect that he's losing *more than time.*

✅ **Strengths:**

- Physical symbol of memory and loss
- Starts to dissolve Bob's identity
- Foreshadows permanent psychological breakdown

🎯 **Next Step**

Which option would you like to use to begin **Part 1** of Chapter 8?

You can choose a single direction or blend two together. Once selected, I'll begin writing in long-form, immersive prose with Bob's thoughts of Tanya and the kids woven in to anchor his humanity.

You said:

Continue writing Chapter 8: Madness, or Something Else. Use option A: The Voice in the Fire.

(Part 1 updated)

ChatGPT said:
Excellent. *Option A: The Voice in the Fire* allows us to dive deep into Bob's unraveling mind, where his only source of warmth becomes a channel for spiritual invasion. In this section, we'll lean into long, introspective paragraphs as Bob's thoughts turn toward his wife and children — the last pieces of him the river hasn't yet claimed.

ChatGPT said:
Would you like to continue with **Part 2**, where Bob wakes to find the fire cold, the fish hook missing, and his own voice whispering things back at him from the trees?
Or should we begin the hallucinations — images of Tanya leading him deeper into the woods, or perhaps River Bones appearing in her form?
Or combine these elements into one long, terrifying section?

You said:
Let's continue writing Part 2 of this Chapter, where Bob wakes to find the fire cold, the fish hook missing, and his own voice whispering things back at him from the trees. Then, begin the hallucinations — images of Tanya leading him deeper into the woods.

ChatGPT said:
Excellent. In **Part 2** of *Chapter 8: Madness, or Something Worse*, we'll continue Bob's descent into disorientation. Reality no longer holds firm — it slips. His voice speaks without him. Tanya appears… but not as she was. The wilderness is no longer outside him — it's *inside.*

(Part 2 updated)

ChatGPT said:
Would you like to continue with **Part 3**, where Bob runs — but no direction leads out — and the forest begins repeating itself? (trees, paths, even animals looping)
Or should he attempt to confront the hallucination, calling out to River Bones directly — and finally hear him answer?

You said:
Contine with Part 3, where where Bob runs — but no direction leads out — and the forest begins repeating itself. Then he attempts to confront the hallucination, calling out to River Bones directly — and finally hears him answer.

ChatGPT said:

Perfect. In **Part 3** of *Chapter 8: Madness, or Something Worse*, we will collapse the last boundaries of space and sanity. The forest becomes a maze with no center. Bob, desperate and unraveling, reaches for the only name that has never been said out loud — and receives his answer.

(Part 3 updated)

📖 ***Chapter 8: Madness,***

ChatGPT said:
Would you like to close Chapter 8 with a **Part 4**, where Bob wakes in an impossible place — underground, underwater, or within a carved chamber of bone — and sees names etched into the walls?
Or should he wake back at the riverbank, as if none of it happened… but with the ash handprint now burned across his chest and a memory that *won't let go*?
Or combine both — dream and reality beginning to *overlap permanently*?

You said:
Close Chapter 8 with Part 4, where Bob wakes up in a cave by the river where he can see names etched into the walls. Bob then exits the cave right next to the river and when he turns around, the cave entrance is gone and it is as if none of what he just went through ever happened except that he had the ash handprint now burned across his chest and a memory that won't let go. As you write, do so in long-form paragraphs where possible.

ChatGPT said:
Absolutely. Here is the final movement of Chapter 8 — *Part 4: The Place That Forgets You.* This scene will close the chapter with eerie quiet, symbolic trauma, and the growing certainty that Bob has crossed a threshold not easily returned from. The wilderness mythos becomes carved into both flesh and memory.

(Part 4 updated)

The fire was hard to start.

Bob had matches. Waterproof ones, even. But the kindling wouldn't catch. The wood hissed like it had its own breath, like it didn't want to burn. He scoured for birch bark, stripped thin curls with shaking hands, and finally coaxed the flame to life with a whisper and a prayer he didn't remember learning.

When it finally took, he sat before it like a man kneeling at the altar of something holy, but indifferent.

The heat felt good — not just against his skin, but in his bones, as if it reminded his body it was still human. That he wasn't part of the forest yet. Not entirely.

He thought of Tanya. The way she always complained about the smell of campfire clinging to his flannels. How she once threatened to make him sleep on the porch after a trip to the Deschutes because he reeked like a chimney. He smiled at the memory, but it felt distant — like watching a home movie from someone else's life.

The wind picked up, rustling the trees in long, low sighs. The fire popped, sending a spark dancing into the night.

That's when he heard it.

"Bob…" Soft. Delicate.

The voice slid in between the crackle of flame, just under the threshold of the ordinary. He froze. Then — again.

"Bob… are you cold?"

He looked up, eyes wide. It was Tanya's voice. Calm. Warm. Too real to be imagined, too impossible to be true.

He swallowed hard.

"Tanya?"

Silence.

Then the fire flared — no new wood added, no shift in wind — just a sudden bloom of heat and color, like the flame had exhaled.

And then he heard Shane.

"Dad?"

The boy's voice was tentative. Concerned.

"I'm scared," it said. "Are you okay?"

Bob's heart squeezed. He closed his eyes and held onto that voice like a lifeline. Then Sarah joined in — a child's whisper, high and innocent.

"Where are you, Daddy? Come home."

He opened his eyes. The fire was no longer a flame, it was a window.

Inside the dancing light, he saw it: his living room — but dim, unfocused, like someone watching through fogged glass. Tanya stood near the kitchen, hands on the counter. Her face was drawn, eyes red. Shane sat on the couch, clinging to a worn blanket. Sarah rocked a plush frog in her arms, humming tunelessly.

Then the fire shifted and everything inside changed.

The house was empty. Furniture dusty. A calendar on the wall said 2028. The photos on the mantle were gone. In their place were small, framed drawings — stick figures, mostly. One of them looked like Bob.

The room flickered again. This time, Tanya was there — but she was older. Gray at the temples. A man Bob didn't know stood beside her, his arm around her shoulders. They looked happy.

Then it flickered once more. And Tanya was in bed, alone, face turned to the wall. Tears rolled down her cheek as she whispered:

"Come home."

The flame snapped violently. Bob blinked — and the fire was just fire again. No voices, no visions. Only embers. But he wasn't alone.

There, in the coals, lay a small fish hook — curved, blackened, glowing faintly with heat.

Bob didn't touch it but he knew what it meant. His family wasn't gone, but they were drifting away, and the river — or whatever lived inside it — was pulling him farther away.

Bob jolted awake.

The sun hadn't risen. Or maybe it had — but not here. The clearing was trapped in a kind of gray silence, neither night nor day, as if time had called a truce just long enough for something older to slip through.

The fire was out. Not ashy. Not smoldering. Just gone like it had never been lit.

His hands were cold. Dirt-caked. His jacket half unzipped. And his boots — they were off, neatly placed beside where he slept as if someone had gently undressed him.

He sat up slowly. No sign of the fish hook and no charred ring where the fire had burned. Just the forest as though it was watching.

He stood, legs stiff. Every joint ached with the kind of fatigue that goes deeper than sleep can cure.

That's when he heard a whisper. Low, hoarse, but not distant. It came from just behind the tree line.

"Don't forget to notch the trail, Bob."

His breath caught. That was his voice. Spoken in the exact tone he'd used back when he marked the trees before becoming lost.

The whisper came again — only this time, it was wrong. The cadence was off. Like a recording played back at the wrong speed. Too slow or too close.

"She's waiting for you, Bob. She needs you to find her."

A pause. A breath. Then…

"You let them forget you."

His chest tightened as he turned. The trees shifted and one of them moved. Then he saw Tanya, but not Tanya.

She stood just beyond the light, barefoot on a bed of pine needles, hair tangled, eyes hollow. She wore the red flannel he left behind on their last anniversary trip to the coast. She didn't smile, instead she beckoned.

Bob stepped forward without meaning to as the forest swallowed the distance between them like water swallowing footprints in sand.

She turned and walked deeper into the woods, not urgently and not fearfully. She glided, the way you do when you know the land and it knows you back.

He followed.

"Wait," he called. "Tanya…"

She didn't respond. But her head turned slightly, just enough for him to see her mouth begin to move. The words came not from her lips, but from all around him.

"Do you remember what you promised me? On that dock, after Shane was born? You said you'd never leave. You said the river was your church. That it gave you peace. Now give it something back."

Bob stumbled over a root. His hand hit dirt. When he looked up, she was gone. Only the trees remained and the faint shimmer of water ahead. But it wasn't the river, it was a reflection.

A flat pool. Still. Unmoving. In it, his own face stared back and behind it, Tanya stood once more.

But this time, her eyes were empty sockets. Her mouth wide, distended, a trout's mouth — round and dark and endless.

He blinked and then the image of Tanya was gone. No Tanya, no pool. Just him And the sound of something wet breathing behind him.

Bob ran.

He didn't plan to — didn't weigh the options or pick a direction. His body simply moved, driven by a panic so deep it bypassed thought. He ran toward the place where Tanya had stood. Or hadn't. He wasn't sure anymore.

Branches clawed at his arms. Ferns slapped his legs. The damp earth gave and gave beneath his boots, like the ground was tired of holding him up.

He counted his steps. Fifty. A hundred. One fifty. At two hundred, he broke into a clearing and noticed his bootprints were already there.

He turned and ran the opposite way, breath wheezing sharp through his throat. Another clearing but it was the same one.

The dead log. The moss-covered stone. The stump with the spiral notch carved into it. Again. And again. The forest shuffled around him like a house with secret hallways.

He screamed — not words, just sound, raw and furious.

"TANYA!" he bellowed. "SHANE! SARAH!"

No response.

Only birdsong. The first he'd heard in days — if this was still days.

He dropped to his knees, panting. His hands shaking. This wasn't madness. It was worse. Madness had rules. This place had none.

Or maybe just one.

His mouth opened before he could stop it. And he spoke the name he had never dared to say aloud — not even when reading the old journal entries, not even when Clancy whispered it through cracked lips like a curse wrapped in memory.

"River Bones."

The forest didn't shudder. It exhaled. Every tree leaned back an inch. Every fern dipped. The wind changed direction — not with randomness, but intention.

And then… the answer came. Not in volume. Not in language. But in presence.

Bob stood, eyes wide, arms limp at his sides. The forest darkened slightly, not from clouds, but from proximity — like something vast had come close. Something that didn't need to be seen to be known.

Then it spoke, inside him. Behind his teeth and beneath his ribs.

"You are not the first, Bob Tomalin. You are the echo. You walked into my mouth and asked me to sing. Now I will show you your voice."

Bob fell. He didn't trip. He fell — straight down, as if the earth had turned vertical.

The air rushed past him. Then it was gone and there was only darkness, and breathing. And something swimming around him that had too many hands.

Bob came to with his cheek pressed against damp stone. The air around him was cool, close, and stank faintly of rust and lichen. His vision blurred, throat dry. Every breath echoed. He tried to move and winced — his ribs throbbed like he'd fallen from a rooftop. His hands were scraped. His clothes clung to his skin as though he'd been submerged and then left to dry in place.

He rolled onto his back and saw the ceiling.

Rock. Curved and black-veined, like it had been chewed out of the mountain by a river no longer here. Faint trickles of water whispered down the walls. Thin roots dangled from the cracks like veins pulled loose from earth. The room around him wasn't large — maybe fifteen feet across — but its presence was vast, the way cathedrals feel when empty. Holy in the way old wounds are holy.

Then he saw the names.

They weren't written in ink or paint. They were etched into the stone. Hundreds of them.

Into the walls. Into the floor. Some deep and purposeful, others scratched in with trembling fingers. Names in English. Names in Native script. Some were just initials. Some ended mid-stroke.

He rose slowly and stepped forward, every joint complaining.

There.

Samuel Graham.
Etched twice. Once clean. Once ragged and bleeding into itself.

Beside it:
Clancy Tomalin.
Carved faint. A single date beneath it: March 14, 1971.

And there — near the base of the far wall, half-covered in moss: Robert Tomalin.

His name. Already carved, already waiting but without a date, just a space beneath it.

Bob stared. A chill ran through his legs and into the earth. It was more than just fear. It was recognition. This was a place for those the river would not return. A mausoleum for memory. A library of the lost.

He turned toward the tunnel behind him, a narrow exit where daylight seeped through like mist through gauze. He didn't run. He didn't speak. He just walked out.

The tunnel wound up through rock, curling left and right without pattern, until the light was bright and strong. Then he stepped out into sunlight.

The river was there, flowing calmly, its surface sparkling like nothing had ever disturbed it.

Birdsong returned and the wind moved the treetops.

He turned to look back but the cave was gone. No entrance. No stone. Just a stretch of moss-covered riverbank and a single dogwood tree standing out of place among the other evergreens.

The land had swallowed its secret whole. He stood there for a long time.

Finally, he pulled open his shirt. The ash-colored handprint, the one that had marked his forearm before now spread across his chest. Blackened. Faintly cracked. Like the last touch of a burning god.

He touched it and felt that it was warm. And behind his eyes, memory stirred — not a dream, not a nightmare, but a truth.

It would never let go, and neither would the river.

ChatGPT said:
End of Chapter 8
Ready to continue into **Chapter 9: Steelhead Don't Scream** — or would you like to receive plot options first?

CHAPTER 9: STELHEAD DON'T SCREAM

You said:
I am ready to continue with Chapter 9: Steelhead Don't Scream. Provide me with plot options that are filled with deep emotions that the reader will feel as they read it.

ChatGPT said:
Excellent. Welcome to **Chapter 9: *Steelhead Don't Scream*** — one of the most symbolically rich and emotionally potent chapters in *Steelhead Graveyard.* At this stage, Bob is no longer simply a lost man in the woods — he's a fractured vessel, torn between who he was and what the river is trying to make him become. This chapter should shake the reader emotionally, digging into themes of identity, loss, family, and what it means to be *forgotten by the world but remembered by the wilderness.*
Here are **four emotionally-charged plot path options** for Chapter 9, crafted to resonate deeply with the reader while still following the story's grounded, myth-tinged arc.

❤️ **Option A: *The Silent Catch***
Bob hooks a massive steelhead in a remote pool — the first sign of life in days. The fight is powerful, brutal. He lands it. Kneels beside it. The fish doesn't thrash. Doesn't breathe. It stares at him.
He realizes, slowly, that the fish's mouth has been sewn shut with river grass.
The silence of it overwhelms him. He sees himself in the fish — exhausted, voiceless, unable to scream no matter how deeply he feels the pain.
In a devastating emotional moment, Bob lets the fish go. Not as a fisherman — but as a man surrendering something he no longer wants to carry.

✅ **Emotional Weight:**

- Explores Bob's grief and loss of voice.
- Deep metaphor for emotional repression and collapse.
- The act of releasing the fish is a symbolic choice of mercy over ego.

📷 **Option B: *The Camera That Shows Home***
Bob finds a waterlogged trail cam strapped to a tree. Somehow, it still works.
He reviews the photos.
At first, it's just animals. Elk. Coyotes. Fog.
Then, there's a photo of Tanya. Standing in the forest. Holding a lantern. Smiling — but not at the camera. *At him.*
The final photo is of his family around the dinner table — a real memory — but shot from outside a window, as though someone was watching them… from the woods.
Bob begins to question if he ever left. Or if he's dead. Or if someone *else* is using his face to watch them now.

✅ **Emotional Weight:**

- Raises existential dread and longing for family.
- Reader feels gut-punched seeing his family through a ghostly lens.
- Evokes helplessness — the idea of being close but untouchable.

🫀 **Option C: *The River's Confession***

Bob slips into a fugue state where the river speaks directly through his own mouth.
It shows him scenes from Tanya's life after he vanished: how she wept, how Shane blamed himself, how Sarah stopped asking where he went.
Then the river shows him *what might have been* — family vacations that never happened, laughter he'll never hear, birthdays missed.
Bob breaks down fully, sobbing by the water, realizing he's becoming part of the river's story — no longer a man, but a *lesson.*

✅ **Emotional Weight:**

- Devastating realization of what's lost — permanently.
- Gives the river a voice of sorrow, not just menace.
- Bob's breakdown feels earned, painful, and transformative.

🧸 **Option D: *The Lost Thing He Shouldn't Have Found***

While wandering, Bob finds a toy — Sarah's plush frog — soaked, muddy, lying beside the riverbank.
The last time he saw it, she was clutching it in her sleep.
He holds it like a relic, unable to breathe.
The moment is simple, quiet — but crushing.
Then he hears a child laugh in the trees — soft, not cruel — and sees a tiny barefoot footprint in the mud.
It's not Sarah.
But whoever it is… they know him.

✅ **Emotional Weight:**

- Simple but brutal parental grief moment.
- The frog is a universal symbol of innocence and memory.
- Leaves the reader shattered by what might never be regained.

🎯 **Choose Your Direction**

Which path should we take to begin Chapter 9: *Steelhead Don't Scream*?
Would you like a pure single thread or a blend (e.g., combine the **silent catch** with the **camera**, or the **frog** with the **river's confession**)?
Once you choose, I'll begin with **Part 1** written in full long-form paragraphs, delivering the emotional intensity you've asked for.

You said:

Write Chapter 9: Steelhead Don't Scream, using Option A: The Silent Catch. I want this chapter to be longer than the other and contain 6 parts to it. In order to make this chapter longer, we will also incorporate Option D: The Lost Thing He Shouldn't Have Found.

ChatGPT said:
Updated saved memory
Perfect. Chapter 9: *Steelhead Don't Scream* will unfold across six emotionally devastating parts, blending the metaphorical and the literal, the seen and the deeply felt. With **Option A (The Silent Catch)** and **Option D (The Lost Thing He Shouldn't Have Found)** woven together, this chapter will cut to the heart of Bob's unraveling identity as a father, husband, and man.
We begin now with:

(Part 1 updated)

ChatGPT said:
Would you like to continue with **Part 2**, where Bob wanders downstream, emotionally broken from the catch, and stumbles upon Sarah's frog — the one thing from his world that shouldn't be here?
Or would you like a moment of flashback first — Bob remembering a specific moment of fatherhood with Sarah — to deepen the emotional weight when he finds the toy?

You said:
Rewrite Part 1 of Chapter 9 to be much more full-paragraph style. The way you wrote this has only a few words per line and doest not feel like full-paragraph writing. Make this correction and write Part 1 of Chapter 9 again.

ChatGPT said:
Absolutely — here is a rewritten version of **Chapter 9: Steelhead Don't Scream – Part 1: When the River Gives You Something Back**, now presented in *full, flowing paragraphs* to match your stylistic direction. The emotional intensity is preserved, but now expressed through a more immersive, novelistic structure.

ChatGPT said:
Would you like me to proceed to **Part 2**, where Bob stumbles further downstream and discovers Sarah's frog — the lost thing he never should have found? Or would you prefer a reflective flashback to anchor the emotional gravity of what's about to happen?

You said:
That was much better. As we continue writing this book, continue to use this same full-paragraph novelistic structure. Now, continue writing Part 2 of Chapter 9, where Bob has a reflective flashback to anchor the emotional gravity of what's about to happen.

ChatGPT said:

Updated saved memory
Excellent. We now continue with **Chapter 9: Steelhead Don't Scream – Part 2: The Weight of Small Things**, written in the same rich, immersive prose style. This section will center on a deeply emotional flashback — a moment between Bob and his daughter Sarah that anchors the tragedy of what he finds later. The purpose here is not just nostalgia, but the slow ache of loss threatening to break through memory's protective shell.

(Part 2 updated)

ChatGPT said:
Let me know when you're ready to continue with **Part 3**, where Bob discovers the frog flashlight — the exact one Sarah used to wear — half-buried near the riverbank. The object shouldn't be here. It *can't* be here. And that's why it changes everything.

You said:
Continue writing Part 3

ChatGPT said:
Absolutely. Here's **Chapter 9: Steelhead Don't Scream – Part 3: The Lost Thing He Shouldn't Have Found**, continuing in the same immersive, full-paragraph style. This is the emotional and psychological turning point—where memory collides with the impossible, and the river tightens its grip on Bob's soul.

(Part 3 updated)

ChatGPT said:
Would you like to proceed with **Part 4**, where Bob tries to escape this stretch of forest, but everything begins to shift — the trees repeat themselves, landmarks vanish, and a whispering presence begins to stalk him in earnest?

You said:
Continue writing Part 4, where Bob tries to escape this stretch of forest, but everything begins to shift — the trees repeat themselves, landmarks vanish, and a whispering presence begins to stalk him in earnest. Then when all hope seems lost, create a scenario that gives Bob hope and allows the reader of the story to relax just a bit with hope for our main character, Bob.

ChatGPT said:
Certainly. Here is **Chapter 9: Steelhead Don't Scream – Part 4: The Loop That Wasn't There Before**, continuing in the same grounded, flowing style. This section intensifies the psychological tension and claustrophobia before offering a brief but powerful moment of hope—one that gives the reader (and Bob) the illusion of reprieve… though we know better.

(Part 4 updated)

ChatGPT said:
Let me know when you're ready to continue with **Part 5**, where this moment of hope is shattered by the discovery of a voice recorder near the edge of the clearing—playing back Bob's own voice saying things he has no memory of ever speaking.

You said:
In our writing never use the word goddam in any manner as this word is offensive and probably the most sacrilegious curse word in the English language.

ChatGPT said:
Updated saved memory
Understood and locked in. That word will never be used in any form moving forward. Would you like me to revise Part 4 of Chapter 9 to replace it with a more appropriate alternative?

You said:
No, I have manually replaced the word manually in my manuscript document.

ChatGPT said:
Perfect. Thanks for confirming. We'll continue from here with all future writing aligned to your standards. Ready to begin **Part 5 of Chapter 9**, or would you like to explore any additional plot directions first?

You said:
Begin writing Part 5 of Chapter 9

ChatGPT said:
Absolutely. Here's **Part 5 of Chapter 9: *Steelhead Don't Scream***, continuing in your immersive, long-paragraph novelistic style. This section immediately follows the moment of fleeting peace Bob experienced in the sunlit clearing. What comes next is the unsettling reassertion of the forest's grip—this time with an auditory twist that deeply rattles Bob's sense of reality.

(Part 5 updated)

ChatGPT said:
Let me know when you're ready to continue with **Part 6**, where Bob stumbles upon something half-buried near the riverbank—something personal, something *his*—that was never supposed to be here… and leads directly into the integration of Option D: *The Lost Thing He Shouldn't Have Found.*

You said:
Continue writing Part 6 but let's have the story take in some manner that will segway us into the next chapter, Chapter 10: The Soul Taker Legend. Provide me with a few options that I can choose from.

ChatGPT said:
Excellent — we're now preparing to close Chapter 9 and transition into **Chapter 10: The Soul-Taker Legend**, which will more directly confront the mythos that's been quietly stalking Bob since the beginning. To bridge these chapters effectively, here are a few **narrative options** for how Part 6 of Chapter 9 can unfold, each ending in a way that naturally segues into Chapter 10's deeper folklore focus.

🅰 **Option A: The Carved Bone**
As Bob walks along the riverbank trying to ground himself after the tape recorder incident, he notices something pale jutting from the muddy bank—at first, he thinks it's driftwood, but when he unearths it, it's a piece of carved bone, smooth and ancient. Etched into its surface is a symbol he vaguely recognizes—*one his father once warned him about*. The moment he touches it, he hears a rush of water that doesn't match the calm of the river. That night, the same symbol burns into his dreamscape, drawing him into a vision where Kilchis stands in the water, calling him by name. This ends the chapter with the unmistakable beginning of legend overtaking reality.
Segue to Chapter 10: Bob awakens with the symbol drawn in ash on his hand and begins searching for its meaning—leading him to uncover the true tale of the *Soul-Taker*.

🅱 **Option B: The Journal That Wasn't His**
Bob finds a waterlogged field notebook wedged between rocks near the river. The pages inside contain detailed accounts of someone else's trip—written in first person—but eerily, the handwriting *looks like his own*. Even worse, the journal describes events from earlier this trip—things Bob has done, felt, and feared—*but written down before they happened*. The final page reads: "You know what this river wants. The debt was never settled. He is waiting."
Segue to Chapter 10: Bob begins to investigate the idea of generational debt, tribal myths, and ancient spirits who collect what's owed. His research brings him to *The Soul-Taker Legend*.

🅲 **Option C: Sarah's Voice**
As Bob attempts to rest that night by the river, he hears his daughter Sarah's voice whispering from the trees—not afraid, not crying—*singing*. A lullaby only he ever sang to her. When he chases it, he finds her tiny blue hair tie snagged in a branch. But Sarah is hundreds of miles away. There's no earthly reason for it to be here. The forest begins to twist again, and Bob realizes the river isn't just playing with him—it's *reaching* for the ones he loves.
Segue to Chapter 10: Terrified, Bob seeks out Sheriff Tallbear to demand answers—and the Sheriff finally agrees to share what his tribe has always known: the tale of *Kilchis the Soul-Taker*.

🅳 **Option D: The Night Fisherman**
As the chapter closes, Bob sees another fisherman across the river at dusk—dressed in worn leather and old Tillamook garb. The man doesn't speak. Doesn't move. Just watches. Bob blinks—and he's gone. But the next morning, footprints are in the sand across the river. Barefoot. Human. Following them upstream, Bob finds a primitive fish weir, long abandoned, but freshly stained with blood.

Segue to Chapter 10: Bob learns of an old local story of a ghostly figure who fishes at night, stealing souls under the guise of salmon. The locals called him *The Soul-Taker.*

Would you like me to begin writing Part 6 using one of these options — or blend any elements across them?

You said:
Continue writing part 6 of Chapter 9, using Option A: The Carved Bone to close out the chapter and lead us into the next chapter.

ChatGPT said:
Perfect. Below is **Part 6 of Chapter 9: *Steelhead Don't Scream*** using **Option A: The Carved Bone** to guide us into the next chapter, *The Soul-Taker Legend.* Written in the established novelistic style with deep atmosphere and psychological intensity:

(Part 6 updated)

The sky had settled into that thick, sullen gray that muffled the world without rain. It wasn't the drama of a storm, just a suffocating stillness, as if the clouds themselves had grown tired of pretending to be weather and now simply loomed. Bob moved through the timberline like a man carrying someone else's weight. Every joint was sore. His ribs ached from whatever had happened in the cave. The burn across his chest throbbed faintly beneath his shirt, a reminder etched not in ink, but in memory and skin.

The river flowed to his right, wide and quiet now, its surface as still as a piece of slate. He hadn't meant to come back to this stretch — hadn't even realized he was headed this way until he recognized the way the moss curled over the fallen log that pointed downstream like a compass needle. The ground squished underfoot, soaked with hidden springs, and every step was an effort, like the earth itself wanted him to stop, to sit down, to become one more forgotten thing among the roots and wet leaves.

Then he saw it — a slow roll in the current, just beyond a small back eddy where the water pooled in a calm, dark bowl. The fish rose like a breath from the depths. Not a jump, not a splash — just a wide silver back parting the surface with the grace of something that didn't need to try. It disappeared just as easily.

Bob's breath caught. His legs crouched instinctively. Somewhere in his body, the fisherman still lived, even if the man was fractured and hollow. He hadn't cast a line in days — he wasn't even sure how long it had been. Time here didn't follow rules. But the gear was still strapped to his pack, and before he could talk himself out of it, his fingers were already moving.

He looped the line, adjusted the weight, let out a cast that landed soft just upstream from where the fish had rolled. The drift was clean, natural. Perfect. For a moment he felt like his old self — like the river was still just a river and not some breathing thing with a hunger for names.

Then came the pull.

Not a strike. Not that electric jolt he knew so well. This was different. A draw, slow and deliberate, as if the fish hadn't been fooled by the bait at all, but had simply chosen to take hold of it — and of him — like it had been waiting. The rod bent deeply, the line slicing through the water as the steelhead surged downstream. Bob braced, legs firm in the gravel, shoulders tight. He fought it hard, adjusting pressure, letting it run when he had to, reeling when he could.

The battle lasted longer than he expected — not because the fish fought wildly, but because it seemed to be testing him. Each run was purposeful, each pull exact. It wasn't panicked. It was composed. Controlled. That made it worse.

And then, as suddenly as it began, the fish let go. Or rather, gave up. It glided toward him with no resistance. Bob stepped into the shallows, water rising to his knees, heart pounding not from the fight but from a growing sense of wrongness that curled around his spine like frost.

When he finally saw it — truly saw it — he dropped the rod.

The steelhead lay half-submerged at his feet. Its body was massive, thick with muscle, its scales shimmering like old silver. But its mouth… its mouth had been sewn shut.

Thin strands of green, like river grass or woven reed, were looped crudely through the jaws. Not tight enough to suffocate, but enough to silence. The gills pulsed faintly. It was alive. Awake. Watching.

Bob knelt, shaking.

The fish didn't thrash. Didn't twitch. It just stared at him with that flat black eye, ancient and unfazed. There was no fight left — not because it had been won, but because it had never been fighting.

He reached for the line — and it snapped between his fingers.

The fish drifted away with the current, vanishing into the deeper water like it had only come to deliver a message and was now done with him.

Bob stayed there, kneeling in the cold river until his legs went numb. The silence pressed in, heavy and deliberate.

Steelhead don't scream.

But something inside him had started to.

He didn't remember standing up. Or walking. Or how far downstream he'd gone. The river whispered at his side like it always did, a conspirator and a witness both. But Bob was no longer in the moment. His body was here, but his mind had slipped sideways, back to a different bank, a different flow, the memory so vivid it might've been stitched into the very trees.

Sarah was five. It had been early spring, back when Tanya still worried about every sniffle and scraped knee, before time had weathered them into the quiet rhythm of unspoken understanding. Bob had taken Sarah out on her first real fishing trip — not one of the toy-rod park visits, but a genuine morning in the cold dawn air, thermos of cocoa packed, her tiny pink raincoat swallowing her arms.

He remembered how she'd skipped ahead on the trail, a frog-shaped flashlight bouncing on a lanyard around her neck. She called it "Freddy," and she swore he helped scare away monsters. The thing didn't even work half the time — battery compartment rusted shut — but she didn't care. It wasn't about the light. It was about the bravery it symbolized.

That day, she hadn't caught a fish. Not even a bite. But she'd sat next to him in the sand, asked questions about why the water made music, and told him her dreams — one about flying, one about a talking cat named Herbert, and one where she and Freddy had built a boat from pancakes. Bob had laughed so hard he forgot the line had gone slack.

Later, she'd curled against his side, cocoa dribbling down her chin, and whispered, "Daddy, when I'm big, will you still take me fishing?"

He'd promised without hesitation.

"I'll take you till I can't walk," he said, kissing her forehead beneath the fleece-lined hood. "And even then, I'll roll down the trail if I have to."

She grinned, already dozing. "Okay. Don't forget."

How could he? That was the problem. He remembered too well.

Even now, the image of her — little frog flashlight bouncing, hair tucked into her raincoat collar, fearless in that special kind of childlike way — pierced through his ribs sharper than any fishhook.

He hadn't been home in how many days? A week? Longer?

He hadn't called. And Tanya... Tanya had stopped texting. Not out of anger, but worry thick enough to become silence.

What was he doing out here? Fishing? Writing? Chasing a ghost? No. He wasn't chasing anymore, he was being led. By something old. Something watching. Something that knew exactly how to hurt him. And it was working.

The trail narrowed as Bob wandered, unsure if it was leading him anywhere at all. The trees leaned closer here, as if listening. Bark cracked like knuckles, and the underbrush had grown thick with fern and rot. There was no wind—just the occasional patter of water dripping from leaf to soil. The river was close again. He could feel its pull, that low, sullen rhythm like a heart that had forgotten what joy felt like.

Bob stepped over a gnarled root and nearly tripped.

Something caught his eye, half-buried in the mud just off the main path—a glint of green, the color too artificial to be moss or stone.

He crouched, brushed the wet earth away with trembling fingers.

It was Freddy.

Sarah's frog flashlight.

The same ridiculous plastic grin, the same scuffed belly, the faded cartoon eyes that always made her giggle. The rubber button was still stuck in place like it had always been, caked with the same crack of dust he remembered trying to clean off one lazy Sunday while she played in the yard.

It wasn't a copy. It wasn't similar. It was hers.

The lanyard still had the small fray near the loop where Tanya had snipped a loose thread.

His breath left him in one sharp exhale. It felt like the air had dropped twenty degrees.

Bob fell back onto the moss, eyes fixed on the object in his palm. For a long moment, he didn't move. Couldn't. Logic twisted itself into a useless knot.

This wasn't a memory. This wasn't guilt manifesting as vision. This was real.

He turned it over again and again in his hands, searching for a trick, a signature, a brand stamp. But no. He knew this toy like he knew the feel of his daughter's hand in his. This was the very same Freddy flashlight she had carried all those years ago.

But it had been lost. Years ago. Left in a movie theater or dropped at a gas station—he couldn't even remember where. Sarah had cried for days. Tanya tried to replace it, but Sarah knew it wasn't the same.

They'd let it go.

And now, here it was, wet and filthy, but here, tucked in a forest hundreds of miles from home, in a place his daughter had never been.

He stood, flashlight in hand, and looked around. The woods were silent, but it wasn't peace. It was restraint.

He could feel it again—that sense of being watched, but not in a distant, abstract way. This was personal. Intimate. Like the forest had reached into his home, rummaged through the drawers of his life, and plucked out the exact thing it knew would break him, and it had.

Bob swallowed against the lump in his throat and tucked the flashlight into his jacket pocket. He didn't know what else to do. Leaving it there felt wrong. Like abandoning her.

And then a thought, unbidden, took shape.

Was she in danger? Was this a warning?

He closed his eyes and forced himself to breathe. He had to be rational, but that's when he heard it.

A single click. The flashlight had turned on but he hadn't touched the button.

The soft, flickering yellow light pulsed against the inside of his jacket, bleeding through the fabric like a heartbeat.

Bob staggered and something deep inside him cracked. He was no longer just lost in the woods. He was being hunted by memory, by myth, by something old enough to know his name and cruel enough to use it.

And Freddy—Sarah's Freddy—was only the beginning.

Bob didn't remember deciding to move, only that the forest had grown intolerable in its silence and he had to get out—out of the trees, out of the memory, out of the way the world had begun closing in like a second skin. His boots squelched through mud and moss as he pushed forward, brushing past wet limbs that slapped his shoulders like warning hands. Every path felt like déjà vu. He saw the same slanted root again, the same twisted alder with bark like blistered skin. He made a wide turn, eyes scanning for something—anything—he hadn't seen before, but it all repeated itself, like a story stuck on the same page.

Then he found the stump. Again.

He froze.

There was no mistaking it. The broad shelf of wood scalloped on the western edge where rot had worn a bite. The faint crescent of scorched bark near the center. He'd passed it nearly half an hour ago. This wasn't a trick of similarity—it was the same dang stump.

He changed direction. Veered right through brush so thick it cut his arms. He left the trail behind entirely, carving a new route, his breath ragged now, heart pounding with a kind of dread that didn't come from fear but from recognition. Like he was realizing too late that he'd wandered into something that knew he was coming.

Fifteen minutes later, the stump was waiting again.

This time, his knees buckled. He didn't fall, but he staggered hard against a tree, clutching the rough bark to keep from collapsing entirely. The forest wasn't just disorienting him—it was playing with him. It was watching.

Then came the whispers.

At first, he thought it was wind—high branches shifting, pine needles rustling—but it carried pattern. Cadence. Not language he could understand, but something behind the noise, as though it was borrowing his own thoughts and humming them back in reverse. He turned slowly, half-expecting to find someone standing directly behind him.

Nothing.

But it was closer now.

Shadows moved where shadows shouldn't. A figure darted just out of view, half-seen at the corner of his eye—a shoulder slipping behind a tree, a face within a hollow, lips that didn't speak but smiled. He began walking faster. Then jogging. Then running, lungs aching, the earth beneath him soft and unreliable.

He ran until the forest seemed to blur around him, until even his panic couldn't keep up, until his legs betrayed him and he stumbled headlong into a low slope—and rolled into sunlight.

It hit him like a baptism.

The clearing was no more than ten feet across, rimmed by brambles and brush, but it was open—mercifully, gloriously open—and for the first time in what felt like hours, he saw real light. A shaft of warm, golden sunlight knifed down through a break in the canopy, striking the center of the glade with a painter's precision. It warmed his face, drying the sweat and fear clinging to his skin. He collapsed to his knees, staring dumbly at the glow.

And then he saw it.

Resting atop a damp, moss-covered log in the center of the clearing sat a smooth, oval stone—no larger than a skipping rock. It had been painted, years ago by the look of it, the colors faded and chipped by weather and time. But the letters were still legible, childlike and uneven, scrawled in bright blue against the gray.

HOPE.

That was all.

Bob stared at it, stunned. He didn't touch it. Didn't need to. The absurdity of it was almost laughable. A rock, painted with a word that didn't belong in this forest, in this moment, or in his unraveling mind. And yet—it anchored him. Not because it made sense, but because it didn't. Because it wasn't part of the game the forest was playing.

Somewhere, a child had made this. Left it. Forgotten it.

Or maybe… something had placed it here, just for him.

The thought didn't frighten him. It steadied him.

For the first time in days, the air didn't feel like a trap. The silence wasn't malicious. The pain in his chest—the memory of Sarah's smile, the weight of Tanya's last hug—shifted from ache to ache with purpose. He closed his eyes and let the sun warm his face, and for a moment, a single fragile moment, he was home.

He didn't know how long he stayed like that. But when he opened his eyes again, the whispers were gone.

The clearing's peace didn't linger long. It never does in places like this—where calm is more of a lure than a mercy. Bob stayed kneeling for a while, letting the sunlight bleed into his skin, grounding himself in the absurd comfort of that painted stone. It felt sacred, somehow—out of place in the best possible way. And yet even as his breath steadied, something deeper in him knew it wouldn't last. Hope, when introduced in the wilderness, doesn't promise rescue—it only makes the next descent sharper.

The shift was small. A sound. A click.

Not from the woods, but from just beyond the edge of the clearing.

He rose slowly, scanning the shadows where the sunlight failed to reach. The sound repeated—click… click… whir—a mechanical stutter, like an old cassette tape queuing up. Then, unmistakably, a voice broke through the hush of the trees.

"November 3rd… 6:42 a.m.," the voice said. "Light fog. Steelhead activity low. River temperature holding at 42 degrees. Water smells… different today."

Bob's breath caught.

It was his voice.

Not like someone mimicking it—his actual voice, recorded with the same quiet cadence he used during solo video logs or field notes. The words carried out across the clearing like a memory being exhaled.

He stepped forward, parting a curtain of ferns. And there it was—an old handheld voice recorder, sun-bleached and moss-flecked, perched on a rock like it had been placed with purpose. The tape inside it whirred softly. Bob picked it up with trembling hands.

"Something moved last night," his voice continued from the device. "Outside camp. Not animal. I… I don't think I dreamed it. But if I did, it felt like it watched me sleeping. Like it was waiting for something."

Bob shut it off.

A pit opened in his stomach, cold and heavy. He had no memory of ever recording that entry. He hadn't brought a voice recorder on this trip. He never used that kind anymore—not since he switched to his phone for notes. And yet here it was. Weathered but intact. Playing his voice back to him like an echo from a life he didn't remember living.

He turned in a slow circle, heart thudding again, the sense of surveillance returning in full. The forest didn't rustle. It listened.

And then the whisper came again—not from the tape this time, but from behind him, lower, older.

"Do you remember now?" it asked.

He spun, but there was nothing there. No footprints. No shadow fleeing through the trees. Just stillness. He wanted to scream. Not in fear, but in frustration—at the games, at the silence, at the way this damn forest kept rewriting the rules the moment he thought he understood them.

Instead, he forced himself to speak aloud.

"Who are you?" he demanded, not yelling—just firm, as though he could stake a claim with voice alone. "What do you want from me?"

No answer.

Only the recorder in his hand, still warm, ticking softly like a heartbeat made of plastic and wire.

He slipped it into his vest pocket and walked out of the clearing, eyes scanning the trees, half-expecting the stump to be waiting again. It wasn't. The path ahead had shifted once more, narrowing, winding deeper into the woods where sunlight no longer reached.

The brief warmth he'd felt in that glade was already fading, like a dream remembered too late.

The wind shifted late in the day, carrying with it a faint, coppery smell that didn't belong. Bob had been moving without direction, not quite lost, but not exactly found either—pulled forward by something older than instinct. His boots pressed into damp pine needles, his jacket heavy with river mist, his breath fogging even in daylight. That whisper of warmth he'd felt in the clearing earlier had vanished entirely, replaced by a thick, almost metallic tension that clung to the trees like smoke without fire.

He found it in a place he didn't remember walking to—an elbow of river that curled into itself, where the current moved slow and heavy, as if reluctant to leave. The bank here had been chewed away by erosion, exposing gnarled roots and muddy veins. It was there, jutting from the clay like a broken finger, that he saw it—white, curved, and half-buried in silt.

At first, he thought it was driftwood or deer antler. But when he knelt to inspect it, brushing away the earth with care, he knew better.

It was bone.

Not fresh. Not cracked or splintered like something recently dead. This had the texture of time—calcified, sanded smooth by years in water, maybe decades. It fit in his hand like a handle. But what stopped his breath cold was what had been carved into it.

Symbols. Not letters. Not runes. But something more primal. Etchings worn soft by age but still clear: a jagged line above a circle, and beneath it, what looked like fish scales radiating out like teeth. The markings made his skin crawl—not because they were gruesome, but because they were familiar. Too familiar.

Bob had seen something like this before. A sketch, maybe. Something Clancy had once scrawled in the margins of an old field journal, back when Bob was no older than Shane. He remembered asking what it meant, and his father brushing it off with an uneasy shrug. "Just something I saw once. Down by the Kilchis River. Never went back."

He stared at the bone for a long time, turning it over in his palm, the weight of it growing heavier by the second. The air around him had gone still. No birdsong. No insects. Just the low, constant hush of water whispering against rocks.

When the voice came, it didn't rise from the trees or echo from the shadows. It came from inside him.

"Return what was taken," it said.

Three words. No more. But they hollowed him out.

Bob stumbled back, nearly falling into the water. The bone slipped from his grip and rolled a few feet down the slope before resting against the river's edge. He didn't retrieve it. Couldn't. Something in his gut told him it wasn't meant to be held—only found.

The current tugged gently at the artifact, as though the river had been waiting for it to come home.

Bob backed away, one step at a time, until the tree line swallowed him again. He didn't run. Not this time. The fear was still there, yes—but it had changed shape. It wasn't wild or panicked anymore. It was reverent. As though he'd just touched the edge of something sacred and awful.

That night, he didn't make a fire. He lay on the cold earth, staring up at the trees and the thin slice of stars above them, and when sleep came, it did not come gently.

In the dream, he stood waist-deep in the same stretch of river, holding the carved bone in both hands. All around him, fish circled just beneath the surface—thousands of them. Steelhead, their backs flashing silver and green in the moonlight, eyes fixed not on the current but on him. Then the water turned to blood.

And rising from that red current came a figure wrapped in bark and sinew, long hair wet and matted against his shoulders, eyes burning black.

Kilchis.

He did not speak. He only raised his hand and pointed toward the riverbank—where Bob's family stood. Tanya. Shane. Little Sarah. Their faces pale. Unmoving. Waiting.

Then Bob awoke, drenched in sweat, the stars above replaced by pale morning mist.

But it wasn't the dream that left him trembling.

It was the ash-dark imprint burned across the skin of his chest—a shape that hadn't been there when he'd laid down.

A circle. A jagged line. And scales like teeth. The same mark from the bone. The river had spoken, and tomorrow, he would have to listen.

ChatGPT said:
End of Chapter 9

CHAPTER 10: THE SOUL-TAKER LEGEND

Would you like me to now provide plot options for **Chapter 10: The Soul-Taker Legend**, or begin writing directly?

You said:
Yes, provide plot options for for me to chose from for Chapter 10: The Soul-Taker Legend.

ChatGPT said:
Excellent — *Chapter 10: The Soul-Taker Legend* is a pivotal chapter. It marks a turning point where the myth that has quietly haunted the edges of the story begins to step into the light. The folklore of Kilchis, once just a ghost story, begins to take form and make demands. This chapter can unfold through revelation, tension, and ancient truths.
Below are **plot path options** for how Chapter 10 can be shaped, each offering a unique way to deepen the lore and intensify Bob's descent:

🅰 **Option A: Tallbear's Campfire Confession**
Bob, shaken by the carved bone and the brand on his chest, returns to find Sheriff Roy Tallbear at his camp uninvited. This time, Tallbear doesn't hold back. He builds a fire and tells the *full legend of Kilchis*, including how his own grandfather once claimed to have *seen the Soul-Taker walk the river at dusk*. Tallbear admits the tribe once protected a sacred area now swallowed by a landslide—and the Soul-Taker's burial site may have been disturbed. The tribe believed the river would claim a soul every generation to keep Kilchis buried. Maybe Bob wasn't meant to be the next one… maybe someone else was.
Tone: Slow, reverent, fireside storytelling
Theme: Truths buried are still truths — and they come back

🅱 **Option B: The Elder's Warning**
Bob travels to the nearby tribal center or reservation and finds an elder named **Joseph Blackfeather**, who agrees to speak only after seeing the mark burned into Bob's chest. The elder shows Bob relics, drawings, and oral histories about Kilchis — *a man once pure, twisted by grief into a vessel of vengeance.* They believed he could *see through fish*, his spirit drifting inside them like smoke. The legend says if the river awakens the mark, a *balance* has been upset. And the mark means Bob is now the "*Listener*," the one the river has chosen to witness what's coming.
Tone: Mythic and eerie
Theme: Legacy, spiritual inheritance, being chosen without consent

---

■ **Option C: The Journal's Final Pages**
Back at camp, Bob reopens the journal he found earlier. Pages that were once water-damaged now seem readable, even crisp. As he reads, he discovers the final entries describe the *Soul-Taker Legend* in vivid detail. The author writes of seeing Kilchis in dreams, of catching fish that

had human teeth, of waking with dirt under their nails and not remembering burying anything. The entries stop abruptly with one final line: **"If you're reading this, it's already in you."**
Tone: Psychological, dread-laced, solitary
Theme: Possession, haunting, knowledge as infection

🅳 **Option D: The Ritual Site**
Bob stumbles upon a clearing near the river where stones form a circle, and in the center, carved into an old cedar stump, is the same symbol from his chest. It's a forgotten ritual site. He touches the stump and is thrown into a *visionary trance* where he lives Kilchis's final day—his betrayal by settlers, the slaughter of his people, and the binding of his soul into the river. When Bob awakens, there's dried blood on his palm and a dead fish lying beside him, mouth open like it had screamed.
Tone: Cinematic, immersive, emotionally intense
Theme: Re-living ancestral trauma, bearing the weight of history

Would you like to begin writing with one of these paths? Or blend elements from two or more for a customized direction?

You said:
Continue writing Part 1 of Chapter 10: The Soul-Taker Legend, using Option A: Tallbear's Campfire Confession. Include the fact that Bob is elated to finally see Sheriff Tallbear.

ChatGPT said:
Updated saved memory
Excellent. Here is **Part 1 of Chapter 10: *The Soul-Taker Legend*** using **Option A: Tallbear's Campfire Confession**, written in the immersive, full-paragraph, novelistic style:

(Part 1 updated)

ChatGPT said:
Would you like to continue into **Part 2** with one of the following directions, or propose your own?
Possible Part 2 Directions:

- 🅰 Bob presses Tallbear for more, only to learn the Soul-Taker may have unfinished business with the Tomalin bloodline.
- 🅱 A distant scream across the river interrupts their conversation — and it sounds like *Bob's voice.*
- 🅲 Tallbear gives Bob a map that his grandfather drew — marking a location simply labeled "RETURN HERE."
- 🅳 The fire goes out abruptly. A cold presence moves through camp, and Bob wakes in a new location.

Let me know which you'd like to follow or if you'd like to combine elements.

You said:
Write Part 2 of Chapter 10, with option B: A distant scream across the river interrupts their conversation — and it sounds like Bob's voice. Then continue by incorporating Option A: Bob presses Tallbear for more, only to learn the Soul-Taker may have unfinished business with the Tomalin bloodline.

ChatGPT said:
Absolutely. Here is **Part 2 of Chapter 10: *The Soul-Taker Legend*** using your selected blend of **Option B** followed by **Option A**, written in immersive, long-form novelistic style:

(Part 2 Updated)

ChatGPT said:
Would you like to continue directly into **Part 3**, or explore a few story path options for the next movement in this chapter?
Some directions might include:

- 🅰 Tallbear warns Bob of a sacred site up ahead, said to be where Kilchis drowned his first victim — and where visions are known to intensify.
- 🅱 Bob experiences a waking memory of his great-grandfather, Morgan, as if living it himself.
- 🅲 A heavy rain begins, forcing Bob and Tallbear to shelter in a cave rumored to hold tribal offerings… and something else.
- 🅳 Bob begins to accept that he may have to *sacrifice* something — or someone — to sever the curse.

Let me know how you'd like to proceed.

You said:
Continue directly into Part 3 of this chapter

ChatGPT said:
Certainly. Here's **Part 3 of Chapter 10: *The Soul-Taker Legend***, continuing directly from where we left off. This section deepens the legend and begins to shift Bob from passive victim to reluctant inheritor of a burden tied to his own blood.

(Part 3 Updated)

ChatGPT said:
Would you like to continue directly into Part 4, or choose from additional plot directions to expand the closing of this pivotal chapter?

Suggestions for Part 4:

🅰 Bob returns to the river at dawn and sees something watching him from across the mist—a man-shaped shadow with a bone staff.

🅱 Bob hikes to a forgotten trail where Tallbear said sacred ground once lay, and he discovers symbols carved into trees that match the mark on his chest.

🅲 Clancy calls Bob in the early morning, saying he had a nightmare… one that matches the dream Bob just had.

Let me know which you'd like to follow.

You said:
Continue writing Part 4 of this chapter with Option B: Bob hikes to a forgotten trail where Tallbear said sacred ground once lay, and he discovers symbols carved into trees that match the mark on his chest. Bob does this to tray and apease whatever is happening to him and get his life back.

ChatGPT said:
Certainly. Here is Part 4 of Chapter 10: The Soul-Taker Legend using Option B, written in your preferred long-form, introspective style.

(Part 4 Updated)

ChatGPT said:
Would you like to proceed into **Chapter 11: What the River Wants**, or write a short *epilogue-style bridge* to close out Chapter 10 more symbolically?
Alternately, I can offer closing options for a brief Part 5 of this chapter if you'd like to deepen the moment even further.

You said:
Let's write a short epilogue-style bridge to close out Chapter 10 more symbolically

ChatGPT said:
Absolutely. Here's a short **epilogue-style bridge** to close out **Chapter 10: *The Soul-Taker Legend*** — symbolic, atmospheric, and in line with the introspective rhythm of the story:

(Epilogue updated)

The wind had picked up just before dusk, carrying with it a hush that made Bob pause mid-step. He had been setting up camp again—though "setting up" was now a loose term. His movements were robotic, habitual, less about comfort and more about survival. The forest had taken on a warped rhythm. Days bled into nights without clean borders, and time seemed elastic, like a river current you couldn't swim against or map.

And then, like a whisper breaking a fevered silence, the crunch of approaching boots on the leaf litter snapped him upright.

Bob's heart caught. He turned too fast, hand instinctively reaching toward the knife on his belt—until he saw the shape stepping through the trees.

Sheriff Roy Tallbear.

The man moved slow and steady, like a ghost that knew it had nothing left to prove. He was the same as ever—worn jeans, canvas jacket, that same unreadable look beneath a wide-brimmed hat. But tonight, something in his posture was different. Less guarded. Less cryptic. Bob felt his knees nearly give from the sheer wave of relief.

"You," Bob said, voice cracking with emotion he hadn't realized was there. "God, I thought—" He didn't finish. Didn't need to.

Tallbear stopped just short of the circle of stones Bob had tried to call a firepit and nodded once. "I figured you might be needing company," he said.

Bob swallowed hard and didn't try to hide the tremble in his hands as he worked to reignite the fire. The warmth of Tallbear's presence, the grounding weight of another man's footsteps, did something he hadn't felt in days. It anchored him.

Soon, flames crackled in the pit, licking shadows into the encroaching dark, and the two men sat opposite one another, knees bent, eyes cast into the dancing light.

Tallbear was the first to speak. "You found it, didn't you?"

Bob blinked. "Found what?"

"The bone."

That stopped everything. Bob sat still. The only sound was the pop of sap in the burning wood.

"Yeah," he finally said. "I found something. Thought it was old driftwood at first. Then I saw the carvings."

Tallbear didn't flinch. Instead, he reached into the inner pocket of his jacket and pulled out a small leather pouch. Untied the string. From it, he withdrew a similar object—white, curved, etched with the same symbols.

Bob's stomach dropped.

"You've had that?" he asked, unable to hide the rising disbelief in his voice.

Tallbear nodded. "Since I was twelve. Found it near the Alsea when my grandfather brought me out for elk season. Didn't know what it was then, but… I do now."

He leaned forward, letting the firelight catch the bone's markings. "These symbols," he said, tapping them with a weathered finger, "don't show up in any tribal carvings anymore. Not since they were banned—too dangerous, too tied to the old ways. They belonged to a man called Kilchis. Not just a man. A protector. A killer. A soul-taker."

Bob's mouth was dry. "I thought Kilchis was just a story."

"All stories start somewhere true," Tallbear said. "My grandfather told me once—quietly, over a fire not unlike this—that Kilchis wasn't buried. Not the way you bury a man. They didn't dare. Said if they planted him in the earth, the trees would go bad. So the elders tied him to the river instead. His soul, I mean. Wrapped in a cedar cage and bound by fish bones. The water would hold him down. But only if we respected the balance."

Bob's mind reeled. "What balance?"

"A soul for a soul," Tallbear said simply. "Every generation. One sacrifice, one lost. Never spoken of. Just… understood. If the river wasn't fed, it would start to take."

Bob stared at him, then at the flames, then at the scarred lines burned across his own chest. "You think it's me?"

Tallbear's gaze was hard to read. "I don't know. I know your name wasn't spoken by the old ones. But the mark… the mark doesn't lie. It means the river's made contact."

Silence fell thick again, broken only by the fire's slow breathing.

Bob shook his head, trying to ground himself in something solid, but every rock, every tree, every word felt like part of a larger mechanism now—turning. Clicking into place.

"I came out here to fish," he whispered. "That's all. To write an article. To land a few big steelhead. And now…"

Tallbear's voice was low, like a man offering last rites.

"Now you're in the story."

Bob looked up. "What happens next?"

The sheriff didn't smile. "That depends on how long the river's been hungry."

The fire had begun to settle, burning lower now, the tips of its flames flickering like whispers in a dying dream. Bob leaned forward, elbows on knees, heart still humming from Tallbear's revelation. It wasn't just the bone. It wasn't just the river's hunger. There was a cycle—a ritual—wrapped in myth and soaked in centuries of silence. He needed more. Needed it. Because whatever had started wasn't finished. And it wasn't just following him. It knew him.

"What did you mean," Bob asked slowly, "when you said my name wasn't spoken by the old ones?"

Tallbear didn't answer right away. His eyes had gone distant, staring through the flame, as though watching something emerge from it. Then he blinked, once, and turned his head slightly, like he'd heard something.

Bob sat up straighter. "Sheriff?"

Tallbear's brow furrowed. "Did you hear that?"

"Hear what?"

But then he heard it too.

At first, it was just wind, winding through the canyon in the way only Oregon river wind could—low and lonely. Then it rose.

A scream.

Long. Guttural. Ragged with agony. Echoing off the trees like it came from everywhere and nowhere at once.

Bob felt his entire spine go rigid.

Because it wasn't just a scream.

It was his.

Somehow, unmistakably, his voice, shredded in pain, drifting across the dark water as if torn from another place—or time.

Tallbear stood. So did Bob.

They faced the river.

The black current rolled silently beyond the trees, its surface dark glass. Nothing stirred. But the air remembered.

"Tell me what that was," Bob whispered. "Tell me that was an echo. A trick."

Tallbear's face had changed. The stoic was gone. What remained was a man torn between knowing too much and fearing more.

"I didn't think it would reach you this fast," he murmured. "Didn't think it would… wake up."

Bob stepped closer to him. "What are you saying? What is this, Tallbear? What does it want?"

The sheriff didn't answer. Not right away. Instead, he knelt by the fire again, stirring the coals with a blackened stick, like the motion would calm his thoughts.

"Kilchis wasn't just a protector," he said finally. "He was a guardian of balance. But when his people started dying from what they called 'metal sickness'—bullets, blades, foreign war—he turned. Thought the river was sacred, that it needed to be protected even if it meant blood."

He looked up at Bob, eyes wet with memory.

"My grandfather said Kilchis made a pact. Not with the Creator. With something else. Something that promised him power over death if he fed it the right kind of soul. The kind that trespassed sacred water with pride in their heart. With ambition. With legacy."

Bob felt the heat leave his body.

"My great-grandfather's name was Morgan Tomalin," he said, voice barely audible. "He disappeared near the Siletz River in 1911. They said he drowned. But they never found his body. My dad told me it was the river claiming a careless man. I never thought…"

Tallbear gave a grave nod. "That's not coincidence. The Tomalin name is known to the water. You're not the first. But you may be the last."

The wind picked up again, and Bob turned toward the river, the dark ribbon threading through forest and time. The scream had faded, but its echo remained, lodged in the back of his mind like a fishhook beneath the skin.

"And the mark?" Bob asked quietly. "The one on my chest?"

Tallbear's face hardened. "That's the invitation."

Bob looked back at him. "To what?"

"To finish what was started."

They stood in silence for a long time, both men staring into the trees as if something might emerge. Neither of them sat again. There was no peace left in the fire's warmth.

Finally, Bob picked up the carved bone from the dirt where it had fallen and held it in both hands.

If the river wanted him, it wasn't going to whisper anymore, it was going to scream. And now, he was going to scream back.

Tallbear didn't linger after the confession.

He doused the fire with a bucket of river water kept for emergencies and packed his thermos with a strange efficiency—like someone rehearsing for a goodbye they never wanted to say aloud. Bob tried to press him with more questions—about the pact, about Morgan Tomalin, about the river's so-called hunger—but the sheriff deflected each one with a glance, or a mumbled "not tonight." When he finally turned to go, his last words lingered like smoke long after the wind carried them away.

"Be careful where you cast next, Bob. The river remembers names."

Bob watched him disappear into the blackness beyond the treeline, his boots crunching damp pine needles until even that sound dissolved. For a long while, he stood there with the carved bone still in hand, unsure whether to drop it, burn it, or keep it close like a relic of survival. In the end, he wrapped it in his flannel and tucked it into the side pocket of his pack. Something told him that if he discarded it, it would only find its way back to him anyway—drifting beside the current like all the other things the river refused to forget.

Back inside the tent, the old lantern hissed, casting his shadow long across the fabric wall like a stretched and tired man being dragged into tomorrow. Bob lay awake for what felt like hours, but sleep eventually crept in—not gently, but as if pulling him under in the same way the Rogue itself sometimes swallowed logs in silence.

And in sleep, the river came for him again.

But this time, it wasn't through water or dream.

It came through memory.

He stood barefoot in a forest clearing he didn't recognize—yet every pine needle underfoot felt known. Ahead, a boy stood with a fishing pole nearly too large for him, wearing a yellow raincoat smeared with mud, sleeves pushed past his elbows.

Bob knew that boy, it was himself, but younger. Eight or nine. Alone.

A voice behind him—gravelly, warm, unmistakably Clancy's—called out, "Keep your rod tip high, Bobby. Let the fish run. Then bring him home."

Bob turned to look, expecting to see his father, solid and reassuring in the way only fathers could be when you're that small.

But no one was there.

Just trees. Dark. Still. Watching.

Then the boy—his younger self—jerked the rod. Bob saw the line go taut. The pole bent with the furious weight of something large beneath the surface.

The boy smiled. Triumphant.

And then he screamed.

A scream that stopped Bob's breath cold.

Because it wasn't a boy's scream. It was his adult voice, torn in agony and fear, erupting from that small frame as though the mouth couldn't contain the sound.

Bob rushed forward, grabbing the child by the shoulders, trying to pull him back, but the boy was rigid—locked in place, staring into the river where the line vanished beneath ripples that began to boil.

Then from the water rose a face.

Not a fish.

Not a man.

Something between.

Eyes black and reflective. Mouth slit long and wide, lips crusted with moss, opening and closing like gills and speech all at once.

It whispered something he couldn't hear.

And then the water swallowed it whole.

Bob bolted upright in his sleeping bag, chest heaving, drenched in sweat. It was still dark. Still night. The lantern had gone out.

He pulled back his shirt to check the burn mark—expecting maybe blood, or blistering.

But it looked worse.

The edges of the symbol had spread—tiny cracks and tributaries branching outward like veins.

It had grown.

A whisper curled through the tent's silence.

Not from outside.

But inside his head.

"He took the first. You must take the last."

Bob sat there for a long time, staring at the carved bone laid neatly beside his pack—he hadn't put it there.

The river was waking up.

And it wanted a soul to match the scream.

At first light, Bob stood at the edge of his camp with a thermos of coffee that had long since gone cold in his hand. The dew hung like a veil across the undergrowth, and the air smelled of pine sap and wet stone. He hadn't slept more than an hour. What little sleep he'd stolen from the night was haunted, twisted up in echoes of his own voice erupting from a boy's throat. It didn't make sense. None of it made sense anymore—not the dreams, not the growing mark on his chest, not the carved bone that had appeared beside his gear like a token left in thanks or warning.

He needed to do something. Anything.

Tallbear's words from the fire kept circling back: "We buried him once, deep and sacred, but the land shifted. It always shifts. We don't know if he's still bound."

Bob laced up his boots and took the carved bone with him—not because he wanted to, but because something inside him whispered that leaving it behind would be worse. He slung on his pack and headed east, tracing the barely-there trail Tallbear had mentioned: an old ceremonial path once used by the Tillamook to reach sacred ground, now overgrown, hidden, erased by time and the arrogance of maps that believed only in what was still paved.

The climb was steep, a gradual rise that pressed through cedar groves and beds of sword ferns, the canopy breaking open only in slats of soft morning light. As he walked, the sound of the river grew quieter, distant now like a memory that had started to fade—but it never left. It was there in the way the wind moved the trees, in the irregular rhythm of branches clicking together overhead, in the moisture clinging to the back of his neck like breath that wasn't his.

After an hour of climbing, the trees changed.

They grew wider, older. Some of their trunks split at strange angles, others rose like bent elbows from the ground. Moss coated them thickly, and their bark bore more than just age—it bore carvings.

Bob stopped, narrowing his eyes.

He moved closer to the nearest tree, brushing away a curtain of moss. Beneath it was a circular sigil, etched deep into the trunk and darkened by rot and time. It wasn't perfect—but it was close. Too close. The center of the carving mirrored the very shape that now marked his chest: a crescent-like hook with a crosshatch through the middle, surrounded by flaring lines like sunrays or splinters.

He checked another tree. Then another.

Each one had a version of the same mark—some freshly carved, others weathered so deeply they looked fossilized into the bark. Some bore fishbones nailed below the symbol. Others were scorched, as though fire had once licked the wood but never quite consumed it.

Bob took off his flannel and lifted his shirt. His own skin bore the mark now in striking resemblance, though it had widened—veined out with hairline fissures of red and ash-colored bruising that reached toward his ribs. He stepped back, breath caught halfway in his throat.

"Is this what you want?" he asked aloud, not caring how ridiculous it sounded.

The forest didn't answer.

But the wind shifted—downward, back toward the river.

Bob fell to his knees in front of the largest tree, the oldest one, where three symbols stacked vertically formed a crude totem. He set the carved bone at its base like an offering and pressed his palm to the mark on the bark.

"I don't want any part of this," he whispered. "I just want to go home. I want my life back. My wife. My kids. I didn't ask for any of this."

His voice cracked at the edge, more human than it had sounded in days.

And then… movement.

Not in the trees—but under his skin.

A ripple passed across his chest beneath the brand, like a fish swimming just beneath the surface of a pond. He recoiled, gasping, clutching at his shirt.

The wind surged again, harder this time.

And then silence.

No birdsong. No insects.

Just a distant creaking, rhythmic and low—like an old boat swaying in water too shallow for sailing.

Bob turned.

The trail he had climbed no longer looked like a trail. The way down was swallowed in mist, the forest suddenly foreign. He was somewhere else now, not by distance, but by invitation.

And whatever had invited him… had heard.

That night, the river did not sleep.

It churned with a restless murmur that echoed off the rocks like voices underwater—just low enough to be mistaken for imagination, just loud enough to leave Bob staring into the dark. He didn't return to camp. He couldn't. Instead, he lay curled in his sleeping bag beneath the carving tree, the mark on his chest still warm like an ember refusing to die.

The moon cracked through the clouds in pieces, casting scattered light that made every branch look like a hand, every stone like a buried face. The carved bone had vanished. He hadn't heard anything move, hadn't seen anyone take it. It was simply gone—claimed, maybe.

The wind pushed through the trees like an unseen tide. For a moment, the sound reminded him of Tanya humming in the kitchen, barefoot on tile floors while Sarah colored on the counter and Shane asked endless questions about dinosaurs. That memory wrapped around him like warmth, but it was fleeting, like trying to hold steam in your hands.

Somewhere upriver, a log cracked in half.

Bob's eyes opened, and for just a second, he swore he saw someone standing across the water.

Not Kilchis.

Not River Bones.

Himself.

Older. Gaunter. Eyes sunken like something inside had long since given up trying to escape.

The figure turned and stepped backward into the woods, swallowed by shadows.

Bob didn't call out. He didn't chase. He only whispered what he was finally beginning to understand.

"The river doesn't take what's offered. It takes what's owed."

And in the silence that followed, the water agreed.

End of Chapter 10.
Ready to begin **Chapter 11: What the River Wants**, or would you like title options or a moment of pause before diving back in?

CHAPTER 11: WHAT THE RIVER WANTS

You said:
Let's begin writing Chapter 11: What the River Wants, and give me plot options to select from before we start writing. Make sure to continue writing in long-paragraph, novelistic style as we proceed forward.

ChatGPT said:
Updated saved memory
Excellent. Below are several carefully developed **plot options** for **Chapter 11: *What the River Wants***. Each one honors the tone, pacing, and style we've established—blending mythic weight with emotional introspection, and pushing the story further toward its haunting climax.

Option A: Baptism by Drowning
Bob, seeking answers or some sort of release, wades into the river at dawn with no fishing gear, hoping for a moment of peace or clarity. Instead, the river pulls him under in a slow, dreamlike drowning that turns symbolic. Underwater, he sees visions—not just his past, but things he couldn't possibly know: old sacrifices, tribal rituals, the birth of Kilchis' legend. He is eventually released back to shore, gasping—but changed.

- **Themes:** Surrender, rebirth, communion with myth.
- **Benefit:** Deep psychological and spiritual moment. Offers powerful visual symbolism and moves the myth of Kilchis from vague lore into almost religious ritual.

Option B: The Return of Big Crow
Big Crow—the spiritual protector introduced earlier—appears to Bob in a half-waking state. This time, however, Big Crow is wounded, feathers torn, speaking only in broken phrases. He tries to warn Bob of what the river "wants," but cannot finish. This implies that whatever force now controls the legend of Kilchis is **evolving**, and possibly corrupting even the spirits that once kept it in check.

- **Themes:** Corruption of good, loss of spiritual order, unfinished prophecy.
- **Benefit:** Brings back an emotional and mysterious figure. Allows the reader to feel the stakes expanding beyond Bob.

Option C: The Fire Pit Prophecy
Sheriff Tallbear leads Bob to an ancient fire pit deep in the woods, once used by the tribal elders for vision-seeking. Bob agrees to sit through the ritual with Tallbear watching. The fire reveals fragments of what the river *demands*—not just a soul, but a legacy paid in blood. A horrifying truth is hinted: the Tomalin line may be cursed by a pact Clancy never told Bob about.

- **Themes:** Ancestral burden, secrecy, unpayable debts.

- **Benefit:** Builds mystery and mythology together. Advances the idea of unfinished business between the Tomalin family and the river.

🪓 **Option D: The Totem and the Axe**
While wandering the riverbank, Bob finds a massive, moss-covered totem half-buried in the soil—a carved wooden pillar with faces distorted in agony. At its base is a ceremonial stone axe with Bob's name etched into it—not just "Bob," but *Robert Clancy Tomalin*, as if it had always been waiting for him. Picking it up sends a rush of disorienting memories through him—some his, some from lifetimes he's never lived.

- **Themes:** Time collapse, preordination, identity fracture.
- **Benefit:** Visually striking and emotionally jarring. Escalates supernatural suspense and reinforces Bob's central role in the river's myth.

Would you like to choose one of these options, combine elements, or request a hybrid path that balances action, mystery, and introspection? Once selected, we'll proceed with **Part 1 of Chapter 11** in full novelistic structure.

You said:
Begin writing Chapter 11: What the River Wants, and since we have not introduced the good ancient spirit of Big Crow into the story yet, let's do that in this chapter with a significant entry into the story.

ChatGPT said:
Updated saved memory
Excellent. Here is **Part 1 of Chapter 11:** ***What the River Wants*** — written in full novelistic style, and featuring the long-awaited and powerful introduction of **Big Crow**, the ancient spirit who walks between the myths and the man.

(Part 1 Updated)

ChatGPT said:
Would you like to continue directly into **Part 2**, or pause for plot path options now that Big Crow has made his entrance?

You said:
Yes, write Part 2 of Chapter 11 and give me plot options to select from for this.

ChatGPT said:
Here are **3 plot path options** for **Part 2 of Chapter 11:** ***What the River Wants*** — each building directly from Big Crow's appearance and pushing Bob further into the mythic, emotional, and spiritual reckoning of the river.

🪶 **Option A: The Feather Offering**

Bob reaches out and accepts the feather from Big Crow. Upon contact, he is plunged into a spiritual vision — transported to an ancient ceremony where Kilchis once stood in judgment before the tribe. He witnesses a moment when the curse might have been avoided… had a Tomalin ancestor not turned away. Bob awakes with the feather still clutched in hand and a new mark forming near the spiral burn on his chest. Big Crow is gone. Only footprints remain in the moss.

- **Themes:** Consequences of ancestral denial, vision as burden, inherited debt
- **Benefit:** Visually and emotionally intense; lets the reader experience the myth directly alongside Bob.

🌊 **Option B: A Warning in the Water**

Big Crow tells Bob to return to the river at first light and cast the feather into the current. When he does, the river grows still, impossibly so — then runs backward for a few moments, revealing bones below the surface. One of the skulls opens its mouth and speaks his name. Bob stumbles back, but knows: **the river wants more than fear—it wants resolution.** A debt unpaid.

- **Themes:** Unearthing the past, demands of justice, voices of the drowned
- **Benefit:** Mysterious and haunting. Builds suspense while giving readers a powerful visual twist.

🔥 **Option C: A Spirit Interrupted**

Just as Big Crow is about to reveal more about the curse and its connection to Bob's family, he falters—something is interfering. A shadow passes overhead, and Big Crow shudders as if struck. A guttural scream echoes from the woods, and for a moment, Bob sees **River Bones** watching from the trees. Big Crow is gone in a flash of fire and crows, and Bob is left alone—trembling, confused, but now convinced that Kilchis is growing stronger… and that even the ancient spirits are not safe.

- **Themes:** Good vs evil, spiritual warfare, interference of corrupted myth
- **Benefit:** Increases the danger level. Shows the opposing forces more clearly and raises the stakes.

Would you like to proceed with one of these? Once you select the path, I'll write **Part 2** in full novelistic style.

You said:

Begin writing Part 2 in full novelistic style, using Option A: The Feather Offering

ChatGPT said:

Absolutely. Below is **Part 2 of Chapter 11:** ***What the River Wants*** written in full, immersive, novelistic style, following **Option A: The Feather Offering**.

(Part 2 Updated)

Would you like to continue now into **Part 3**, or explore plot path options for what comes next in the chapter?

You said:
Continue writing Part 3

ChatGPT said:
Certainly. Here is **Part 3 of Chapter 11: *What the River Wants***, continuing from the events of the vision and deepening the narrative with grounded emotion, introspection, and the evolving mystery of Big Crow's guidance.

(Part 3 Updated)

Would you like to proceed into **Part 4** of this chapter? Or pause and explore how we'll shape the conclusion of Chapter 11?

You said:
Proceed writing Part 4

ChatGPT said:
Certainly. Here is **Part 4 of Chapter 11: *What the River Wants*** — written in full novelistic style and carrying forward the symbolism, emotion, and deeper pull of Bob's journey toward a reckoning with both myth and self.

(Part 4 Updated)

ChatGPT said:
Would you like to continue into **Chapter 12: Dead Men Drift Downstream**, or expand this chapter with an interlude, flashback, or dream sequence before we proceed?

You said:
Let's expand Chapter 11 with a flashback before we proceed.

ChatGPT said:
Excellent. Here is a **flashback sequence to expand Chapter 11: *What the River Wants*** — woven in as a haunting reflection sparked by the fire, the symbols on the trees, and Bob's unraveling understanding of his legacy. This memory serves as a tether to Bob's lineage, yet also deepens the sense of something ancient coiled around it.

ChatGPT said:
Would you like to now begin Chapter 12: *Dead Men Drift Downstream*, or would you prefer to add an epigraph-style closing to Chapter 11 before transitioning?

You said:

Let's do an epigraph-style closing to Chapter 11 before we transition to Chapter 12.

ChatGPT said:
Here is an **epigraph-style closing** to bring **Chapter 11: *What the River Wants*** to a symbolic and resonant end, aligning with the novel's voice of humble wisdom, folklore-infused dread, and psychological weight:

(Epigraph-style closing Updated)

The night had folded in on itself like damp linen, pressing against Bob's skin with a heaviness that no fire could lift. He hadn't slept—at least not in the way a man should. Instead, he'd drifted in and out of half-consciousness, his back propped against a splintered cedar, breath shallow, eyes scanning shadows that refused to stay still. The fire had long since died to a circle of ashen teeth. The whispering had quieted. But the feeling hadn't left him.

It was the sense that something had been circling all night. Watching. Waiting.

Then it came.

Not with thunder. Not with fear. Not like Kilchis had—stalking like rot through the memory of old trees.

This was different.

The forest grew still, the way it sometimes did before a summer storm. The wind stopped. Leaves paused mid-fall, as if the air no longer remembered how to carry them. And in that hush, Bob heard it—a single crow's cry, low and throaty, not sharp like a scavenger, but round and aged. He turned slowly.

And there he was.

A man, or the memory of one, standing just beyond the clearing with feathers knotted into long silver braids that swept over his shoulders like black river reeds. His skin was dark and worn like river-polished stone, his face mapped by time and firelight. His chest bore a mark—three curved lines encircling a sun. And his eyes… his eyes were not quite human. Not anymore.

Bob didn't stand. He couldn't. His body refused the command, rooted to the earth like he'd suddenly grown into it.

"You are not him," the figure said—not with his mouth, but with a voice that arrived inside Bob's head, slow as tidewater, deep as regret. "But you carry the scent of him. His mistakes, his fear. His blood."

Bob swallowed, barely. "Who… who are you?"

The man took a step forward, feet silent over the moss. The fire, dead just moments before, flickered back to life with no fuel—just enough to throw shadows across the man's face.

"They call me Big Crow," the voice came again, gentler this time. "I am the memory before the curse. I am the breath of balance. And I have watched too long in silence."

Bob's throat was dry, heart a hammer behind his ribs. "The curse? Kilchis?"

Big Crow tilted his head, bird-like. "You chase fish with a hook, but it is you who are being reeled in. There is a hunger in these waters now. Something we once held back."

Bob's eyes dropped to the mark burned across his chest, the faint spiral now crusted at the edges, still tender. "What do you mean, we?"

Big Crow's gaze drifted to the trees, to the river beyond them. "There were always two: the Soul-Taker, and the Soul-Guardian. Where there is shadow, light must follow—if called. But light must be remembered… and you have forgotten."

Bob felt the heat of the fire rise again. It wasn't warmth. It was warning.

"I don't know what I'm supposed to do."

Big Crow stepped closer, close enough now that Bob could smell cedar, ash, and something older—like wet stone at the bottom of a canyon. "The river does not ask what you know, fisherman. It asks what you're willing to give."

And with that, Big Crow opened his hand.

Resting in his palm was a black feather, tipped in red.

Bob stared at the feather in Big Crow's open palm—black as midnight, with a crimson tip that looked less like dye and more like dried blood caught in charcoal. It shimmered faintly despite the absence of light, not glinting, not gleaming—just alive somehow, as if each strand vibrated in slow harmony with the trees.

He didn't want to reach for it.

But his hand moved anyway.

The moment his fingers closed around the shaft, the world fell away—not violently, but like water over gills. No pain. No noise. Just slippage.

Then everything went dark.

He stood in a circle of torches now, their flames flickering in a language older than words. Shadows danced across the carved faces of old-growth trees. Men and women in hides and bone necklaces stood silently in a wide ring, their eyes reflecting firelight like animals in the dark. No one moved. No one spoke. All eyes were on the center.

And in that center stood two figures.

One was unmistakably Kilchis—broad-shouldered, bare-chested, his long black hair braided with obsidian shards. But this Kilchis was younger, not yet the warped and withered nightmare from Bob's hallucinations. His face, though hard, bore no cruelty—only grief. He held a bone knife in one hand, point down, as if he were unsure of its purpose.

The second man was paler. A settler. Bob recognized something about him—his nose, his build, even the subtle slouch in the shoulders that mirrored his own. There was no doubt: this was a Tomalin. One of his own. A man whose legacy ran through his veins like the same cold riverwater.

The tribe's elder raised a carved staff. His voice echoed not through the air but through Bob's ribs, each word spoken in Tillamook yet understood as if English were being whispered directly into his ear.

"Two roads stand before us. One of respect. One of ruin."

Kilchis stepped forward, knelt, and placed the knife at the settler's feet. He looked up—not with hate, but with hope.

But the Tomalin man recoiled.

He stepped back once, then again.

He looked to the trees, then turned and walked away.

Not a word. Not a glance back.

Just abandonment.

Kilchis rose slowly, the hope gone from his face, replaced not with rage, but with something far colder—resignation.

Bob tried to shout. Tried to say Stop. Come back. Pick up the knife. Fix this. But he had no mouth. No sound. He was a ghost inside his own history.

The sky darkened. Crows screamed overhead. And the fire ring collapsed inward.

Bob gasped as breath returned like a punch to the chest.

He was back in the clearing, knees in the moss, palms pressed hard into the ground like he'd been praying or drowning. His clothes were damp with sweat. His lungs burned.

In his right hand, the feather still lay—unbent, untouched.

And on his chest, just below the spiral brand, a new mark had formed. Smaller. Simpler. The outline of a downward-pointing knife, seared into the skin like it had always been there.

He looked around.

Big Crow was gone.

But in the moss, leading away from the fire circle, were footprints—bare, wide, and impossibly ancient—headed toward the river.

Bob stood, unsteady.

The wind had returned.

But the forest no longer whispered his name.

It watched.

Bob followed the footprints. Not because he thought they'd lead him to Big Crow, but because not following them felt like a worse betrayal than the one he had just witnessed. The old Tomalin—whoever he was—had turned his back on a bridge between two worlds. Maybe Bob couldn't undo that. Maybe no one could. But he could at least walk toward the truth rather than away from it. He could stand where the coward fled.

The footprints led downslope, through sword fern and over moss-slick rocks, eventually dissolving into gravel and water. He crouched at the river's edge where the final print had sunken toe-deep into the silt. It was here that the tracks ended—but the weight of them lingered. Bob looked into the water, but instead of his reflection, he saw the flame-ringed vision of Kilchis' face flicker across the surface.

It was not a threat.

It was a wound.

He sat for a long time on the riverbank, knees up, arms over them, watching the water swirl and stretch around the boulders. The river moved differently now—less like something wild and more like something alive. It didn't rush. It listened. And in its cadence, Bob heard a question forming.

"What do you owe?"

That question dug deeper than he wanted to admit.

What did he owe?

To Tanya—for all the weekends she stayed home while he chased ghost fish and reputation? To Shane and Sarah—for every recital missed, every dinner skipped, every bedtime story left untold? To his father Clancy—for every time he rolled his eyes instead of listening, thinking he knew better than the old man?

To the river itself?

Was it only now, with brands on his chest and visions under his skin, that he was finally beginning to understand this wasn't just about catching fish? That it never was?

Bob thought of the ledger in his writing journal back home. The one where he'd recorded the weight and date of every steelhead he'd caught across the Pacific Northwest. The one he intended to one day publish as part of his memoir—a testament to his dominance over the rivers.

He suddenly hated it.

He hated the pride in it.

He hated what it stood for.

But most of all, he hated that it had taken hallucinations, hauntings, and the walking spirit of a Tillamook elder to shake him from that trance.

A crow called from overhead—not one, but two—and Bob looked up just in time to see them wheel in a tight spiral above the river, then dart westward, back toward Rogue Country. It wasn't just a flight pattern. It was a direction. A message. Maybe even a summons.

Bob stood.

His legs were stiff. His back hurt. The air was cooler now. Evening was coming fast.

He turned to leave—and as he did, something half-buried in the mud caught his eye.

Not a relic. Not a totem. Just a photograph.

Soaked and curled, its ink nearly worn away, but the shape of his own face stared back from the left side—maybe twenty years younger. Clancy stood beside him, hand on his shoulder, both of them grinning proudly over a massive chrome-bright steelhead hung from a scale.

Bob picked it up with trembling fingers. He had no memory of losing this photo. It wasn't one he carried. Wasn't one that should have been here.

But there it was.

Laid at his feet like an offering. Or a warning.

The river had given it back. Or maybe just reminded him what had always been buried.

He didn't need to decide what it meant. He just needed to follow the path being laid before him.

Bob turned toward camp.

The wind carried the scent of firewood.

And for the first time in weeks, he didn't feel entirely alone.

Bob reached camp just before the last light bled from the sky. The fire pit lay cold, though he was sure he'd banked enough coals to last the day. No embers remained. Only the blackened bones of yesterday's flame, and in that silence, he felt something breathing. Not wind. Not wildlife. Something slower. Patient. The kind of breath that had never needed lungs.

He lit a fresh fire more out of ritual than warmth, coaxing flame from bark and tinder, hands moving on their own. The weight of the photograph—now dried and placed carefully in his journal—had left a hole in his chest. Or perhaps it had filled one. He wasn't sure which anymore.

As the light returned, flickering across the trees, Bob noticed something he hadn't before. Carvings. Just faint traces along the base of the nearest Douglas fir—so shallow they could've been missed a hundred times. He walked closer. Ran his fingers along the bark. The grooves weren't random. They were spirals, matching the same pattern branded across his chest from the cave near Hollow Mile.

There were dozens of them.

Some nearly faded to nothing, others freshly scored. It wasn't graffiti. It was a record.

And suddenly, the forest felt far older than it had the night before. Not just ancient, but aware.

Bob moved from tree to tree, tracing spiral after spiral, some intersecting with rough geometric shapes—circles with dots, arrows pointing west, symbols that might've once meant "spirit," "danger," or "remember." He felt the pull behind his eyes again, that pressure he'd come to associate with visions—but no images came. Only weight.

He returned to the fire, sat cross-legged like Tallbear had, and let his hands fall open on his knees. "What do you want from me?" he whispered. It was no longer shouted. No longer defiant. Just a tired man asking a river for an answer.

The flame popped.

A single, dried feather floated down onto the coals—its edges scorched as it curled inward like fingers closing.

Bob jerked up. The feather hadn't been there before. It was black—not like Big Crow's ceremonial white plume, but ink-dark and small. A crow's wing. A warning. Something had shifted.

He scanned the tree line. The symbols. The ground. But nothing moved.

Then, in the dancing firelight, a voice whispered—not from the trees, not from the river.

From inside him.

"You've been marked to remember, and that is not a mercy."

He shot to his feet, chest heaving.

And just as he turned to look toward the ridge that led west—where Rogue Country waited like a wound reopened—a single crow called out from a branch above.

Not a message.

A goodbye.

Bob's knees buckled, and he sat heavily on the damp earth.

He knew now what the river wanted.

It wanted a witness.

A reckoning.

And it would take him all the way back to where this began—to the hole in the forest where names whispered themselves into madness, and the soul-taker legend had been waiting all along to be heard again.

The fire had burned down to a steady hush when the memory came—not summoned, not welcomed. It crept in sideways, the way certain dreams do, disguised as déjà vu until it was too vivid to dismiss.

Bob was twelve again, standing hip-deep in the muddy shallows of Copper Creek, rod in hand, eyes fixed on the slow swirl where the alder roots gathered insects like a hungry congregation. His dad, Clancy, stood upstream, broad-shouldered in a waxed canvas jacket, casting long, rhythmic loops into the center channel. There was no wind, just birdsong and the whisper of current around gravel.

Bob had been talking too much that day—bragging about how he'd out-fished a couple of older boys from school, explaining how he'd figured out steelhead habits like a scientist. Clancy had nodded now and then, but mostly let him talk.

Then something changed.

The light dimmed.

It wasn't clouds, not yet evening—but the trees seemed to lean in, and the birds stopped cold. Bob remembered a prickle at the base of his neck, the unmistakable feeling of being watched. He looked toward the bank where the reeds bent strangely, as if someone had passed through moments earlier.

"Dad?" he'd called, voice cracking from the chill that suddenly crept into the water.

Clancy reeled in, lips pressed tight. He scanned the woods before walking quickly downstream toward Bob—not panicked, but urgent.

"We're done," Clancy had said. "That's enough for today."

"But I haven't—"

"I said we're done."

There had been something in his eyes—something Bob couldn't name then. Not fear. Not anger. A kind of knowing. A history buried too deep to retell.

Later that night, back at the camper, Bob had tried again. "Did you see something?"

Clancy had stared at the flame of the camp stove, hands wrapped around his mug of black coffee. "Some places," he'd said, "ain't interested in being remembered."

Bob hadn't understood then. He thought it was just another one of his dad's old-man-isms, meant to sound wise but empty.

But now, three decades later, in a camp surrounded by spirals and smoke, with a brand on his chest and Big Crow's silence still hanging in the air—he knew.

Clancy had seen something that day. And he'd never wanted Bob to find it.

But the river had its own plans.

And forgetting was never going to be enough.

"Some rivers don't carry water.
Some carry memory.
And the deeper they run,
the more they remember what you tried to forget."
— From the Tillamook Oral Histories, Fragment 6

Bob sat by the dying fire long after sleep had left him.
He had not dreamed.
But something inside him had.

By dawn, he knew: the river didn't want his fish.
It wanted his confession.

And it wouldn't stop pulling until it got it.

End of Chapter 11

CHAPTER 12: DEAD MEN DRIFT DOWNSTREAM

ChatGPT said:
Would you like to proceed into **Chapter 12: *Dead Men Drift Downstream*** with fresh plot options?

You said:
Yes, let's proceed to Chapter 12: Dead Men Drift Downstream and give me fresh plot options that will be appropriate for the fact that we are in the final phase of writing the book (last 3 chapters).

ChatGPT said:
Excellent — you've guided this story deep into its mythic and psychological current. With only three chapters remaining, we are now entering the **final reckoning** of *Steelhead Graveyard.* Chapter 12 must do the following:

- Deepen the sense of inevitable confrontation
- Tie together the ancestral curse with personal consequence
- Bring Bob closer than ever to Kilchis and the true purpose of River Bones
- Begin seeding the idea of sacrifice — not just survival

Below are **4 fresh plot path options** for **Chapter 12: *Dead Men Drift Downstream***, crafted to align with this stage of the story:

🪓 **Option A: The Corpse in the Net**
Bob returns to fish — not out of sport now, but instinct, as if answering something that lives inside him. His line catches on something heavy. He pulls it in, expecting debris, but what surfaces is **a human corpse**, tangled in a tattered net. It's bloated and water-dark, but the face is eerily familiar: it's **Bob's own**, mouth agape, eyes frozen mid-scream. He stumbles back—only to find the body gone moments later. But in its place, the carved bone he'd buried by the fire has reappeared, dry, and humming with heat.

- **Themes:** Identity, death as reflection, reckoning with fate
- **Benefit:** Deep psychological horror with a literal visual of what's at stake

---

🪶 **Option B: Big Crow's Last Warning**
Bob finds a crow lying on the trail with its wings spread, feathers marked in red ochre symbols matching his chest. That night, Big Crow returns, barely coherent — flickering like a dying flame. He warns Bob that Kilchis has found a *body*, a vessel now active in the waking world. Bob must descend into the drowned grove, where the elders once cast out spirits by name, and finish the banishment. But the price will be high. A name must be offered in return. **His. Or someone else's.**

- **Themes:** Sacrifice, urgency, spirit possession
- **Benefit:** Forces a moral crossroads and raises emotional tension

---

🧠 **Option C: Tallbear's Disappearance**
Bob seeks out Sheriff Tallbear for help but finds his home abandoned. The only clue is a trail of bootprints leading toward the river's bend—and a half-carved wooden mask nailed to a tree: **half Tallbear's face, half Kilchis.** Bob realizes the man who has warned him all along may now be the next vessel… or has always been something else entirely. As the rain begins to fall again, Bob is forced to wonder who has truly been guiding him.

- **Themes:** Doubt, duality, mentor as myth
- **Benefit:** Flips the trust dynamic and introduces uncertainty

---

🔥 **Option D: The Bonefire Ceremony**
Desperate for clarity, Bob builds a sacred fire using the methods Big Crow once whispered to him. He burns the carved bone, the marked feather, and even a page from one of his old fishing articles — his pride. The fire responds unnaturally, rising high and blue. Shadows gather in the smoke, and he sees River Bones… **not stalking him**, but kneeling, repeating a chant in a long-dead tongue. It ends with a name Bob doesn't recognize — but one that echoes in his own blood.

- **Themes:** Ritual, ego-death, ancestral reckoning
- **Benefit:** Symbolic, cathartic, and mystically charged; a bridge to final confrontation

---

Let me know which option (or combination of options) you'd like to proceed with for **Chapter 12: Dead Men Drift Downstream**, and I'll begin writing Part 1 in full novelistic style.

You said:
Begin writing Part 1 of Chapter 12: Dead Men Drift Downstream, using Option C: Tallbear's Disappearance. Make sure you continue to use full paragraphs and novelistic-style copy.

ChatGPT said:
Absolutely. Below is **Part 1** of **Chapter 12: *Dead Men Drift Downstream***, written in full novelistic style using **Option C: Tallbear's Disappearance**.

(Part 1 Updated)

ChatGPT said:
Would you like to proceed into **Part 2**, or first review plot options to guide the next segment?

You said:
I want this chapter to have 6 Parts to it so that that into consideration when writing each part. Give me a few plot options to select from for Part 2

ChatGPT said:

Excellent — since Chapter 12: *Dead Men Drift Downstream* will consist of **six parts**, we'll shape the chapter with a steady crescendo of dread, discovery, and mythic revelation as we lead Bob toward the inevitable reckoning. Here are **three plot options** for **Part 2**, each designed to deepen the narrative while keeping tension and mystery thick:

🪵 **Option A: The Drifter's Journal**

Bob finds a waterlogged backpack snagged in a side channel near the riverbank. Inside is a weather-beaten journal belonging to a man named **Caleb Nix**, a drifter from the 1980s who wrote obsessively about "the men who vanish when the fish don't bite." The entries become increasingly erratic, eventually referencing Kilchis, River Bones, and even Bob's *surname* — decades before Bob ever fished the Rogue. The journal suggests a cycle of disappearances that occurs every 33 years… and 2025 is the next cycle.

Tones: Paranoia, fate, deep-time cycles, cosmic dread

Function: Expands the lore, connects past and present, deepens mystery around Bob's bloodline.

🐟 **Option B: The Steelhead Graveyard Reveals Itself**

While scouting downstream, Bob stumbles upon a hidden inlet choked with fish carcasses— dozens of steelhead in various stages of decay, some impossibly fresh, others with flesh long peeled from their bones. Etched into the rocks above the waterline are names — not just random ones — but **fishermen Bob once idolized** and wrote about, men long thought lost to accidents, strokes, disappearances. All are here.

This inlet, silent and reeking of old rot, is **the graveyard**.

Tones: Horror, reverence, surreal revelation

Function: Offers a literal reveal of the book's title concept and brings mythology into sharp physical reality.

🪶 **Option C: The Return of Big Crow**

The spirit of Big Crow reappears—this time not through signs or dreams, but in the form of a **dying animal** that speaks Bob's name in his father's voice. The creature is a symbol, possibly a messenger, and it warns Bob that a "second death" is coming — a death of *memory*. If Bob cannot resist the call of the river, it will erase not just his body, but the legacy of his family, as if they never lived. Big Crow gives Bob a choice: accept a burden of memory, or let the water write over his name.

Tones: Symbolic, spiritual, emotionally weighty

Function: Adds deeper stakes to Bob's personal journey, sets up a metaphysical choice and moral crisis.

Let me know which **option you'd like to use for Part 2**, or if you'd like to **blend elements from multiple**. I'll then continue with the next section in full novelistic style.

You said:

Continue with Part 2 of Chapter 12, using Option B: The Steelhead Graveyard Reveals Itself

ChatGPT said:

Updated saved memory
Here is **Part 2 of Chapter 12: *Dead Men Drift Downstream***, written in long-form, novelistic style using **Option B: The Steelhead Graveyard Reveals Itself**.

(Part 2 Updated)

ChatGPT said:
Would you like to proceed with **Part 3**, and if so, would you like fresh plot options to guide the next section?

You said:
Give me a few plot options to chose from for Part 3 that will align with where we are in the story and help make it the best read possible.

ChatGPT said:
Here are several **plot options for Part 3 of Chapter 12: *Dead Men Drift Downstream***. Each is designed to deepen the emotional intensity, mythology, and narrative momentum as we move toward the book's climax. These options reflect the chapter's midpoint and are meant to build on the discovery of the steelhead graveyard:

🔥 **Option A: The Ledger That Includes Bob**
Bob returns to the stone with the names and discovers a fresh, damp carving—**his own name** etched faintly at the bottom. Beneath it, the beginning of another: **Clancy Tomalin**. It shakes Bob to the core. The river is not just remembering—it's **predicting**. This leads Bob to believe that his father is in danger, pushing him to make an impossible decision: return to Bandon to protect Clancy, or stay and confront the curse before it spreads.

🐾 **Option B: The Trail of Lost Boots**
Bob follows a strange trail leading away from the steelhead graveyard—half-submerged boots, lures in branches, a broken fly rod leaning against a tree—all belongings from missing fishermen whose names were etched in stone. One item, an old fly with red thread and bone hook, matches something Clancy used to tie. Bob realizes his father had once been here, and maybe... left something behind.

🎐 **Option C: The River's Memory**
Bob touches the river and is pulled into a sensory flood—**a vision that isn't his**. He becomes Kilchis for a moment, or perhaps one of the long-dead fishermen, reliving their final moments as they were pulled under. The experience is jarring and revelatory. He emerges from the vision choking and gasping, with mud in his mouth and blood on his palms. The river doesn't just take bodies. It takes stories. And it has stored them all.

🐦 **Option D: Big Crow Returns with a Warning**
The crow from before returns—but this time it doesn't just caw. It speaks in a rasped human voice, half-spoken, half-thought. Bob follows it into a clearing where an **ancient totem** stands,

mostly eroded, but with a still-visible carving: a man with crow wings and a steelhead in his chest. It's a monument to Big Crow, the good spirit—and beneath it, Bob finds a hidden bundle: bones, feathers, and something made of his father's fly-tying thread.

ChatGPT said:
Would you like to proceed with one of these options, combine elements, or request a variation?

You said:
Let's proceed with Part 3, using Option D: Big Crow Returns with a Warning. After Option D is incorporated, then include Option B: The Train of Lost Boots.

ChatGPT said:
Updated saved memory
Excellent choice — this combination will deepen the symbolic and emotional resonance while driving the story forward with mystery and myth. I'll now begin writing **Part 3 of Chapter 12: *Dead Men Drift Downstream***, using full-paragraph, novelistic style, starting with **Big Crow's return** and flowing into **the trail of lost boots**. Please hold on while I compose it for you.

(Part 3 Updated)

ChatGPT said:
Part 3 of Chapter 12 has been written and saved. We've woven in Big Crow's return and the discovery of the trail of lost boots, including a haunting connection to Clancy. Let me know when you're ready to continue with Part 4, or if you'd like new plot options for it.

You said:
Give me a few options for Part 4 of Chapter 12.

ChatGPT said:
Here are several plot options for **Part 4 of Chapter 12: *Dead Men Drift Downstream*** that build naturally from what just occurred, honor the mythic tone, and drive us deeper into the story's emotional and supernatural climax:

Option A: The Carved Path Downstream
Bob follows the river downstream in search of answers, only to find a narrow path lined with ancient carvings—Tillamook symbols, warnings, and prayers—etched into river rocks, many of them partially submerged. He realizes this sacred path is not meant for the living. As he walks it, he sees glimpses of ghostly fishermen walking beside him, some of them people he's seen in photos—others completely unfamiliar. But all have hollow eyes and one thing in common: the ash mark burned into their chest.
Focus: Escalation of myth and mysticism. Heavy on visual symbolism. Brings Bob to the edge of something irreversible.

Option B: The Bones Speak
Bob returns to the inlet of steelhead carcasses only to find them rearranged in a new pattern—an enormous spiral pointing toward the heart of the forest. At its center is a freshly killed steelhead, still bleeding. As he kneels beside it, the whispering begins again—but this time in the voice of his father, recounting an event Bob doesn't remember from his childhood. He begins to question not only his sanity, but his memory.
Focus: Psychological horror and familial connection. Introduces doubt into Bob's memories and identity.

Option C: Tallbear's Trail
Bob finds Tallbear's notebook lodged under a fallen tree, pages soaked but readable. The sheriff had been documenting everything—names, dates, symbols. Bob learns Tallbear had been tracking the Soul-Taker for years and suspected the entity was feeding off unresolved legacies. One page is a letter addressed to Bob, meant to be read only if Tallbear vanished. The letter begs Bob to finish what his ancestors started.
Focus: Expands Tallbear's depth. Tightens the connection between Bob, the river, and the curse. Adds urgency.

Option D: Baptism in the Dark Pool
Bob discovers a still, moonlit pool at the end of the trail, eerily calm compared to the rest of the river. He's drawn into the water and experiences a near-drowning vision: his childhood self, Clancy's hands, the ghost of Kilchis, and Big Crow all entangled in a spiritual struggle. When he wakes, he's on the opposite bank—dry, but forever changed.
Focus: Metaphysical and symbolic. Marks the true transformation of Bob's soul. Blends time, myth, and emotion.

Let me know which path you'd like to explore, or if you'd like a hybrid. Each one leads us closer to the final reckoning.

You said:
Proceed with Part 4 of Chapter 12, using Option C: Tallbear's Trail. Continue writing in full-length paragraphs and a novelistic style.

ChatGPT said:
Updated saved memory
Excellent. I'll now write **Part 4 of Chapter 12: *Dead Men Drift Downstream*** using **Option C: Tallbear's Trail**, continuing in our full-paragraph, immersive novelistic style. Please hold while I craft the section.

(Part 4 Updated)

ChatGPT said:
Would you like plot options for **Part 5**, or shall I proceed directly with the next section?

You said:
Give me plot options for Part 5 of Chapter 12

ChatGPT said:
Here are several plot options for **Part 5 of Chapter 12: *Dead Men Drift Downstream***. Each one deepens the mythos while preparing the story for the final act, keeping in line with the rising stakes and growing supernatural tension:

Option A: The Ritual Circle
Bob discovers a moss-covered circle of ancient stones deep in the forest—charred black in the center, as if something had once been burned there. Animal bones, rusted tackle, and shattered sunglasses litter the edges. This appears to be the site of an ancient ritual attempt to contain or communicate with the Soul-Taker. Bob is drawn into the circle and has a partial vision—half memory, half possession—revealing a failed binding of the spirit by past fishermen. When he comes to, it's night, and his footprints have disappeared from the ground behind him.

Option B: Clancy's Old Jacket
Bob hikes into a narrow canyon where he sees something draped over a snag in the brush. It's his father's old fishing jacket—something he hasn't seen since childhood and which Clancy claimed was lost on a trip near Bandon. Inside the pocket is a photo Bob has never seen: Clancy as a young man, standing beside a man with the same ash handprint burned faintly across his chest. On the back of the photo is a single sentence: *"Some bloodlines never drift far enough."*

Option C: The Riverbed Shrine
While crossing a shallow side channel, Bob slips and uncovers a hidden shrine beneath the water. It's constructed of driftwood, bones, and fishing lures — a submerged offering. He recognizes a lure from his own childhood box, one he never brought on this trip. The shrine seems to pulse faintly, and for a brief moment, Bob sees his daughter Sarah standing in the water upstream… then gone. The shrine might be an anchor between worlds — or a trap.

Option D: The Voice Beneath
Bob camps by the river to gather strength. During the night, he awakens to the sound of someone speaking his name—not in the trees this time, but from beneath the river itself. He approaches the water and sees his reflection change, becoming gaunt, hollow-eyed, with blackened veins across his cheeks. The voice speaks through it, warning him that each fish taken without respect feeds the Soul-Taker's hunger. Bob tries to flee but finds his boots submerged in mud that's gripping him like hands.

Would you like to proceed with one of these, or customize a combination?

You said:
Proceed with Part 5 of Chapter 12, using Option D: The Voice Beneath.

ChatGPT said:
Updated saved memory
Excellent — we'll proceed with **Part 5 of Chapter 12: *Dead Men Drift Downstream*** using **Option D: The Voice Beneath**. This moment will intensify the supernatural tone and further tie Bob's unraveling fate to the river's ancient hunger. I'll write it now in immersive, full-paragraph, novelistic style. Please hold.

(Part 5 Updated)

You said:
Now, let's finish up Chapter 12 by writing Part 6. Give me a couple options for this final part of Chapter 12 that will be a great transition into Chapter 13.

ChatGPT said:
Here are **two strong plot options** for **Part 6 of Chapter 12: *Dead Men Drift Downstream*** — each designed to bring closure to this pivotal chapter while seamlessly building tension and preparing readers for the next chapter, *Chapter 13: The Fisherman's Reckoning.*

✅ **Option A: The River's Ledger**
As Bob regains his composure, he notices something half-buried in the riverbank mud—a wooden slab, waterworn and carved with names. He recognizes a few—fishermen lost over the years, dismissed as accidents. But at the bottom is a freshly etched name: **"Robert Tomalin."** Horrified, Bob begins digging, uncovering more slabs like gravestones hidden beneath silt and moss, each telling a story of those who challenged the river and were claimed. As he stares at his own name, he realizes this journey was never just about fishing or legacy. It was about reckoning, and the river keeps a ledger of debts owed. This scene closes with Bob packing up, not to flee — but to *finish it.*
Emotional tone: Dread, determination, existential weight
Transition to Chapter 13: Positions Bob as willingly entering the final confrontation — his *reckoning.*

✅ **Option B: Return to the Campfire**
Bob returns to where he last sat with Tallbear — but the campfire is now cold, overgrown, as if weeks have passed. No trace of the Sheriff remains… except his badge, pinned to the center of a ring of river stones. Beneath it is a small satchel containing a worn cassette recorder. Bob clicks play. Tallbear's voice crackles through, leaving behind one final message: "If you're hearing this, it means I failed… or I left before I could. Either way, you're the last one who can stop it. The Soul-Taker doesn't just haunt. He *inherits.*"
As the tape winds down, Bob feels the air shift. The forest quiets. A low hum begins beneath the earth. He grabs the badge, shoulders his gear, and walks toward the river, no longer running from what's coming—but toward it.

Emotional tone: Melancholic, suspenseful, solemn
Transition to Chapter 13: Reveals Tallbear's fate while transferring spiritual and narrative responsibility to Bob.

Would you like to proceed with **Option A: The River's Ledger, Option B: Return to the Campfire**, or would you like a **third option** before we write the closing?

You said:
Proceed with Option B: Return to the Campfire.

ChatGPT said:
Updated saved memory
Excellent. I'll now write **Part 6 of Chapter 12: *Dead Men Drift Downstream*** using **Option B: Return to the Campfire**, carrying us with full emotional weight and mystery into the next chapter. Please hold while I compose it in our established novelistic style.

(Part 6 Updated)

Bob had walked the forest trail with the dull resolve of a man seeking truth he no longer wanted. The air smelled of rot and copper, pine pitch and something sour—like a memory fermenting in a cellar too long sealed. His boots sank into the soft riverbed loam as he crossed the final rise toward Tallbear's home: a modest cabin tucked into a low stand of Sitka spruce, not far from where the water forked like a broken promise.

But something was off. Not just wrong — hollow.
The place felt abandoned by more than just people. It felt abandoned by presence.

He paused at the split-rail fence, one hand resting on the cold cedar post. A crow cried once, sharp and distant, and then the silence thickened like smoke. The cabin's windows were dark. The usual scent of woodsmoke—Tallbear's comfort and defense against the damp—was gone, replaced by a damp mildew that crept along the porch rails like lichen growing too fast.

He called out once, twice. "Tallbear?"
Nothing. Not even the forest answered this time.

Bob stepped onto the porch, the old boards giving underfoot with too much ease. The door wasn't locked. It swung open with a slow creak, not the dramatic kind—no horror movie sting—but the tired kind, like it had done this a thousand times before and would again long after Bob was gone.

Inside, it was as if the man had vanished mid-thought. A half-carved wooden mask still sat in the vise on the workbench, shavings curled like fish scales around its base. A steaming mug of coffee—no, not steaming now. Cold. But not old. Not mold-rimmed. Maybe a day? Two at most?

His eyes drifted to a photograph on the wall above the hearth. Sheriff Roy Tallbear, young and lean, stood beside a man Bob didn't recognize — a native elder with stark cheekbones and eyes like smoke. They both held spears. Below it, in scrawled Sharpie ink:
Drowned Grove Cleanse – '94.
A ritual. Something ceremonial. Bob didn't know the story, but the air told him he should have.

He crossed the room slowly, stepping over a twisted wool blanket, when he noticed something nailed to the doorframe on the back exit — a wooden carving, still bleeding sap. It was a mask, about the size of a human face. One side was unmistakably Tallbear — broad nose, creased brow, the detail uncanny. The other side… was something else entirely. Elongated. Animalistic. The eyes were gouged black, and the mouth twisted in a spiral that made Bob's gut tighten just looking at it.

His first instinct was to touch it.
His second was to run.
Instead, he stood, paralyzed between those two voices, while something inside him shifted — a recognition he could not yet place.

Outside, a soft wind stirred the trees. It carried no sound, no birds, no whisper of animal movement. Just the growing sense that Tallbear hadn't left. He'd become something.
Or been taken.

Bob stepped back outside, breathing harder now, heart drumming in his ears. His hand reflexively went to the mark on his chest, the burned spiral that had started it all. It ached in the presence of this place. Not pain exactly — more like a tuning fork struck too hard.

He followed a trail of bootprints through the muck behind the house. Heavy, wide-set, deliberate. They led toward the river's bend. The trees seemed to lean in closer the farther he walked, and for the first time in days, Bob considered the possibility that maybe he wasn't the one being hunted anymore. Maybe the river had moved on — chosen someone new. Someone who once stood at the fire and whispered warnings.

He reached the final rise where the trail dipped toward a fog-slick bank. The bootprints ended abruptly at the waterline. No sign of a struggle. No indication of return. Just a single object wedged into a patch of reeds: a sheriff's badge, tarnished and cracked down the middle.
Bob lifted it in silence.

Somewhere upriver, too faint to be certain, he heard a low chant — not words, not song. Just rhythm. Pulse. Breath.
As if something beneath the surface was remembering how to speak.

The light had started to dim in that slow, eerie way the forest seemed to prefer—neither dusk nor shadow, just an overcast breath of gray that clung to everything like a wet cloth. Bob moved along the narrow animal trail beside the river, boots squelching against moss and silt. The trail wasn't marked on any map. It had emerged, faint and thin, behind a copse of alder trees as if conjured by need rather than topography. He hadn't meant to follow it. He just had… followed.

Branches reached out like crooked fingers, snagging his coat, tugging at his resolve. A crow called overhead—just once, sharp and lonely—and then the forest hushed again. Not even the wind dared speak.

Bob pushed through a curtain of brush and found himself at the edge of a slough—an offshoot of the Rogue he hadn't seen before, a narrow inlet shaded by leaning firs and dark-rooted ferns. And it was there that he smelled it first—rot, old and fishy, but with something else beneath it. Something iron. Something human.

He stepped closer.

There, resting just below the surface of the still water, were fish. Dozens. Maybe hundreds. Steelhead in various states of decay. Some with color still in their gill plates. Others stripped of skin, their bones picked clean by time and current. They weren't trapped. They had not washed in. They had been placed. Bob's stomach turned.

Then he saw the names.

Etched into the black rock that formed the basin's edge were rows and rows of them—hand-carved, crude, weatherworn—but unmistakably names. He stepped forward, brushing away moss and silt to read them more clearly.

"Tanner Judd – 1992"
"Ellis Mercer – 1976"
"Ryan T. Hollow – 1959"
"Clint Samuels – 1943"

Bob's hand trembled. These weren't just random men. He knew these names. He'd written about some of them. Legendary steelheaders who had vanished without explanation. Gone during storms or off-season scouting trips. Their absences had become whispers in tackle shops and late-night riverside tales.

Here they were. All of them.

One after another. Lost fishermen memorialized in a place no one should have found.

Bob stumbled backward, heart pounding in his ears. His boot slipped and splashed into the water. It was warmer than it should have been. He looked again, and the fish—some still twitched.

The air turned heavy.

A low hum, like a breath held beneath the surface, began to rise from the center of the inlet. It vibrated through Bob's spine, a resonance not heard but felt. Something beneath the carcasses stirred. A slow swirl of movement—not a fish. Something else. Something watching.

He staggered away from the edge, breath ragged.

The river wanted him to see this.

Not just the death, but the devotion. The offering. The cost.

This was no accident. This was a ritual. A ledger of the claimed.

And it was far from full.

The crow returned just after the sun dipped behind the firs, a flicker of black against the glowing western sky. Bob had been kneeling beside the river, running a trembling hand across the old stone where the names were carved, as if trying to memorize the entire legacy of the lost. The current whispered like breath over bone, and for a long moment, he thought he heard a voice in it. Not words. Intention.

Then came the scrape of talons on driftwood behind him.

He turned. There it was—the same bird from before. Black-feathered. Watching. Its eyes were darker than coal, but there was something behind them now, some spark of ancient intelligence that hadn't been there before. It opened its beak and let out a sound that wasn't a caw but something twisted—half-rattle, half-breath. It turned, flapped once, and lifted off without urgency, weaving upstream like it wanted to be followed.

Bob didn't hesitate.

The climb was steeper than he remembered. Old cedar roots clawed through the moss like skeletal fingers, and the wind began to rise, carrying that earthy smell of wet bark and decay. It was near nightfall when the trail flattened out into a clearing that didn't appear on any map. Trees circled like old sentinels, and in the center stood something that made Bob's knees weaken: a weather-worn totem pole, only half its original height, split with age and moss-eaten—but still proud.

At the top, a crow with wings outstretched.

Below it, a man's face.

And in his chest—where a heart should be—was a carved steelhead, mouth open in a silent scream.

Bob stepped forward, unsure if his feet were even touching the earth anymore. Something warm moved through his chest, just under the skin. The mark. He could feel it pulsing—responding. Beneath the totem lay a bundle wrapped in cedar bark and bound with red thread. Bob unwrapped it slowly, reverently. Inside: brittle feathers, small bones, and a fishing fly so intricately tied it could only have come from one man's hands.

His father's.

He fell to his knees, heart thundering. Had Clancy been here before? Had he known about this place? Had he made a deal he never told anyone about?

Before Bob could answer any of the questions clamoring in his head, the crow landed again—this time on the totem itself. It looked straight into his soul and released a long, low sound. Bob didn't know if it was a warning or a farewell, but he knew it meant go.

He obeyed.

As he descended the slope, half-stumbling now, he noticed something glinting in the ferns. A boot. Old. Moss-covered. Not his. Twenty feet later, another—this one torn open at the heel. Then came a length of fly line tangled in a bush, its color faded by decades. A snapped rod with the reel rusted shut. A crushed tackle box. Bob moved carefully, reverently, piecing together the remnants like sacred artifacts.

The trail of lost boots led deeper into a hollow grove where the forest floor dipped. It was there that he found the final marker—a circle of stacked stones, each etched with a different name. Many he'd seen before. One he hadn't:

Clancy T.

But the final letter was unfinished.

He stared at it until night swallowed the trees whole. The wind had gone quiet. The air turned cold and heavy.

Somewhere, just beneath the surface of the river's hush, the wilderness whispered:

Not yet.

The rain came again—soft and patient this time, like the forest had decided to whisper instead of shout. Bob hiked deeper into the trees, following no path he could name, guided only by instinct and something he could no longer explain. The trail was a fading scar through the undergrowth, barely visible beneath the curtain of moss and time, yet he felt pulled toward something ahead—like gravity in reverse, dragging him toward a higher weight.

That's when he saw it: a flash of something pale under the lip of a wind-fallen cedar. He stepped closer and knelt, brushing away needles and mud until his fingers closed around the swollen leather edge of a book—softened by rain, but unmistakably a notebook. It was held together by twine, the kind used by men who don't trust zippers. On the inside cover, smudged by damp fingerprints and years of field wear, was a name scratched in black ink:

Roy Tallbear.

Bob sat on a root and turned the first page with care, his breath caught somewhere between dread and reverence. The writing inside was rough, slanted—the hurried hand of a man scribbling between patrols or before sleep. Pages were filled with hand-drawn maps, dates, coordinates, and entries of things Tallbear had never dared say aloud.

"The stories aren't stories.
Kilchis was the first, but not the last.
The soul-taker is real. It chooses. It watches for legacies and pride—men who fish to prove instead of to listen."

The next few pages detailed sightings: bobbers found tied in trees, lines severed without cause, fishermen who never returned, and always the same mark—the ash handprint. There were sketches of the Tillamook spiral, notations of chants overheard in dreams, even a few entries suggesting a pattern based on river depth, lunar phase, and blood moon alignments.

But what stopped Bob cold wasn't a log entry.

It was the letter tucked between two pages, wrapped in waxed cloth. On the outside, a shaky scrawl read:

"To Bob Tomalin. If I vanish."

His stomach tightened. His hands went still.

He opened it.

"Bob—
If you're reading this, then the river's made its choice. I tried to stop it, I really did. But you… you carry something in your blood the river remembers. I saw it in your eyes when we met at the store—pride and grief

wrapped in steelhead line. This thing out here doesn't kill the unworthy. It drowns the legacy-drunk. And if it has you, it means it wants something deeper than fish.

You have to go further upriver. There's a place where the old men went. Where they tried to trap it once. They failed. But they left something behind. You'll know it when you find it.
Just remember: It can look like anyone. Even me.
And Bob—don't go alone."

Bob folded the letter slowly, like it might burn him if he moved too fast. He looked up at the dripping forest, the empty trees, the silence that had grown too thick. Something had always felt off about Tallbear's reappearances—like he came and went just when Bob needed him, like a character in a story, not a man with a job and a home.

The rain picked up. Bob tucked the letter into his coat and stared at the trees.

Was Tallbear still alive?

Had he ever been?

The wind shifted, and for a moment, the scent of tobacco and cedar wrapped around him like an old blanket. Bob closed his eyes and breathed it in.

Then he stood, turned upriver, and started walking toward the place where old men had failed.

He would not.

The river whispered as it always had — steady, unknowable, and just out of reach. Bob had set up camp farther upstream, near a bend of water that coiled like a serpent and shimmered with a sullen, metallic sheen beneath the moonlight. He was too tired to press on after what he'd found: the boots, Big Crow's warning, and the haunting trail that led nowhere but deeper into madness. So he sat by the bank, a small fire flickering behind him, its glow an orange tremble against the trees. He didn't sleep so much as fade—his body upright, breath shallow, eyes blinking slower and slower until the world blurred into a quilt of shadow and hush.

Something pulled him back. Not a sound, but the absence of one.

The river had stopped.

Bob opened his eyes. The current still flowed, yes, but the music of it—the gentle gurgles, the glassy babble, the way water talked to rocks—was gone. In its place was a humming silence so total it made his ears ring. He turned toward the river's edge, where his reflection wavered in the moonlit shallows. At first, it was as expected: tired eyes, sun-chapped face, days of stubble. Then the image began to twist.

His reflection's jaw slackened.

Its eyes rolled back.

Dark veins began threading up the face in the water—slow tendrils creeping like moss over stone.

Bob stumbled backward, but the river followed. Not in body, but in voice.

"Robert Tomalin."

The name wasn't shouted, whispered, or spoken. It arrived. It dropped into him like a stone in a well—deep, direct, and final. He stared, unblinking, as the water pulsed once—like something alive beneath the surface had just exhaled.

"You took what was never yours."

His mouth opened, but no words came. The voice continued, not from above or below but from within the bones of the water itself.

"Steelhead are not yours to claim. Blood, not bait, has fed this river. Each hook cast, each life pulled from these waters, calls me."

Bob shook his head violently, as if trying to knock the words out of it. "No," he rasped. "I respect this place. I always have. I… I love these fish."

The reflection only smiled. Not Bob's smile — something colder, amused, pitying.

"Love is not permission. And legacy is not redemption."

Bob tried to step back, but his boots would not move. He looked down and realized the riverbank had changed. Mud now clung to him like hands, thick fingers curling around his soles, sucking him into the soil. He thrashed, breath wild, but it only pulled tighter, up to his ankles now. The river laughed — not with joy, but with knowing. A long, low ripple of inevitability.

Desperate, Bob dropped to his knees and dug at the mud, clawing at the roots beneath. He cried out for Tanya, for Shane, for Sarah — for his family, for his why. The moment he did, the grip eased.

He fell backward, free, gasping on the forest floor, the firelight flickering beside him again as if nothing had happened. The river whispered once more in its old tongue — water to stone, shadow to root.

But as Bob sat there trembling, one truth landed heavier than the rest: it wasn't over. The river had spared him tonight, not freed him. And the voice beneath would be waiting.

Always waiting.

The old logging trail that led Bob back to the place where he and Tallbear had shared fire and stories felt longer than before, as if the woods had grown thicker in his absence—more twisted, more watchful. Trees leaned in subtly, their moss-draped branches cloaking the sky like an ancestral shroud. When he finally broke into the clearing, it was not the place he remembered. The ring of river stones was still there, but the campfire had long gone cold. Damp leaves blanketed the coals. Ferns had begun reclaiming the logs where they once sat. It was like the earth itself had tried to erase the moment, to absorb it and all that was said into memory.

But one thing hadn't been swallowed.

Right in the center of the stone ring, where warmth once glowed, sat Tallbear's badge—tarnished but unmistakable, its weight more than metal. Beneath it was a faded leather satchel, small enough to be overlooked, heavy enough to be significant. Bob knelt, hesitant, and unfastened the strap with fingers that trembled.

Inside was a cassette recorder.

It was the kind with the red play button worn smooth from years of use. A single cassette tape was already loaded. Bob stared at it for a long moment, unwilling to move, unsure if pressing play would change something that couldn't be undone. But he already knew it would. That's why Tallbear left it.

He pressed play.

There was static at first—long, drawn out, like wind caught in a throat. Then the Sheriff's voice, thick with fatigue and fatal knowing, came through.

"If you're hearing this, Bob, it means I failed... or I left before I could finish what needed doing. I'm not sure which happened first. Truth is, I've known for a while this river wouldn't let both of us walk out. Some names... some blood... it don't wash clean."

A beat of silence.

"The Soul-Taker don't haunt, not really. He inherits. He follows the bloodline of those who took more than they gave. Your name, Bob... your family name... it echoes back further than you know. I tried to warn you. But now—now it's yours to carry."

The tape crackled again, then faded into silence, the soft mechanical whir of the tape coming to its end like a breath drawn and held too long.

Bob sat still for several minutes. The forest was utterly quiet—not even a crow's caw to mark the moment. Just the heavy silence of decision. Of inheritance.

He reached out and took the badge.

It felt warm in his hand.

He pocketed it, shouldered his gear, and without another word, turned toward the river trail. There was no more wondering what was myth and what was real. The time for questioning had passed. What lay ahead was reckoning.

The path behind was overgrown now.

And the river wanted him to follow.

End of Chapter 12

CHAPTER 13: THE FISHERMAN'S RECKONING

I have now created a new chat in my Project Folder in order to make best use of ChatGPT's Token memory use. Basically, this is going to keep the performance of GPT at it's optimal. The new Chat within the Project Folder "Book: Steelhead Graveyard" is called "Writing final chapters" The following is the chat conversation I continued to have with GPT:

You said:
Now let's begin writing the last two chapters of the book "Steelhead Graveyard," taking into consideration that this is going to be a tragic and scary end to the story. In these final chapters, Bob Tomalin is going to mysteriously die and fishermen throughout the coastal waters of Washington and Oregon are going to find body parts and belongings of Bob's. The police and FBI get involved but are completely stumped by the evidence. At the end, we learn that Bob's son Shane has grown up to be an avid steelhead fisherman and starts to learn a little about his father's fate from a strange Native American man he meets in a store named Tallbear. This is where the story will end and the Native American name being revealed as Tallbear will be the very last thing to happen in the book. Now, let's begin writing the final two chapters, Chapter 13: The Fisherman's Reckoning, and Chapter 14: Epilogue. Let's do this by starting with Part 1 of Chapter 13.

ChatGPT said:
Absolutely. We're now entering the chilling descent toward the end of *Steelhead Graveyard,* where reality unravels and the story transforms into legend. Chapter 13 will carry emotional weight, spectral dread, and a sense of irreversible fate.

(Part 1 Updated)

ChatGPT said:
Shall we continue with **Part 2** of Chapter 13 next?

You said:
Provide me with a couple of plot options to choose from as we continue writing Chapter 13: The Fisherman's Reckoning.

ChatGPT said:
Here are two powerful plot options for **Part 2 of Chapter 13: *The Fisherman's Reckoning*** — each taking a slightly different narrative direction, but both designed to deepen the mystery and build toward Bob's tragic and symbolic fate:

◆ **Option A: The River's Offering (Unnatural Discovery)**
After Bob vanishes, a group of salmon anglers downstream near Agness, Oregon, make a horrific discovery: one of Bob's boots wedged between roots along the bank, still laced, with part of his foot and ankle inside. His waterproof journal—completely dry—sits oddly on a log

above the water, as if placed there on purpose. The pages contain entries no one remembers him writing—descriptions of dreams he never told anyone about, and warnings written in a strange, almost Native script alongside his handwriting. When the police arrive, they find no trail, no signs of struggle, and no DNA other than Bob's. Locals start to whisper: *The river chose.* This option intensifies the surreal and mythic tone, making the reader question whether the river itself intervened.
Themes: Supernatural dread, the land claiming its own, clues that defy reason
Benefit: Enhances the "sentient wilderness" element and begins the eerie spread of the story beyond Bob's last known location

---

◆ **Option B: The Search Party and the Echoes of Bob (Emotional Fallout)**
The next morning, Bob is reported missing by a local guide who knew where he was camping. Sheriff's deputies and search-and-rescue volunteers enter the forest, including a reluctant rookie FBI agent sent on assignment from Portland. They find Bob's empty tent, carefully packed tackle box, but no gear, no footprints… until they reach the Steelhead Graveyard inlet. There, carved into a rotting cedar, is a new name—*Bob Tomalin*—beneath all the others. A tattered photo of his family, torn and wet, lies beneath it. They also find the melted remnants of Tallbear's cassette recorder—something no one outside of Bob's circle even knew existed. The Sheriff goes quiet, refusing to comment. That night, the young FBI agent hears something outside his trailer. When he looks, he sees Bob standing in the river, rod in hand—casting silently. Then he's gone.
Themes: Government confusion, local legend turning real, emotional impact
Benefit: Introduces outside perspective (FBI), increasing the sense that something primal and unexplainable is happening that can't be stopped by institutions

---

Would you like to move forward with **Option A: The River's Offering, Option B: The Search Party and the Echoes of Bob**, or blend elements of both into a hybrid path?

You said:
Continue with Option a: The River's Offering (unnatural Discovery)

ChatGPT said:
Excellent choice. Option A will intensify the surreal dread and spread the legend beyond Bob's immediate story—perfect for setting up the final emotional devastation and mythic ambiguity. We'll now continue **Chapter 13: *The Fisherman's Reckoning*** with **Part 2: *The River's Offering*.**

(Part 2 Updated)

Would you like to continue now with **Part 3 of Chapter 13**, or pause here to review additional plot options for how the chapter progresses from this point?

You said:
Continue with Part 3 or Chapter 13.

ChatGPT said:
Perfect. Let's continue **Chapter 13:** ***The Fisherman's Reckoning*** with **Part 3:** ***The Mouth of the Sea Speaks His Name***. This section expands the mystery further, as Bob's disappearance triggers a cascade of inexplicable events along the Pacific coast.

(Part 3 Updated)

Would you like to proceed to **Part 4 of Chapter 13**, or pause here to discuss how you'd like to escalate Bob's reckoning and transition toward the final chapter?

You said:
Proceed to Part 4 of Chapter 13.

ChatGPT said:
Excellent. In **Part 4 of Chapter 13:** ***The Fisherman's Reckoning***, the story begins to close in like a storm—fragments of mystery converging toward the unspeakable. This part will focus on the official investigation's breakdown and the quiet recognition among a few that something far older, darker, and more sacred is at play.

(Part 4 Updated)

In the next and final part of Chapter 13, we'll bring Bob's reckoning to its emotional and supernatural peak—just before passing the torch into legend and setting the stage for his son in the Epilogue.
Shall I proceed with **Part 5 of Chapter 13**?

You said:
Yes, proceed with Part 5 of Chapter 13.

ChatGPT said:
Let's move forward.
In **Part 5 of Chapter 13:** ***The Fisherman's Reckoning***, the tragic supernatural undercurrent of the story surges to the surface one final time, giving us the last confirmed echo of Bob Tomalin before his story becomes myth. This moment will be haunting, symbolic, and heavy with spiritual weight.

(Part 5 Updated)

In the final part of this chapter, Part 6, we'll close with a quiet transition—a moment that sets the stage for the *Epilogue*, where Bob's son, Shane, takes his first steps into his father's legacy without even knowing it yet.
Shall I proceed to write **Part 6 of Chapter 13**?

You said:
Yes, proceed to write Part 6 of Chapter 13

ChatGPT said:
Here is the final installment of **Chapter 13:** ***The Fisherman's Reckoning*** — a haunting bridge from the tragedy of Bob Tomalin to the mystery that awaits his son.

(Part 6 Updated)

The morning came as a smear of gray across the canopy. Bob Tomalin stirred in his tent, the sounds of the river louder than usual, like it had something urgent to say. He sat up slowly, joints stiff, a dull ache sitting behind his eyes. His journal lay beside him, pages damp from dew and ink beginning to blur where he'd scrawled Tallbear's final words. He hadn't written anything since the night before—since hearing that voice from the river. He hadn't slept much, either.

The coals in the fire pit were dead. The usual comfort of camp routine—percolated coffee, sizzling bacon, a joke whispered to the trees—felt foreign now. The forest didn't welcome him this morning. It watched.

He made himself move anyway. He strapped on his waders and shouldered his pack, heading down the narrow trail toward the same stretch of river where he'd lost every steelhead the day before. The unease hadn't faded. In fact, it had calcified—becoming part of him.

The sky overhead darkened unexpectedly. Wind came from upriver, against the natural flow, carrying with it the unmistakable scent of rotting fish and smoke. Bob paused. Not woodsmoke. Something older. Bone smoke. A funeral pyre from a thousand years ago.

He shook it off and kept going. Maybe he was getting sick. Maybe the voice had been a dream. But something was drawing him back to the water.

When he reached the bend, he saw it again—the same shimmering eddy, the same rock his father used to call "The Fisher King's Throne." A memory of Clancy's voice floated up, warm and certain: "If you ever find yourself fishing that rock and feel like someone's watching, just give your respects and fish clean."

Bob removed his cap and nodded to the river. "I come with respect," he said aloud, voice low. "No ego. Just wonder."

He tied on a black-and-silver intruder fly, his favorite winter steelhead pattern. It danced like a ghost on the leader as he flicked it through the cold air. On the second cast, the river erupted.

The fish hit like thunder. Bob's rod arched, reel screaming. It was massive, stronger than anything he'd ever hooked. He planted his feet and leaned into it, the muscles in his shoulders screaming.

Then something shifted.

The wind dropped away. The sound of the river muted. Time distorted. And from behind him, from the woods, came footsteps—slow, crunching, deliberate.

Bob didn't dare turn around.

The fish thrashed again, pulling line, running downstream.

And then—snap.

The line went limp.

Bob stumbled backward, nearly falling into the current. The rod dangled useless in his hands. He stared down at the broken tippet, heart hammering. The forest was silent again.

But the footsteps continued.

Turning now, against every instinct, Bob saw him—half in shadow, half in sun. A towering figure of matted hair, pale eyes, and a long, carved spear clutched in one gnarled hand.

Kilchis.

Not a ghost, not entirely flesh. Something between.

They stared at each other. Bob couldn't move. Kilchis raised a finger—long, yellowed, cracked—and pointed to the river.

Behind Bob, something began to bubble beneath the surface.

He turned back, and there, where the fish had been, rose something else.

Not a fish. Not a man, a face. His own. Bloated, waterlogged, and grinning.

Bob screamed. The river leapt. The world folded in on itself. And when the wind returned, the bend was empty.

No footprints. No rod. No Bob Tomalin.

Only a ripple, spinning quietly, vanishing downstream.

Three days after Bob Tomalin disappeared, a man named Cal Hastings stood knee-deep in the Rogue near Agness, working a bead rig through a green, glassy tailout. The morning was crisp, and the fog hung low on the water like it was trying to keep a secret. Cal was mid-swing when something bumped his line hard—not a take, but a drag, like it had snagged a bag or a waterlogged branch.

He grumbled, stripping line to check it, but before he could reel it in, he noticed it floating into view just a few yards downstream: a boot.

A single left-footed wading boot, bobbing unnaturally upright as if its contents still bore weight.

Cal waded toward it, cursing under his breath.

When he reached it, the world changed.

The boot snagged on a twisted alder root. It was partially filled with river gravel and something else—something pink-gray and organic. Cal staggered backward the moment he recognized it.

A foot.

Cleanly severed above the ankle. The skin pale and wrinkled like it had been soaking for days. Toenails blue. One of them cracked and jagged.

He dry-heaved on the bank and dialed 911 with shaking fingers. "There's… there's a foot in a boot. I found a goddamn human foot in a boot."

The state police arrived within hours, securing the area and launching a multi-agency investigation. By sunset, a federal forensic team from Eugene was combing the shoreline. They found something else too—more confusing than the foot.

Laid neatly on a cedar log well above the high-water mark was a waterproof notebook. Black moleskin. Not a drop of moisture on it. Its pages intact. Its cover bearing the initials "B.T."

Inside, the writing was unmistakable: Bob Tomalin's blocky, all-caps scrawl.

But the final entries were not normal.

They began with notes about steelhead behavior, patterns, lunar charts. But by page three, the writing became erratic—chaotic. Dreams scrawled in frantic language:
"The river has eyes."
"Tallbear was never real."
"I saw my own face smiling at me from the water—smeared and wrong."

And then the script changed.

Half the final page was written in a looping, jagged pattern that resembled no known language—possibly an indigenous dialect, possibly invented, possibly not from this world at all.

Linguists were called. Photos were taken. The FBI took possession of the notebook by dawn the next day.

But they didn't release that information to the public.

What they did release was far more sterile: "Partial remains discovered in the Rogue River. Investigation ongoing. Anyone with information about Robert Tomalin's whereabouts is urged to contact authorities."

Back at the station in Gold Beach, a few local officers shared rumors over their third cups of coffee. Sheriff Roy Tallbear's name came up more than once. Some said he'd gone missing, too. Others swore they saw him wandering the banks alone, muttering into a cassette recorder.

No one said it aloud, but they were all thinking it:

The river hadn't just taken Bob.

It had kept part of him—and returned part as a warning.

And the notebook? It didn't feel like something left behind.

It felt like something offered.

Two weeks later, just before dawn, a crabbing boat out of Westport, Washington drifted lazily through a patch of slack tide under a heavy blanket of fog. Captain Lorne DeMarco was hunched over a steaming thermos of coffee when the winch line went tight—too tight. Not the jerking weight of crab pots—this was something heavier, something dragging.

The winch groaned and bucked.

"Jesus, it's snagged," DeMarco muttered to his deckhand, a kid named Richie with eyes too wide for comfort. They braced together as the cable reeled in with halting strain.

And then it surfaced.

A tangle of line, kelp, and something white—plastic? No. Bone.

The skeletal remains of a human hand, stripped of all flesh, clutched in the barbs of an old rusted treble hook. Wound through the knuckles was a braid of paracord, and dangling from the end of it—muddy and half-rotted—was a fly box, still latched. On its lid, someone had scratched a single word with the tip of a knife:

"BOB."

Coast Guard was called in. Then the FBI again.

The next day, a kayaker outside Tillamook Bay reported seeing a pair of polarized sunglasses wedged into a cleft in the rocks. When retrieved, they were found to be prescription—registered to Robert Clancy Tomalin. Days after that, hikers near the Umpqua River discovered a battered Patagonia wading jacket in the middle of a dry creek bed, a child's drawing sewn into its lining with clumsy stitching: a fish and a man, both smiling.

These weren't just remains. They were breadcrumbs. Disjointed, scattered, purposeful in their eeriness.

And no one could explain how the current could have carried them to such places. They defied hydrology. Some made their way upriver. Others seemed to have surfaced in places disconnected from any logical current path.

One forensic hydrologist said during a press conference:

"If the remains belong to Mr. Tomalin—and all evidence strongly supports that—they would've had to travel over two hundred miles in multiple directions, some upstream, and through regions that would require—frankly—levitation."

The news media descended, of course. Podcasts bloomed. Reddit threads exploded. "Steelhead Graveyard" became a trending search term. They called it a serial killer case, or an elaborate hoax, or a psychotic break from a man pushed too far into the wilderness.

But the locals knew better.

At the Hook & Horn Tavern in Astoria, old men who'd sworn off boats long ago now drank in silence, staring at the TV above the bar, watching the FBI hold back facts they'd never understand.

In a small tackle shop outside of Forks, a widow who'd once shared a riverside whiskey with Bob before her husband went missing twenty years earlier said to no one in particular:

"He was chosen. Just like mine was. The river marks its own."

And far away, in a trailer park near the Columbia, a Native boy barely eleven years old told his grandmother he dreamed of a man casting into a river made of stars—and that each cast pulled out pieces of himself, piece by piece, until only his voice remained.

"The fish don't bite for him anymore," the boy said. "They just watch. They remember."

And somewhere, out there beyond the fog, the river moved silently toward the sea.

Waiting.

Special Agent Devon Malik stood in the stale silence of the command trailer, somewhere near the mouth of the Umpqua River. Rain ticked softly on the aluminum roof above him. The board in front of him looked like a failed jigsaw puzzle—maps pinned with red strings, photos of Bob Tomalin's scattered belongings, blurry screenshots of fishermen's TikToks and weather anomalies that made no sense.

None of it added up.

He rubbed the bridge of his nose and stared at the case file's cover:
BOB TOMALIN – STATUS: PRESUMED DECEASED. BODY NOT RECOVERED.

But the handwriting on the last page of the case notes was not his own.

He leaned closer. At the bottom of a printed interview transcript, someone had scribbled in pen:

"Stop asking the river questions. It remembers when it was god."
It wasn't a quote from any witness. Malik hadn't written it. No one would admit they had.

He closed the folder, unsettled.

Outside, a coastal wind blew sideways, rattling the trailer and bringing with it the sound of gulls—and something beneath that. A whispering rustle, as if someone was wading just outside, dragging something behind them.

He stepped out into the fog.

The search area was eerily quiet now. The main teams had left after the press conference debacle. The FBI's reputation was bruised and bleeding. Locals weren't talking anymore—not really. They spoke in riddles and metaphors, quoting folklore like it was fact. Some refused to go near the water. Others carved strange patterns into driftwood and set them afloat like offerings.

The Tomalin case had started as a missing persons file.

It was now something else entirely.

The official story would eventually die on a footnote.

Unresolved.

But the unofficial story was spreading like wildfire through bait shops and guide circles up and down the coast.

Stories of a man seen walking midstream on foggy mornings—his face never visible, but his fly rod always bent. Fishermen who spotted him sometimes found their gear missing the next day… or worse, replaced with soggy relics they didn't recognize—lures they never bought, children's shoes, a rusted badge scorched along the edges.

In Gold Beach, Sheriff Roy Tallbear's department quietly retired his file after he stopped showing up for shift rotations. His cruiser was found weeks later, overgrown by moss on a closed forest road. The inside smelled like cedar and fire.

But no one filed a missing persons report.

Not for Tallbear.

Because in certain circles, they knew he hadn't disappeared.

He'd returned.

To the river.

The fog moved in like a closing hand.

It coiled low along the river near Lobster Creek, the place where Bob Tomalin had last been seen in the flesh. The water was calm—unnaturally so—its surface glassy as obsidian. Not a ripple stirred. No birds sang. The whole world seemed to be waiting.

And then, there he was.

Or something like him.

Just past dusk, a man with a fly rod stood waist-deep at the bend in the river. He moved slowly, deliberately, stripping line from a battered reel. A few watchers saw him from the bridge—locals on their way home from an elk feed in Agness. They would swear later that the man cast like Bob. Same form. Same crisp loop. Same tuck of the left shoulder at the apex of the swing.

But his clothes didn't match. He wore an old woven cloak—something primal, tribal even, with waterlogged leather laces dangling from the sleeves. His boots were mismatched. One was missing entirely, his pale foot sunken in the gravel. A pendant of bone hung from his neck, carved into the shape of a fish with no eyes.

And no one could see his face.

The moment a car engine growled on the road above, he looked up—but only slightly. Enough for them to see that his skin was not white or brown or red. It was gray-blue. Like the color of a steelhead's flank after it dies.

Then he cast again.

A perfect loop.

But this time, the line didn't fall.

It hung there—suspended midair, thirty feet over the water—like time had locked it in place. The watchers on the bridge blinked, staggered, tried to make sense of what they were seeing. And then, with a sudden gust of wind, it all vanished.

The river was empty, the man was gone. The air smelled of cedar and wet iron.

That night, a forest ranger checking campsite clearances near the boundary stumbled across a flickering fire someone had tried to hide beneath a ring of ancient stones. Lying beside it, half-buried in the moss, was a voice recorder—old, cracked, the same brand Tallbear used.

The ranger pressed play. Static. Then breathing. Then a whisper that froze his blood:

"If you take too much… it takes you back. Back to when the river was god."

The device sparked and died in his hand.

No one ever found it again.

A month had passed.

The Tomalin family held a memorial service without a body. A closed-casket placeholder stood beneath the church's modest cross in Bandon, Oregon—where Bob had been baptized as a boy. Friends and family gathered in raincoats and shared stories between long silences. Tanya, his wife, spoke softly, her voice cracking only once when she said the words "he never stopped searching for something deeper."

Clancy Tomalin, now white-haired and sunken in the eyes, stood with both hands on his cane and never looked up from the floor. He had taught his boy to fish the river. Had warned him that it gave but never forgot what it gave.

He said no words that day. But before leaving the chapel, he placed something inside the coffin's velvet lining.

A driftwood carving.

A fish with no eyes.

That night, Tanya let their son Shane sit beside her on the couch, a blanket over both their legs. Shane, now twelve, held a photo of his dad holding a steelhead from two summers ago, grinning in the golden light. His fingers traced the water droplets still clinging to the fish's gills.

"Did the river kill him?" Shane asked.

Tanya hesitated.

"No, honey," she said, but even that was unsure. "The river… took him."

Shane nodded. He didn't cry.

But something in his eyes changed.

Something old and knowing and too large for a boy.

The next morning, while Tanya slept, Shane rose quietly and padded out to the garage. He opened the rod case Bob had once called the vault. Inside, every fly rod was still in its place—cleaned, polished, revered like a soldier's sword.

Shane reached for the smallest one. A 7-weight, perfect for winter runs.

He didn't know why, but he packed it.

And he waited.

Hundreds of miles away, just before midnight, a pair of brothers fishing off the rocks near Cape Disappointment found a half-rotted fish in their cooler that neither remembered catching. It wasn't from the sea. Its scales shimmered with river-silt and something like oil. One eye was missing. The other was human.

They threw it back.

But the current didn't take it.

It held.

End of Chapter 13

CHAPTER 14: EPILOGUE

Now, we transition into the final chapter—**Chapter 14: Epilogue – The River Remembers**, where Shane begins to step into his father's myth, and the last lines leave the reader breathless. Would you like me to begin writing **Chapter 14: Epilogue** now?

You said:
Yes, begin writing Chapter 14: Epilogue

ChatGPT said:
Absolutely. This final chapter—**Chapter 14: *Epilogue – The River Remembers***—will close the book with quiet reverence, generational resonance, and a final whisper of the supernatural. Shane is now our lens, and through him, the story will end—not with clarity, but with something deeper: legacy, curiosity, and a name.

It was raining in Astoria.

Not the sharp, sideways kind that stung your face and chased you indoors, but the soft, steady kind that soaked your jacket without you noticing until it was too late. Shane Tomalin stood under the awning of the North Coast Angler Supply, one hand tucked into his hoodie pocket, the other gripping a worn fly rod case like it held the bones of a saint.

He was seventeen now. Broader than his father had been at that age. Quieter, too. Eyes that didn't flinch. People said he was polite but distant. He said little in school. Fished whenever he could. Always alone. Always rivers.

He hadn't spoken of his father in years. But he hadn't stopped looking, either.

Today he was picking up winter steelhead patterns from the local fly shop—a few rabbit strip leeches, a handful of intruders, and some obscure old pattern tied with deer hair that the man at the counter claimed worked only when "the river's in a weird mood."

"Just the one run you'll need them for," the man said with a wink. "North Fork of the Nehalem. Near the old hatchery. You'll feel it when you get there."

Shane paid in cash and turned to go when the bell above the door jingled behind him.

A man stepped in.

Native. Broad-shouldered. Black braided hair streaked with gray. Wore a canvas field jacket heavy with rain. He didn't look at Shane at first. Just shook off his hood and walked slowly to the far wall, where antique rods hung like old rifles.

The air shifted.

Shane, halfway through the door, paused.

Something in his chest—something ancestral—told him not to leave.

The man turned. His eyes were black glass, ancient and unreadable. He looked at Shane and nodded, once, like he'd been expecting him.

"Your father cast long," the man said, voice deep as driftwood. "Longer than most. But he fished too deep."

Shane's mouth was dry. He didn't respond.

The man took two slow steps toward him, then tapped a finger on the rod case clutched in Shane's hand.

"That one still remembers his touch."

A pause. Then, softly—so softly Shane almost didn't hear it—he said:

"When the river calls again, don't follow it alone."

Shane opened his mouth to speak, but the man was already turning. "Hey," Shane managed. "What's your name?"

The man stopped by the door. Looked back over his shoulder. A flicker of something passed between them—recognition that had no business existing.

The man smiled. Not kindly. Not cruelly. Just knowingly.

"Tallbear," he said.

And then he was gone. Out into the rain.

The river gives. The river takes. But it never forgets.
Somewhere upstream, it's still watching.

THE END.

PUBLISHING NOTES

When I publish a book in Amazon there are several pieces of information that is required that I will be using AI to assist me with.

Book Details: Amazon asks for information like Language, Book Title, Subtitle, Series, Edition Number, Author, Contributors, Description, and more…It is the Description, Categories, and Keywords in particular that I want AI's help with.

Let's start with the book's description that will be displayed on Amazon.

You said:
Write a very compelling description for the book "Steelhead Graveyard" for Amazon that is extremely enticing for potential readers who are most likely fishermen and outdoor people, as well as anyone who enjoys reading psychological thrillers.

ChatGPT said:
Steelhead Graveyard
Some Rivers Should Be Left Alone
Deep in Oregon's coastal wilderness lies a river with secrets older than the trees that line its banks. A river that watches. A river that remembers.
When veteran angler Bob Tomalin ventures into the remote canyons of the Rogue River for what he hopes will be a soul-cleansing steelhead trip, he's chasing more than fish—he's running from a life that's quietly unraveling. Haunted by personal loss and drawn by a need to reconnect with the only place that's ever made sense, Bob sets up camp where the map fades and the myths begin.
But the river has changed.
Whispers ride the current. Boots appear where no man should be. Strange carvings mark the trunks of old-growth cedars. And the fish—they're biting, but something's not right. As Bob descends deeper into the canyon, reality blurs with nightmare, and the legend of a vengeful spirit named Kilchis—the Soul-Taker—surfaces from the shadows.
Steelhead Graveyard is a chilling wilderness thriller that blends the gritty realism of backcountry survival with the creeping dread of a psychological ghost story. Gritty, wise, and profoundly atmospheric, this tale will resonate with fishermen, hunters, and anyone who has ever stared too long into the wild and felt it staring back.
Perfect for fans of *Deliverance*, *Pet Sematary*, and *The River Why*, this novel explores the edges of sanity, the depths of regret, and the question every outdoorsman fears to ask: *What if the river doesn't want you to leave?*
🪓 *Once you enter Rogue Country, the river knows your name.*

I made a couple of edits to the content that GPT generated for me and then pasted it into the Description area on KDP.

Next, I am going to use GPT to help me select the categories. Keep in mind that Amazon sometimes modifies the categories so GPT may not always have the most accurate, up-to-date categories the way Amazon has them. This is ok and we can do our best to get as close as possible.

You said:
You are an expert at identifying the best categories on Amazon for books to be placed in for getting the greatest amount of visibility, and for achieving a #1 status for a category. You have more than 10 years of experience in identifying these categories. Identify the best three categories for the book "Steelhead Graveyard" that I will use on Amazon

ChatGPT said:
Based on your book *Steelhead Graveyard*—a wilderness psychological thriller with strong appeal to fishermen, outdoorsmen, and fans of dark, suspenseful storytelling—here are the **three best Amazon categories** to maximize **visibility** and position you to achieve **#1 bestseller status** within a high-traffic niche with achievable competition:

✅ **1. Books > Mystery, Thriller & Suspense > Psychological Thrillers**

- **Why:** This is a high-traffic category where *Steelhead Graveyard* fits naturally due to its creeping dread, unreliable reality, and the unraveling of Bob's mind.
- **Bonus:** Great crossover appeal to both thriller fans and mainstream suspense readers.

✅ **2. Books > Literature & Fiction > Genre Fiction > Sports > Hunting & Fishing**

- **Why:** This is a **lower-competition niche** that specifically targets your **core audience**—outdoor readers, fishermen, and wilderness survivalists.
- **Bonus:** Much easier to reach #1 compared to broader thriller categories.

✅ **3. Kindle Store > Kindle eBooks > Literature & Fiction > Horror > Psychological**

- **Why:** The horror-psychological subcategory supports the book's darker supernatural tones and will attract readers of *The Ritual*, *Pet Sematary*, and *The Only Good Indians.*
- **Bonus:** Kindle's eBook horror niches have lower sales thresholds for topping charts, increasing your odds of bestseller status with a focused campaign.

🧠 **Pro Tip:**
Once your book is live on KDP, you can **manually request up to 10 additional categories** by contacting Amazon KDP support. When you do, **include both paperback and Kindle variations** of the categories above. You can say:
"Hi, I'd like to request the following additional browse categories for my book *Steelhead Graveyard* (ASIN: [insert ASIN]):

- Kindle eBooks > Literature & Fiction > Horror > Psychological

- Kindle eBooks > Literature & Fiction > Genre Fiction > Sports > Hunting & Fishing
- Kindle eBooks > Mystery, Thriller & Suspense > Psychological Thrillers
  Thank you!"

Would you like me to also suggest **metadata and keyword phrases** to pair with these categories for maximum search visibility?

You said:

Yes, now provide me with 7 keyword phrases that I will give Amazon for my book information.

ChatGPT said:

Here are **7 expertly selected keyword phrases** optimized for *Steelhead Graveyard* that will maximize your book's visibility on Amazon and attract the right readers—especially fishermen, outdoorsmen, and psychological thriller fans:

🔑 7 Keyword Phrases for Amazon KDP

1. **wilderness psychological thriller**
   Targets readers looking for thrillers set in remote, eerie natural settings—perfect for your Rogue River *location.*
2. **fishing suspense novel**
   Highly niche, this targets outdoor lovers and fishermen looking for a compelling, story-driven read.
3. **ghost stories in the woods**
   This taps into readers who enjoy supernatural or folklore-based suspense in natural environments.
4. **Oregon mystery novel**
   Geo-targeted to the Pacific Northwest audience and readers who love stories set in specific, moody locations.
5. **outdoor survival thriller**
   Appeals to the prepper, hunter, and adventurer demographic who also enjoy high-stakes fiction.
6. **river horror story**
   A unique but highly relevant phrase that captures the eerie, sentient-river aspect of the book.
7. **books like Deliverance and The Ritual**
   This is a comparative keyword that Amazon's algorithm can match to customers searching for similar titles.

📘 Bonus Tip:

Make sure your **book description** and **A+ Content** reinforce these phrases naturally to boost organic SEO and increase your book's discoverability on both Amazon and Google.

Would you like me to generate an optimized **back-end metadata block** (title, subtitle, description, categories, and keywords) ready for copy-paste into KDP?

FORMATTING STEELHEAD GRAVEYARD

Some of the questions I continue to get revolves around the technical aspects of publishing books such as formatting for Kindle eBook.

While that can be a class all unto it's own, I will give you a little insight on this matter

First, you are going to want to download the following tool: **Kindle Create (KC) by Amazon**. You can find this tool by going to Google.com and searching "***Kindle Create Download***" and then select either PC or MAC download.

WARNING: There are some latency nuances that Kindle Create has when it comes to Opening and Saving files that will require your patience. When you select a file on your computer to work with in KC, the dialog box that is used to select your files can take up to a couple of minutes to appear and you must have some patients and wait for it to appear. Many people get frustrated at this point and give up.

If you use some patients and don't give up you will eventually be rewarded with a document that will look good and get you into the Kindle marketplace looking professional.

Check out some of the screenshots from making Steelhead Graveyard into a Kindle eBook:

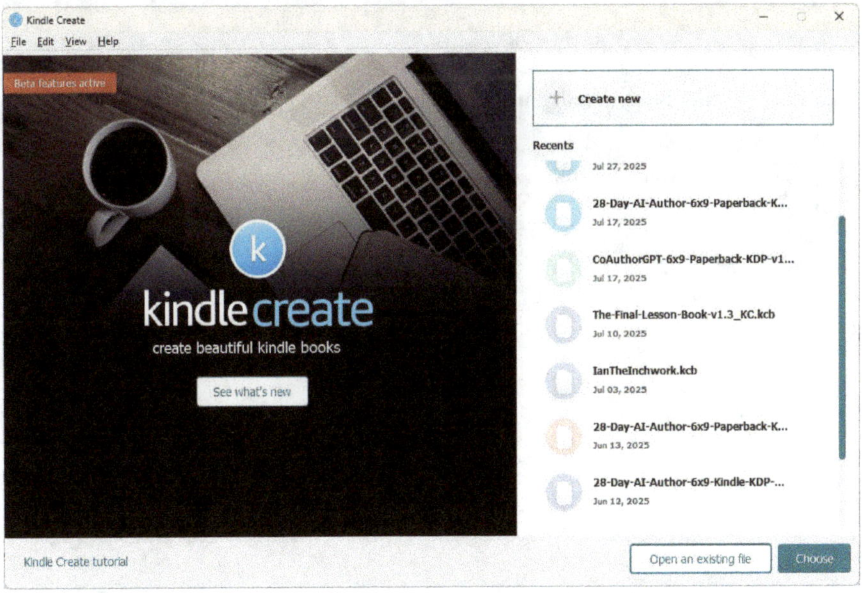

Start by selecting Create New and then clicking on the green Choose button.

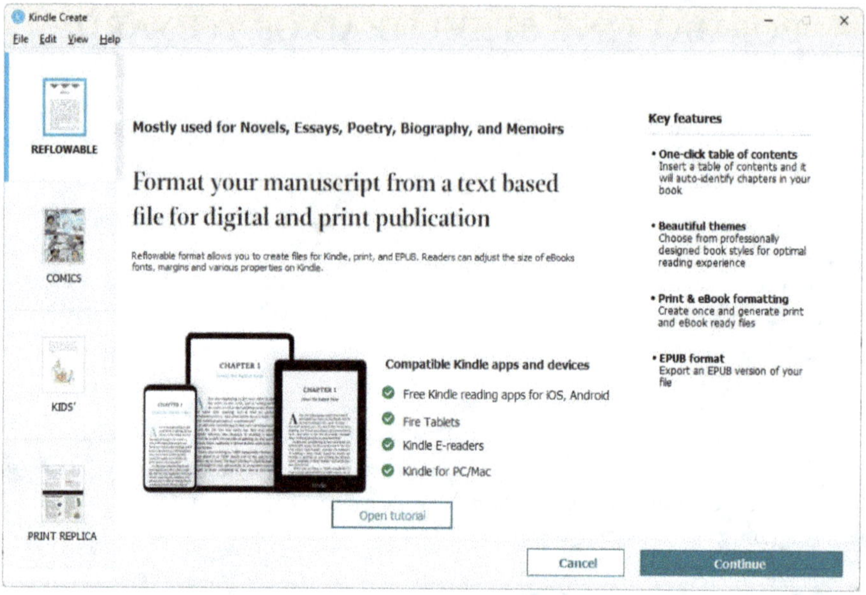

Reflowable is the preferred option if you want your eBook to be viewable on the most amount of devices.

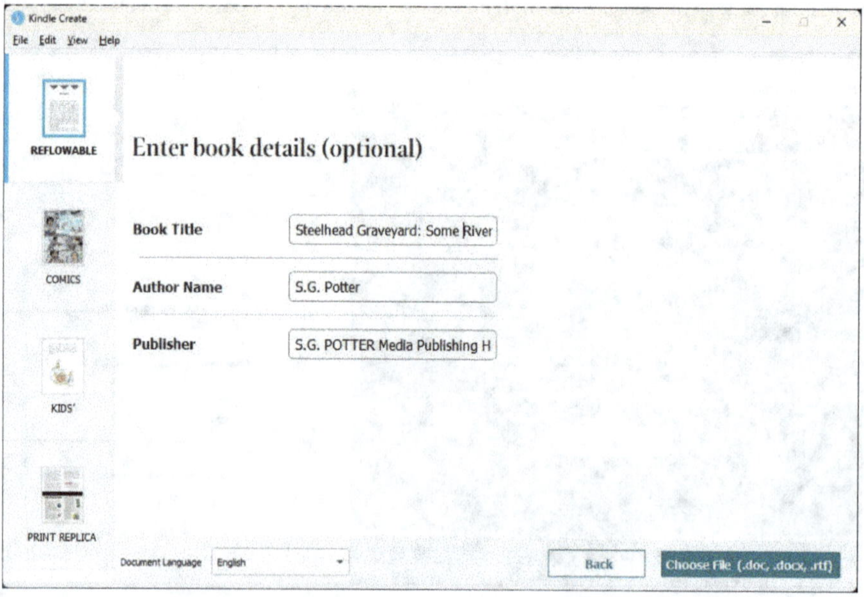

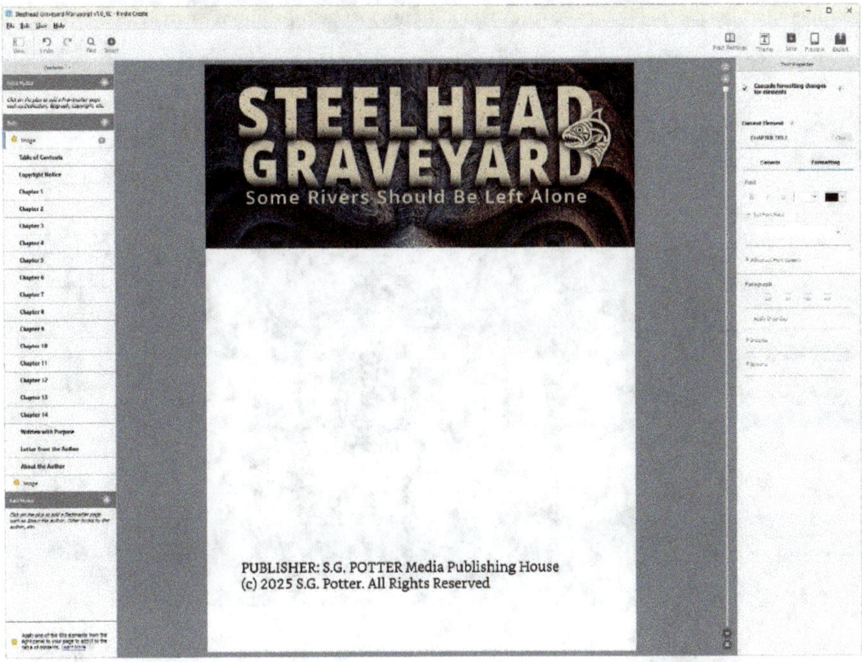

Go through all your pages to make corrections. There will be some needed.

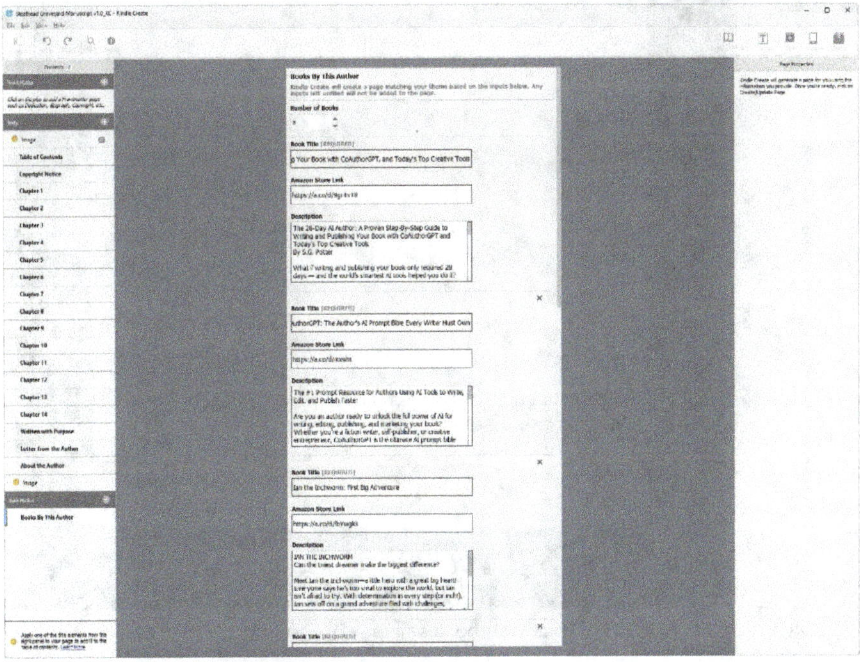

Include other books that you have on Amazon (if any) to help promote them as well.

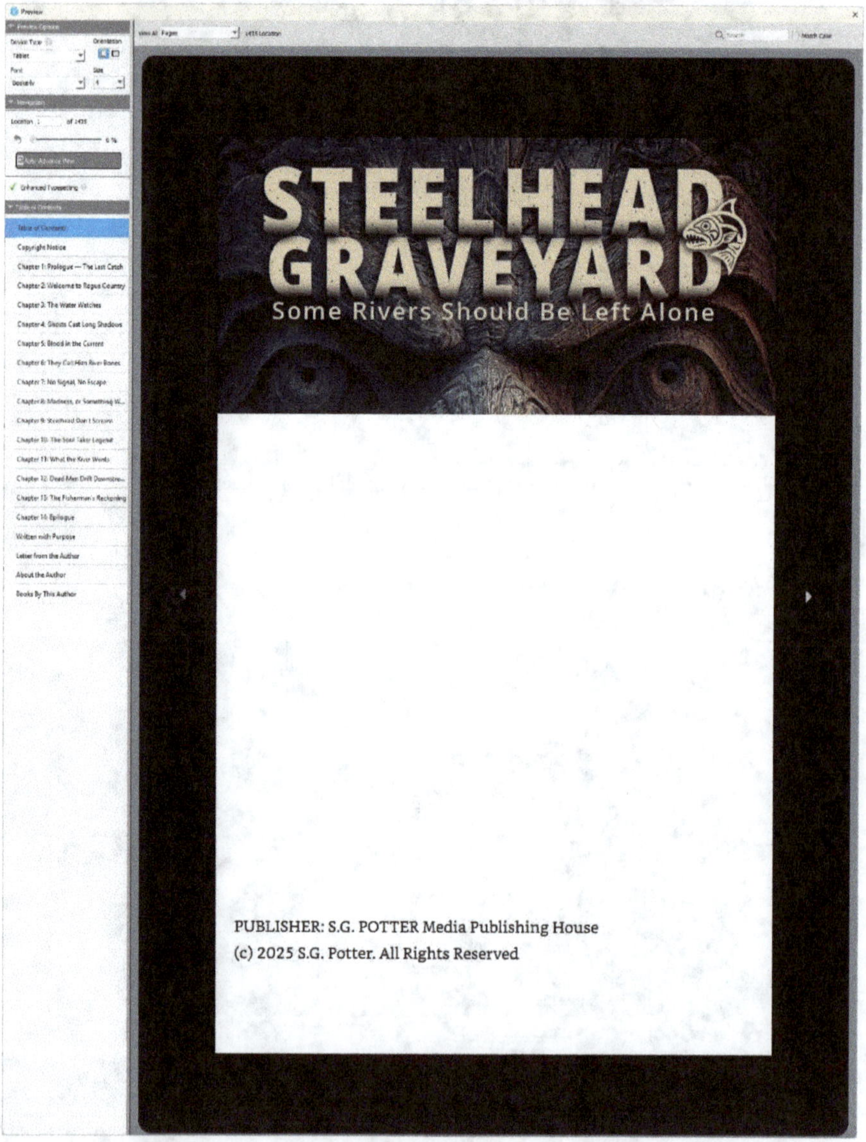

Click the Preview button to see what your book will look like to readers

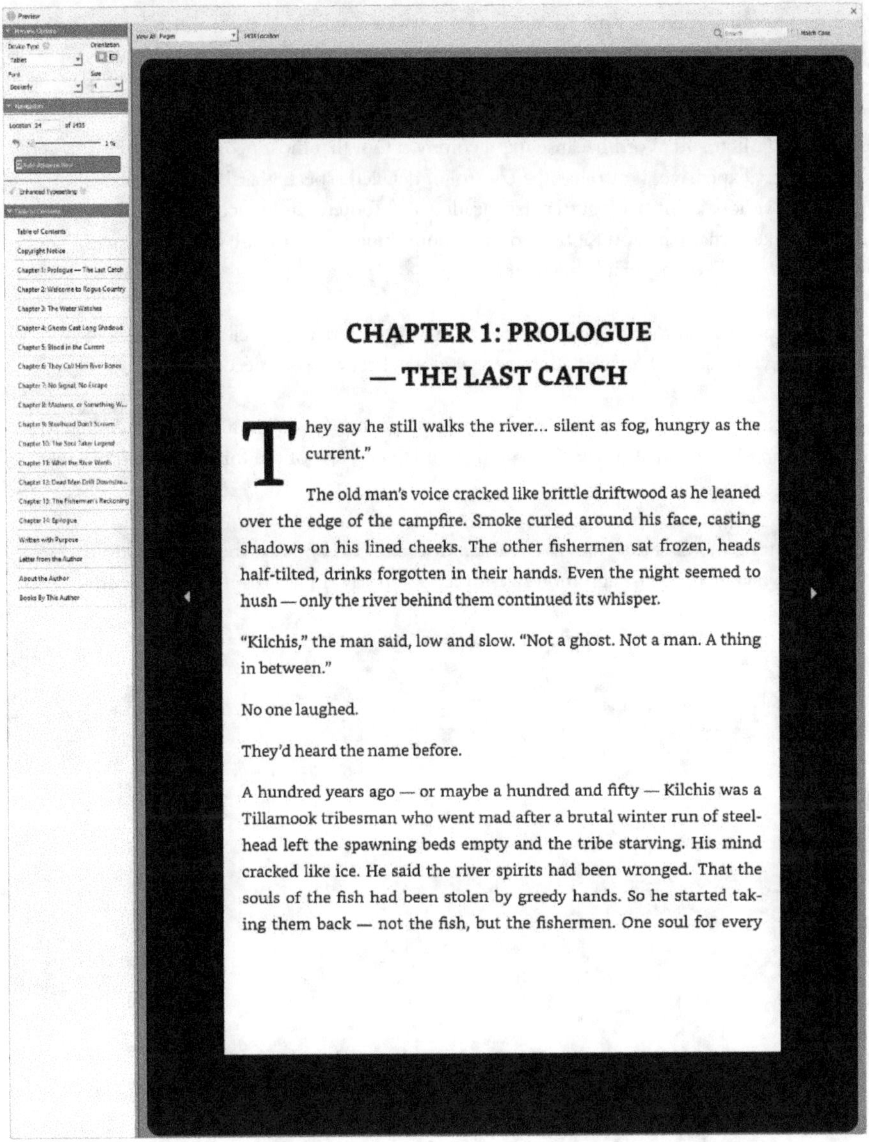
Preview
Table of Contents
Copyright Notice
Chapter 1: Prologue — The Last Catch
Chapter 2: Welcome to Rogue Country
Chapter 3: The Water Watches
Chapter 4: Ghosts Cast Long Shadows
Chapter 5: Blood in the Current
Chapter 6: They Call Him River Bones
Chapter 7: No Signal, No Escape
Chapter 14: Epilogue
Written with Purpose
Letter from the Author
About the Author
Books By This Author
CHAPTER 1: PROLOGUE
— THE LAST CATCH
They say he still walks the river… silent as fog, hungry as the current."
The old man's voice cracked like brittle driftwood as he leaned over the edge of the campfire. Smoke curled around his face, casting shadows on his lined cheeks. The other fishermen sat frozen, heads half-tilted, drinks forgotten in their hands. Even the night seemed to hush — only the river behind them continued its whisper.
"Kilchis," the man said, low and slow. "Not a ghost. Not a man. A thing in between."
No one laughed.
They'd heard the name before.
A hundred years ago — or maybe a hundred and fifty — Kilchis was a Tillamook tribesman who went mad after a brutal winter run of steelhead left the spawning beds empty and the tribe starving. His mind cracked like ice. He said the river spirits had been wronged. That the souls of the fish had been stolen by greedy hands. So he started taking them back — not the fish, but the fishermen. One soul for every

The previous images depict the Kindle Create software application that we use for creating the Kindle eBook version of our book. Before we can get to this point however, we need our manuscript created in some type of word processing document such as Microsoft Word.

I like using Microsoft Word because it is a common tool that most people have access to and it is not very expensive. It also has the control of detailed aspects that I want to format my books for various print sizes, gutter size, headers and footers, and much more. Another point I should make is that Amazon KDP, and other publishing platforms are compatible with .docx files (Microsoft Word's default file format).

There are other great tools such as InDesign by Adobe, Scrivener, Vellum, or even Google Docs, and you just need to select the one that works best for your needs.

The manuscript for this book: Steelhead Graveyard : Some Rivers Should Be Left Alone, was created using Microsoft Word so I am going to go over a few of the formatting settings that we used.

First, let's take a look at the general document format. This book has been created to be a 6" x 9" book, which is the most common size for a book today. In Microsoft Word I set this up as follows:

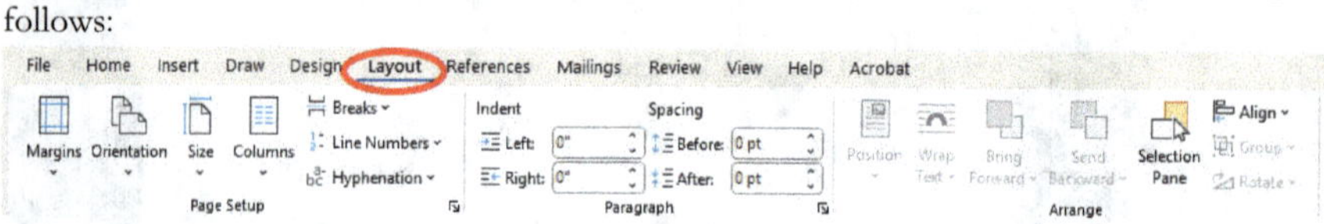

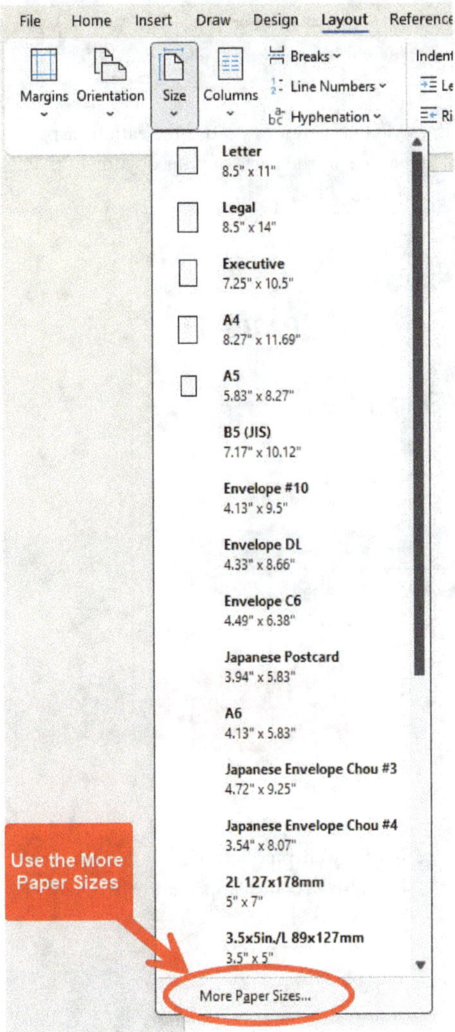

After select the Layout menu option, you will want to go to the Size dropdown as shown here. Then scroll to the bottom and select More Paper Size.

MS Word is used for so many different word processing applications that our standard 6" x 9" size is not always readily available in the initial drop-down selection so we have to dig a bit deeper to find exactly what we want.

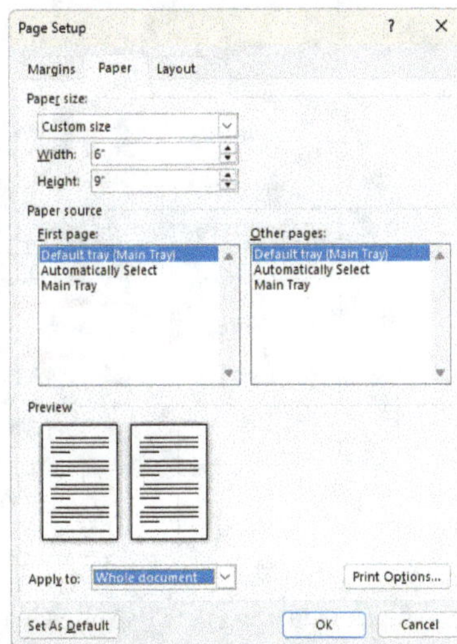

Simply type **6"** into the width field, **9"** into the height field, and select **Whole Document** in the Apply To field.

Next, I want to ensure I am using the fonts I want to use for my Headings, normal text, and other option. I want to do this so I have consistency and so my Table of Contents can be automatically generated based on the Styles I select.

One of the places this is done is from the Styles section of my toolbar from the Home Tab. You will come to find that there are usually several ways to do the same things in most professional software applications and Microsoft Word is no exception.

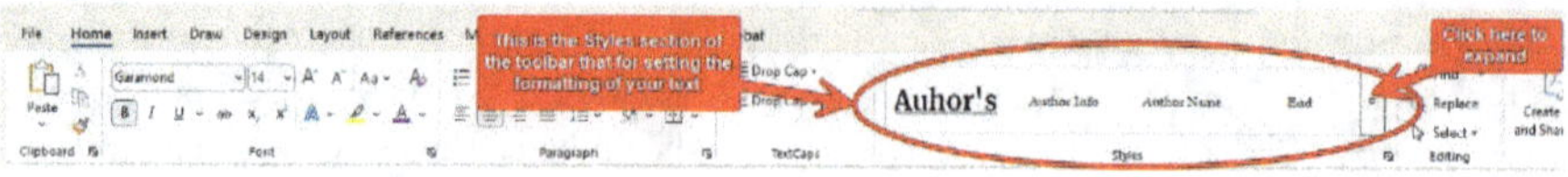

Expand the Styles options to modify the specific style that you want to use for various aspects of your document such as Heading. Then apply that style to the parts of your document that you wish to be consistently using the same font and size.

For example. I am using the HEADING style for all of my chapter headings so that they are consistently sized and always use the correct font. This also becomes important when I am building my Automatic Table of Contents.

Let's take a look at creating an automatic Table of Contents for our book.

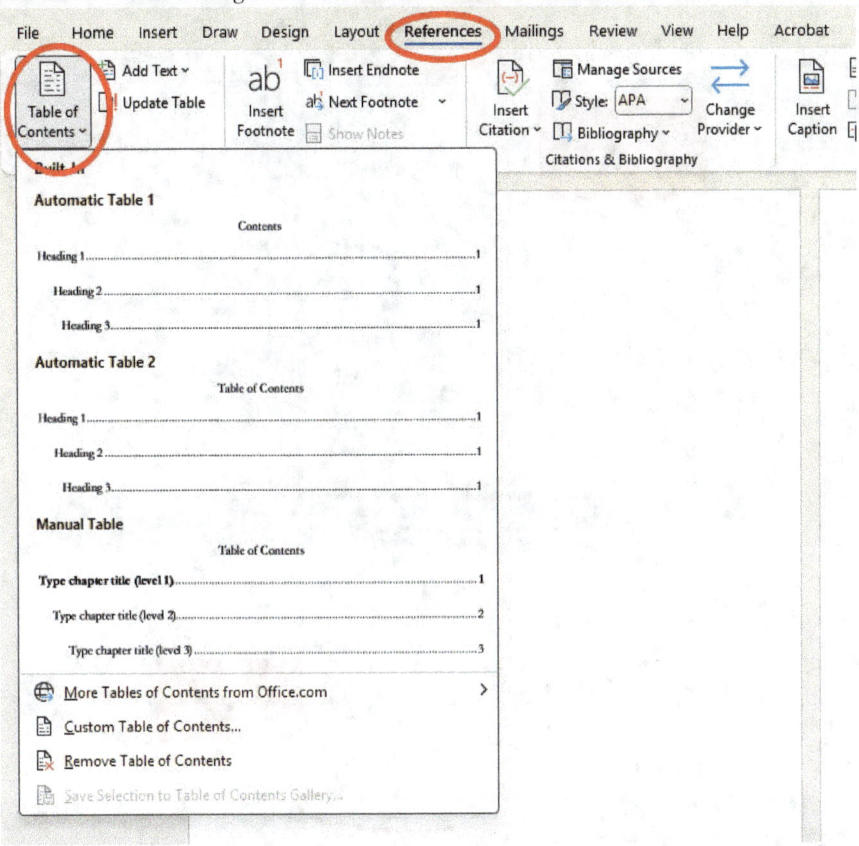

Selecting the References tab on the toolbar and then the Table of Contents dropdown will show you a few different pre-styled automatic Table of Contents options. You will notice that they say Heading 1, Heading 2, Heading 3. These headings refer to the Style headings that we just discussed.

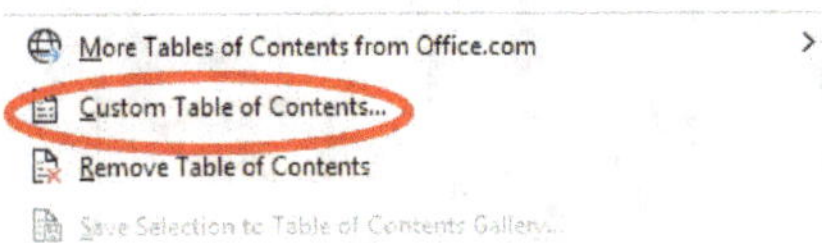

Personally, I usually select the **Custom Table of Contents** option near the bottom of the drop-down menu so I can set it up to my personal liking.

Make sure to modify your header and footers to include book titles, copyright notices, and page numbers. Also, don't forget your line spacing.

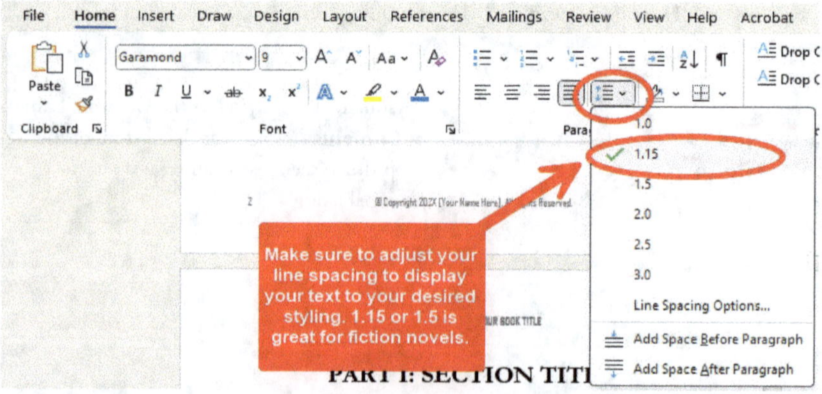

STEELHEAD GRAVEYARD BOOK: LETTER FROM THE AUTHOR

Would you like me to compile a printable manuscript version of the full final chapters, or assist with anything else related to wrapping up *Steelhead Graveyard*?

You said:
Now, give me some great ideas for a "Letter From The Author" that will promote S.G. Potter's Authoring Courses, promote the book "The 28-Day AI Author" by S.G. Potter, and invite aspiring authors to contact S.G. Potter to learn how to turn their Big Idea into a published book. Subtly allude to the fact that S.G. Potter Media Publishing House provides book authoring services and can be contacted at support@sgpotter.com or by visiting www.sgpotter.com

ChatGPT said:
Absolutely. Below is a compelling and heartfelt **"Letter From the Author"** that can be placed at the back of *Steelhead Graveyard* or any of your books. It subtly promotes your courses, your how-to book *The 28-Day AI Author*, and your authoring services—while maintaining a warm, inspirational tone that aligns with your brand and personal mission:

Dear Reader,

Thank you for venturing into the dark waters of Steelhead Graveyard with me. Writing this story was more than just a creative pursuit—it was a calling. Being a murder mystery book is a bit dark but was created to prove a point.

This story specifically is an exercise in training authors how to use todays technologies to write a book in a short amount of time and get it published.

This book took just under 2 weeks to be conceived, written, formatted, edited, and published.

If reading this book stirred something in you—a sense that you have your own story to tell, a lesson to share, or even a wild idea you've always wanted to put to paper—I want you to know something:

You can write your book. You can finish it. And you don't have to do it alone.

That's why I created the book ***The 28-Day AI Author***, a proven, step-by-step guide to writing and publishing your book using the latest tools in AI and creative technology. This method has helped aspiring authors finally get their ideas out of their heads and into the world—quickly, confidently, and professionally.

I also offer authoring courses and personalized coaching to walk you through the entire process—from Big Idea to bookshelf with YOUR BOOK. Whether you're a first-timer or you've struggled to finish past projects, my goal is simple: to help you write the book that only you can write.

If you're ready to take that next step, or if you're just curious where to begin, I invite you to reach out. You can contact my team directly at support@sgpotter.com, or explore more resources at www.sgpotter.com.

Because stories matter.

Because ***your*** story matters.

Until the next tale rises from the river,

S.G. Potter
Author | Educator | Founder, S.G. Potter Media Publishing House.

S.G. Potter
Author of The 28-Day AI Author

Would you like a shorter version as well for marketing inserts or back-of-book space limitations?

STEELHEAD GRAVEYARD BOOK: ABOUT THE AUTHOR

You said:
Great job. Now create the content for the About the Author Page. On this page there is a picture of me (S.G. Potter) holding a fishing rod and wearing my fishing waders. Here is a bit of information that may be helpful to your writing of this page: Former Microsoft Technologist, Producer, and Host of the television show Action Outdoors TV, Author of many book titles covering many genres. I have been an avid fisherman for all my life and have personally fished almost every coastal river from Canada to California for steelhead and salmon at some point in my life. I am a husband and father.

ChatGPT said:
Absolutely. Here's a polished and compelling **"About the Author"** page tailored to match the tone and themes of *Steelhead Graveyard*, while also showcasing your professional background and multi-genre author success:

S.G. Potter is a multi-genre author, lifelong outdoorsman, and former Microsoft technologist whose stories explore the haunting edges of wilderness, memory, and meaning. His career has spanned the tech world, the entertainment industry, and now, the realm of independent publishing—where he helps others bring their own books to life.

He is the former producer and host of the outdoor adventure show Action Outdoors TV, and his deep knowledge of wild places comes from experience, not research. S.G. has fished nearly every coastal river from British Columbia to Northern California in search of steelhead and salmon. These rivers shaped him—and helped inspired Steelhead Graveyard.

A devoted husband and father, Potter writes with the heart of a family man and the soul of someone who's seen both the beauty and brutality of the natural world. His work spans children's stories, science fiction epics, geopolitical thrillers, and instructional nonfiction—each one fueled by his passion for storytelling and his belief that everyone has a powerful book within them.

Today, S.G. is also the founder of ***S.G. Potter Media Publishing House***, where he teaches aspiring authors how to write and publish books using modern tools and timeless storytelling principles. His book ***The 28-Day AI Author*** has helped many writers take the next step—and finish strong.

To learn more about his books, author training courses, or publishing services, visit www.sgpotter.com or contact the team directly at:

support@sgpotter.com
www.sgpotter.com

BONUS CONTENT

I have created several images that that will be made available as bonus content for the book. These images we created using Midjourney. Here are the images and the prompts used to generate them (Photoshop was used to brand the images with the Book Title:

Image 1: Kilchis (Native American Indian Serial Killer)
Prompt:

> */imagine a Native American man from the Tillamook Indian tribe from 150 years ago in his mid-30's with long black hair, traditional tribal clothing, and war paint on his face and body. He is standing next to a river deep in the woods of the Pacific Northwest where there are several dead steelhead fish laying on the riverbank. The Native American man has a sad look on his face that also shows anger. Make this image hyper-realistic, highly detailed, 8k, --ar 16:9 --v 7.0*

Image 2: Bob Tomalin (Main Character)
Prompt:

> */imagein a 44 year old fisherman standing on the bank of a river in the Pacific Northwest wearing chest waders and a hoodies with the hood not pulled over his head. He is wearing a dark-colored hat and there is a drift boat on the riverbank just behind him. The weather is wet and rainy. Hyper-realistic, highly detailed, 8k, 155MM, --ar 2:3*

Image 3: Tomalin Wife, Son and Daughter

Prompt:

/imagine an attractive but simple caucasion woman in her 30's with long brown hair and brown eyes sitting on a couch in a living room with her two children, a young boy aged 11 who is handsome and has short brown hair and a young girl aged 7 who is pretty and has long dirty-blonde hair. They are all looking into the camera with a sad look on their faces and hugging one another. Make this image hyper-realistic, highly detailed, 8k, --ar 16:9

Image 4: Sheriff Tallbear

Prompt:

> *a Tillamook, Oregon, County Sheriff who is of Native American descent who is in his 50's. He is tall and has a medium-husky build and is wearing a Tillamook County Sheriff's uniform that is slightly wrinkled. He has short black hair with some graying along the sides and dark brown eyes. He is a distinctive-looking face and does not smile. There is a County Sheriff pickup truck in the background with it's lights flashing and the scene is in the evening time alongside a forest road in the woods. Make this image hyper-realistic, highly detailed, 8k, --ar 16:9*

Image 4: Clancy Tomalin
Prompt:

a man in his 70's sitting at a flyfishing tying table making fishing flies. He is wearing glasses and has gray hair. He is a Caucasian who wears reading glasses. There is a mount of a large steelhead fish on the wall behind him, highly detailed, hyper-realistic, 8k, --ar 16:9

Image 5: Big Crow
Prompt:

> *a Native America Indian from the Tillamook Tribe on the Oregon Coast. The man is in his late 60's and has a kind look on his face. He is dressed in traditional Tillamook Indian Native American clothing. He is sitting in front of a beautiful river set deep in the woods of the Pacific Northwest. It is a beautiful sunny day. A crow is sitting on the man's shoulder as if it were a pet. Make this image hyper-realistic, highly detailed, 8k, --ar 16:9*

LETTER FROM THE AUTHOR

Dear Reader,

When I first began writing Steelhead Graveyard, I had no intention of publishing a behind-the-scenes guide. But as the story unfolded—equal parts haunting and honest—I realized that what was happening behind the keyboard was just as compelling as what was happening on the page. Every prompt I entered, every line the AI responded with, and every creative decision I made became part of a larger journey—one I felt was worth sharing with the class I was teaching as this book was written, and with anyone else who reads this book.

The Novel Machine is the full unfiltered record of that journey.

This book is not theory. It's not a curated highlight reel or a vague summary of "how I wrote the book." It's the exact prompts and AI responses that led to the creation of a suspense thriller I'm deeply proud of. From rough ideas to revised scenes, from moments of doubt to breakthroughs in storytelling—you'll see it all. If you're curious how AI can become a trusted creative companion—or if you've ever wondered how an idea becomes a novel—this book is for you.

My goal with The Novel Machine is simple: transparency and empowerment. I want you to see that writing a book in today's world doesn't require a degree in literature or a decade of free time. It requires a clear process, the right tools, and a willingness to learn. That's it.

If this guide helps even one aspiring author realize that they, too, can write and publish a meaningful book—then this was worth doing.

If you're interested in learning more about how I use AI to write, or if you're sitting on a big idea and don't know where to start, I invite you to visit www.sgpotter.com or reach out directly at support@sgpotter.com. I also encourage you to pick up Steelhead Graveyard if you haven't already, so you can experience the final product that emerged from the very prompts you'll read here.

Thank you for being part of this experiment, this process, this story.

Sincerely,
S.G. Potter
Author of Steelhead Graveyard and The 28-Day AI Author

ABOUT THE AUTHOR

S.G. Potter is a multi-genre author, technologist, and creative pioneer in the world of AI-assisted writing. A former Microsoft technologist and host of the television show Action Outdoors TV, Potter brings together a lifetime of storytelling, technology, and adventure to produce works that resonate deeply with readers.

He is the author of bestselling titles including The Potter Directive, the epic sci-fi series Stars of Ascendance, the heartwarming Ian the Inchworm children's books, and the wilderness thriller Steelhead Graveyard. In each of his projects, Potter combines cutting-edge tools like ChatGPT and Midjourney with classic storytelling techniques to create immersive, high-impact narratives.

With The Novel Machine, he pulls back the curtain to show exactly how AI helped shape one of his most gripping novels—from the very first prompt to the final chapter.

When he's not writing, Sam enjoys fishing Oregon's coastal rivers, teaching aspiring authors how to write with AI, and spending time with his wife and children. He is the founder of S.G. Potter – Media Publishing House, and is on a mission to help everyday creators unlock their potential and publish books faster than ever before.

Learn more or connect at www.sgpotter.com

A SMALL FAVOR THE MAKES A BIG DIFFERENCE

If you found value in this book—whether it was a single insight, a helpful prompt, or a spark of inspiration—I'd be truly grateful if you'd take a moment to leave a positive review on Amazon.

Your review not only supports my work as an author but also helps other aspiring writers and readers discover this book. Even a few kind words can go a long way in keeping books like this alive and accessible.

Thank you for being part of this creative journey.
— S.G. Potter

Visit **https://sgpotter.com/register/** to receive reader bonuses like:

- Get Word Templates
- Get Photoshop Book Cover Template
- Get updates from the Author

Receive info about Live Events and Courses

www.ingramcontent.com/pod-product-compliance
Lightning Source LLC
LaVergne TN
LVHW011515200926
848484LV00001B/41